CONNECTED COMMU
Creating a new knowledge

MW00341627

CO-PRODUCING RESEARCH
A community development approach

Edited by Sarah Banks, Angie Hart, Kate Pahl
and Paul Ward

First published in Great Britain in 2019 by

Policy Press
University of Bristol
1-9 Old Park Hill
Bristol
BS2 8BB
UK
t: +44 (0)117 954 5940
pp-info@bristol.ac.uk
www.policypress.co.uk

North America office:
Policy Press
c/o The University of Chicago Press
1427 East 60th Street
Chicago, IL 60637, USA
t: +1 773 702 7700
f: +1 773-702-9756
sales@press.uchicago.edu
www.press.uchicago.edu

British Library Cataloguing in Publication Data
A catalogue record for this book is available from the British Library

Library of Congress Cataloging-in-Publication Data
A catalog record for this book has been requested

ISBN 978-1-4473-4076-8 paperback
ISBN 978-1-4473-4075-1 hardcover
ISBN 978-1-4473-4078-2 ePub
ISBN 978-1-4473-4079-9 Mobi
ISBN 978-1-4473-4077-5 ePdf

Cover design by Hayes Design

Contents

List of images and tables

Images

Tables

Notes on contributors

Andrea Armstrong is a researcher at Durham University, UK, currently working on the dynamics of trust in physical places/digital spaces. She was Research Associate for *Imagine North East*.

Shabina Aslam is a theatre maker and has been a creative producer and radio drama producer. She is undertaking a PhD at the University of Huddersfield on 'Bussing Out', the 1960s and 1970s policy of the educational dispersal of black and Asian children.

Sarah Banks is Professor in the Department of Sociology and Co-director of the Centre for Social Justice and Community Action, Durham University, UK. She teaches and researches in the fields of community development, professional ethics and participatory action research. She coordinated the historical work package for *Imagine* and was particularly involved in *Imagine North East*.

David Bell has a background in the interdisciplinary field of 'utopian studies', and now works as a coordinator for Radar, Loughborough University's contemporary arts programme.

Anne Bonner is Chief Executive of Riverside Community Health Project in Benwell, Newcastle, UK. She works alongside a committed team addressing the effects of inequalities on the lives of people who live in the West End of Newcastle. Riverside undertook a project on 'playing with change and ideas' for *Imagine North East*.

Milton Brown is Chief Executive of Kirklees Local TV, which documents stories in Huddersfield and Dewsbury and surrounding areas. He is taking a PhD at the University of Huddersfield on the experience of African-Caribbean people in navigating identity in post-war Britain.

Lisa Buttery is an artist-in-residence and trainer with Boingboing where she designs illustrations and artwork, and co-produces books, films, exhibitions and conference presentations around visual arts, mental health and resilience (see www.boingboing.org.uk). Her artwork is an important way of coping with mental health issues and raising awareness of mental health issues in young people.

Josh Cameron is Principal Occupational Therapy Lecturer, University of Brighton, UK. His interests include collaborative approaches to adult resilience, including the return-to-work experiences of workers with mental health problems, and combining the expertise and knowledge of people with lived experience, practitioners and academics for research and practice development. He also volunteers for the social enterprise Boingboing (see www.boingboing.org.uk).

Prue Chiles is an architect and Professor of Architecture at Newcastle University, UK. She combines research and teaching with architectural practice, using the design process and 'research by design' to work collaboratively with people and communities. She conducted the Park Hill study along with Louise Ritchie and Paul Allender from the University of Sheffield, UK.

Andrew Church is Professor of Human Geography and Associate Pro-Vice-Chancellor of Research and Enterprise, University of Brighton, UK. His highly interdisciplinary and collaborative work focuses on human–nature relations and interactions to better understand how to manage change into the future.

Suna Eryigit-Madzwamuse is Senior Research Fellow and Deputy Director of the Centre of Resilience for Social Justice, University of Brighton, UK. Her work focuses on promoting the wellbeing and resilience of children, young people and their families, taking into account biological and contextual risk and protective factors from a developmental perspective. She also volunteers for the social enterprise, Boingboing (see www.boingboing.org.uk).

Yvonne Hall was formerly a community researcher at the Cedarwood Trust, Meadow Well Estate, North Shields, UK, where she coordinated the 'Imagining community at Cedarwood' project for *Imagine North East*. She is now studying for a degree in History with Creative Writing.

Patrick Harman is Executive Director of the Hayden-Harman Foundation, which focuses on community development efforts in High Point, North Carolina, USA. He also teaches courses on the non-profit sector at Elon University, USA. He provided assistance to *Imagine North East* during his Fulbright fellowship.

Angie Hart is Professor of Child, Family and Community Health and Director of the Centre of Resilience for Social Justice, University of

Brighton, UK. She teaches professional health and social care courses and undertakes participatory research into resilience and inequalities. Angie directs a community interest company, Boingboing, supporting children, families and practitioners (see www.boingboing.org.uk).

Elizabeth Chapman Hoult is a Lecturer in the Department of Psychosocial Studies at Birkbeck, University of London, UK, where she directs the MSc in Education, Power and Social Change. She uses literary theory and literary analysis to deepen understandings of individual and community resilience, hope and imagined futures.

Luke Johnston is a detached youth worker with Phoenix Detached Youth Project in North Shields, UK. His main areas of work are detached work, developing street spaces, working with young men's issues and education around social media safety. He coordinated an intergenerational graffiti art project for *Imagine North East*.

Elias Kourkoutas is Professor of Psychology and Special Education, University of Crete. His research explores ways to develop meaningful resilience-based inclusive practices that help teachers, parents and students with special educational needs, social, emotional and academic difficulties, and those at risk for school exclusion, overcome difficulties and be successfully included.

Ben Kyneswood was researcher at Warwick University for *Imagine Coventry* and is currently Lecturer in Sociology at Coventry University, UK. His work involves using community photographic archives to challenge dominant narratives and established thinking. His company, Photo Archive Miners, recently published the photography book *Masterji* and exhibits worldwide.

Clare Levi works with older people at the Search project based in Benwell, Newcastle, UK. She coordinated the 'Growing old in West Newcastle' project for *Imagine North East*.

Susanne Martikke leads on research at Greater Manchester Centre for Voluntary Organisation (GMCVO), a voluntary sector support organisation. She has more than 12 years' experience of conducting research with and about the voluntary sector. Some of this research has been in partnership with academics at local and national universities. She is now working on a collaborative studentship in Sociology at the University of Manchester.

Onyeka Nubia is a pioneering and internationally known historian, writer and presenter who reinvents perceptions of history. Onyeka is a renowned speaker, committed to the study of comparative research. He is a Visiting Research Fellow at Huddersfield University and the Director of Studies and writer in residence at Narrative Eye. He has published a number of books including *Blackamoores: Africans in Tudor England, their presence, status and origins* (Narrative Eye, 2013).

Kate Pahl is Professor of Arts and Literacy at Manchester Metropolitan University, UK. Kate's original discipline is English and she now works in communities drawing on arts methodologies. She was previously based at the University of Sheffield, where she was the Principal Investigator of the *Imagine* project.

Elizabeth Pente was awarded her PhD from the University of Huddersfield in 2018. Her research is concerned with public history and post-Second World War urban decline and regeneration. She is co-editor of *Re-imagining contested communities* (Policy Press, 2017).

Natalie Pinnock-Hamilton MBE is a Huddersfield-based community activist, who has been involved in numerous community development projects. She is a leading force in Building African Caribbean Communities (BACC) and Reach Performing Arts.

Steve Pool trained as a sculptor and now works as a visual artist in multiple media to help people realise ideas, often making physical objects or changing environments. He has an interest in stories, space and co-produced research. He is now a Doctoral student at MMU exploring the Artists Residency as research method.

Anne Rathbone is a University of Brighton PhD student working on co-produced research on resilience with young disabled adults. She is also Senior Training and Consultancy Manager and co-production lead for Boingboing Resilience CIC.

Louise Ritchie works at the Department for Lifelong Learning at the University of Sheffield, UK, and has extensive experience as a researcher on community research projects.

Mandeep Samra is an oral historian, artist and heritage activist, part of Let's Go Yorkshire. She led Sound System Culture and Let's Play Vinyl, both funded by Arts Council England. She developed the project that led to the publication of *Sound System Culture: Celebrating Huddersfield's sound systems* (One Love, 2014).

Kath Smith works for Remembering the Past, Resourcing the Future (RPRF) in North Shields, UK. She coordinated training and support in oral history skills for the North Shields projects for *Imagine North East*.

Kim Streets is Chief Executive of Museum Sheffield, UK. In the *Imagine* project she collaborated with the team to conduct a series of interviews on the experience of the residents of the newly regenerated neo-brutalist Park Hill flats in Sheffield to produce a film about their lived experiences, which can now be viewed in Weston Park Museum in Sheffield.

Ruth Taylor works for Pendower Good Neighbour Project, based in Benwell, Newcastle, UK. She coordinated the 'Time traveller' project with young people for *Imagine North East*.

Natalie Walton was Head of Learning at The Hepworth Wakefield, a major contemporary art gallery in Wakefield, Yorkshire, UK, which opened to the public in 2011. In the *Imagine* project she worked with a group of young people from a rent deposit scheme and used the gallery collection and the building as a starting point to explore conversations about the past, present and future.

Paul Ward was Professor of Modern British History at the University of Huddersfield, UK, from 2006 to 2018, when he became Professor of Public History and Community Heritage at Edge Hill University, Ormskirk, UK. He is the author of four books, including *Britishness since 1870* (Routledge, 2004). He coordinated the democratic work package in *Imagine*.

Beverly Wenger-Trayner is a learning consultant specialising in communities of practice and social learning systems. Her expertise encompasses both the design of learning architectures and the facilitation of processes, activities and the use of new technologies. She has also been the Creative Director of an Open Source platform for networked communities. She worked with the social work package of *Imagine*.

Etienne Wenger-Trayner is a globally recognised thought leader in the field of social learning and communities of practice. He writes books and articles for practitioners in organisations that want to base their knowledge strategy on communities of practice. His work is influencing a growing number of organisations in the private and public sectors. He worked with the social work package of *Imagine*.

Series editors' foreword

Around the globe, communities of all shapes and sizes are increasingly seeking an active role in producing knowledge about how to understand, represent and shape their world for the better. At the same time, academic research is increasingly realising the critical importance of community knowledge in producing robust insights into contemporary change in all fields. New collaborations, networks, relationships and dialogues are being formed between academic and community partners, characterised by a radical intermingling of disciplinary traditions and by creative methodological experimentation.

There is a groundswell of research practice that aims to build new knowledge, address longstanding silences and exclusions, and pluralise the forms of knowledge used to inform common-sense understandings of the world.

The aim of this book series is to act as a magnet and focus for the research that emerges from this work. Originating from the UK Arts and Humanities Research Council's Connected Communities programme (www.connected-communities.org), the series showcases critical discussion of the latest methods and theoretical resources for combining academic and public knowledge via high-quality, creative, engaged research. It connects the emergent practice happening around the world with the longstanding and highly diverse traditions of engaged and collaborative practice from which that practice draws.

This series seeks to engage a wide audience of academic and community researchers, policy-makers and others with an interest in how to combine academic and public expertise. The wide range of publications in the series demonstrate that this field of work is helping to reshape the knowledge landscape as a site of democratic dialogue and collaborative practice, as well as contestation and imagination. The series editors welcome approaches from academic and community researchers working in this field who have a distinctive contribution to make to these debates and practices today.

Keri Facer, Professor of Educational and Social Futures,
University of Bristol

George McKay, Professor of Media Studies,
University of East Anglia

Preface and acknowledgements

This book is one of the many products of a five-year collaborative research project, *Imagine — Connecting communities through research*. It was funded by the UK's Economic and Social Research Council (ESRC) through the Connected Communities programme (grant no ES/K002686/1) and had a focus on civic engagement (how people get involved in the lives of their communities). It involved research partnerships between people from communities of place, interest and identity largely based outside universities, and academics largely based within universities. In this book we explore and develop what we call a 'community development approach' to the co-production of research, drawing on our experiences with the *Imagine* project.

We are very grateful to the chapter authors for the work they put into their contributions to the book. Many of the chapters were written by teams of authors, requiring considerable energy and commitment to share perspectives, struggle with differences and develop common understandings. We would also like to thank the many people who were part of the *Imagine* project but who are not co-authors in this book. They contributed significantly to the practical work and thinking on which this books draws, and have been responsible for many other outputs including films, artworks, poems, booklets, articles and books (see www.imaginecommunity.org.uk).

We are particularly indebted to Angela Warren for keeping the *Imagine* project together over the last few years by looking after the finances and administration. Without her calm and efficient organising skills we would not have had the spaces for dialogue and collaborative thinking that have led to this book. We would also like to thank Sarah Hollely and Fern Merrill, who supported us through organising communications and events, and members of the Advisory Board for the project, who offered invaluable support and advice, including Keri Facer (sometime Chair), Sophie Duncan, Alison Gilchrist and Morag McDermott.

Sarah Banks, Angie Hart, Kate Pahl and Paul Ward
May 2018

ONE

Co-producing research: A community development approach

Sarah Banks, Angie Hart, Kate Pahl and Paul Ward

Introduction

This book focuses on a 'community development approach' to the co-production of research. By this we mean research undertaken collaboratively by several parties that values multiple perspectives and voices; contributes to creating and developing communities of place, interest and identity; builds collective capacity for action; and works towards social change.

The contributors were all involved in a five-year research project, *Imagine – Connecting communities through research* (see www. imaginecommunity.org.uk). The Economic and Social Research Council (ESRC) funded the project, focusing on exploring the contexts in which civic engagement takes place – that is, how people become engaged in civic life. The chapters in the book draw on the authors' experiences as academics, artists, community activists, residents, service users, third sector employees and research students in the co-production of research; some of our identities are such that we belong to more than one of these categories.

In this chapter we discuss the field of co-production in research and how we understood this within the *Imagine* project. We also describe our understandings of the processes and practices of community development; how co-produced research can contribute to community development; and how community development principles and practices can enhance co-produced research. One of the contributions of the book is to offer a way of thinking about the co-production of research as a process of community development that provides a link between knowing and doing.

The *Imagine* project involved academics working with a range of people in different roles, including artists, museum educators, youth workers, community workers, activists, local residents, teachers, young people and policy-makers. The project drew on a number of disciplinary areas, including history, social sciences, arts practice, architecture and literary theory. Hence the chapters in this book reflect a broad conceptualisation of ways of knowing and working across universities and communities. We propose a community development approach to the co-production of knowledge that draws on modes of engagement that are themselves rooted in a number of traditions, including community activism (Lees, 1975; Ledwith and Springett, 2010) and communities of practice (Wenger, 1998; Hart et al, 2013) as well as socially engaged arts practice and community arts (Kester, 2011; Bishop, 2012).

We, the co-editors of the book, are all academics working in UK universities, yet we come from varied backgrounds and offer perspectives from different disciplines and lived experiences. For example, Sarah Banks has a background in community development work and the study of philosophy, social history and social work; Angie Hart is a practising mental health professional and the adoptive parent of children with complex needs; Kate Pahl used to be an outreach adult literacy worker and has a background in English literature; and Paul Ward is an academic historian and political activist.

In this chapter we bring these academic and community perspectives together to present our visions of co-produced research. Sarah Banks and Angie Hart are more social sciences oriented with a focus on making change happen with people in communities, while Kate Pahl and Paul Ward are more engaged in arts and humanities approaches. What we share is an interest in how to make research more collaborative, with research projects carried out not just by academics, but devised, framed, investigated and disseminated collectively by people who often have less access to the research resources that universities provide. This is frequently due to structural reasons, such as discrimination based on class, gender, ethnicity or difficult life circumstances. Yet people from outside the university have different knowledge, skills and expertise, based on their lived experiences, that academics sometimes lack. Some of these types of expertise might be less obvious than others, and specific strategies are needed to offset people's perceptions that certain kinds of expertise matter more than others.

We bring understandings of co-production that are slightly different, and here we present the different facets of our approach. We stress our commitment to a community development approach through a shared understanding of co-production as a process, not just as a product. It can be dialogic and collaborative (Banks et al, 2013), drawing on people with varied identities who come together in a community of practice around shared issues (Hart et al, 2013). It can involve developing shared research questions and undertaking a collaborative ethnographic study, following Campbell and Lassiter's (2015) approach. It can be informed by arts methodologies that privilege emergence and tacit and embodied ways of knowing (Pahl et al, 2017). People can bring shared perspectives to uncovering hidden histories in a co-producing history approach (Lloyd and Moore, 2015; Ward and Pente, 2017).

Although this book includes a wide range of contributors and the chapters have been co-authored in a variety of ways, the four lead academic investigators of the *Imagine* project took on the overall coordinating and editorial role. Although our original plan was to establish a mixed group of co-editors, the reality of people's time commitments and resources meant that we decided in the end that we would take on the editorial role, with our community partners prioritising their time for contributing to the writing of the individual chapters. We also had more resources (via the ESRC and our universities) to spend time editing and coordinating the writing.

The *Imagine* project

The *Imagine* project was concerned with the social, historical, cultural and democratic context of civic engagement, with a focus on imagining different communities and making them happen. It was framed within the concept of 'Connected Communities' – the name of the Research Councils UK (a strategic partnership of seven research councils, now subsumed within UK Research and Innovation) programme within which the project was located (for an overview, see Facer and Enright, 2016). *Imagine* had four overarching research questions, starting from the basic understanding of communities as collectivities of people with some, but not necessarily all, characteristics in common, who may (but do not always) come together for – at least perceived – mutual benefit. The four overarching questions were:

- How can connected communities be conceptualised, researched and promoted so that they have the potential to accommodate and benefit from social, cultural and economic differences and diverse opinions and practices?
- What does the record of civic engagement (understood in its broadest sense) to date tell us about how and why the social, historical, cultural and democratic context matters to the degrees of success achieved by projects that aim to build connected communities?

- Within the process of promoting engagement in community initiatives by as wide a range of social groups as possible, can imagining better futures play a role in capturing and sustaining enthusiasm and momentum for change, and if so, what is that role?
- Is the landscape of community research being transformed by developments in the research methodologies employed in the arts and humanities and social sciences, particularly the promotion of co-produced research and creative, collaborative, participatory and inclusive methods?

The chapters in this book relate particularly to the last question about co-produced research and collaborative methodologies and methods, although their substantive content is also relevant to the other questions.

In order to explore these questions from different perspectives, *Imagine* was organised through four different work packages: 'social', coordinated by Angie Hart; 'historical', coordinated by Sarah Banks; 'cultural', coordinated by Kate Pahl; and 'democratic', coordinated initially by Graham Crow, who was also the Leader of the consortium until 2014, and then by Paul Ward. Paul also coordinated a strand that looked at history across the project, and developed, jointly with Kate, work in Rotherham with a focus on histories and cultures. Each work package comprised people from many different community organisations, several universities and other institutions such as art galleries, local authority services, the NHS and museums. Our work combined a focus on revisiting past projects and looking at them anew (this was particularly strong in the case of revisiting the community development projects of the 1970s; see Chapters 2 and 8) and a focus on imagining better communities – which led to imaginative, poetic and artistic work that captured new identities and new visions for the future, as evidenced by the work of the arts projects in Rotherham (Campbell et al, 2018). In our work, there was a shared commitment to co-production across the consortium, a desire for social change and the opportunity for us to deepen our research in relation to both of these, including developing new theoretical approaches (see, for example, Pente et al, 2015; Hart et al, 2016; Bell and Pahl, 2018).

In this book we unpack how this shared focus happened, uniting our work through the idea of a community development approach to co-producing research. By this we mean that we look closely at the processes and practices of co-production. This might mean exploring how community–university partnerships work (Chapter 3), or how a writing retreat is structured and developed (Chapter 4). It constitutes a focus on structure, on freeze-framing the processes of co-production to make them transparent and accountable. However, it might also be about how people work together to imagine better futures. One of our questions was concerned with how the arts can help re-imagine the future differently. A community development approach to co-production can be about the ways of knowing within communities that can surface through a stronger focus on process rather than simply looking at outcomes.

We come to the book, then, with a shared focus on imagining different communities and making them happen, and also on methodological understandings of the process of co-production in action. We are interested in the 'how' as much as the 'why'. *Imagine* was an experiment, which lasted for five years and produced many different outputs – books, exhibitions, poems, films, quilts, stories, songs and paintings – but the focus was on change, community and co-production as a process. This book celebrates and critically examines that process.

Co-production of research

Co-production of research entails people from different settings and backgrounds doing research together. Rather like the term 'participatory research', it has a descriptive meaning that goes beyond the literal interpretation. It is not used simply to refer to research conducted by more than one person or by academics from different disciplines; it is usually used to refer to research undertaken by 'professional researchers' (often based in a university) and people who have a direct interest in, or experience of, the issue being researched.

As the prefix 'co-' implies, there is usually an active process of working together with some degree of collaboration and cooperation. Principles of equality and democracy are therefore central to our vision of co-produced research. People may make different contributions to the research, involving different amounts of time and effort at different points in the research process. However, all contributions are regarded as equally valuable. 'Co-production' refers as much to the spirit and philosophy of the research as it does to the mechanics of doing it. It entails a conscious awareness on the part of all co-researchers that some people may have more experience and expertise in particular areas and that this should be acknowledged and shared. People come to the research from different positions of status, power, wealth, ability and confidence.

The idea of co-production as a philosophy that involves a commitment to values of equality and democracy is important. It is this philosophy that guides the actual practice of the research, which may vary greatly according to who is involved, and for what purpose. For example, a group of young people with learning disabilities, one or more arts practitioners and university researchers, will collaborate very differently from a group of experienced community activists, one or more community workers and university researchers. There is a tendency to talk in terms of degrees of co-production, which might lead us to say the research done by the first group was lower down the ladder of co-production because the arts workers and university researchers are as much facilitators, trainers and supporters as they are co-researchers. However, 'co-production' is relative to context, and what makes research 'co-production' is the conscious use of expertise in ways that are as empowering and respectful as possible. So, in research with people with learning disabilities, the use of inclusive methodologies is very important – in order to support and enable as much participation as people are able and comfortable to give.

Our approach to co-production is firmly rooted in a participatory paradigm (Reason, 1998), focusing on equality, democracy and the creation of positive change. Our view of co-production of research is that it is a generic concept that embraces a variety of more specialised types of research with different names, including 'participatory', 'inclusive' and 'action' research. We use it to refer to all types of research that are done together by people from different backgrounds and experiences based on a participatory worldview, with a commitment to principles of equality and democracy. It draws on many traditions, of which we mention just three here in order to highlight some of the influences on our practice and the key values associated with different approaches:

- *Participatory research:* The term 'participatory' gives strong emphasis to the idea of people actively taking part. This approach was particularly developed and is used in the fields of international and community development – although it is also used much more widely and is often combined with action research as participatory action research, or PAR (see, for example, Fals Borda, 1987; Kindon et al, 2007; McIntyre, 2007) (*key value: democracy*).
- *Inclusive research:* This term is more common in the fields of disability and social care, including research involving service users, and gives emphasis to ensuring research projects are accessible to as wide a range of people as possible and that people are supported to participate (see Walmsley, 2008; Nind, 2014) (*key value: equality*).
- *Action research:* This was developed particularly in organisational contexts, education and also community development (where

PAR is common), and has a focus on achieving positive (social) change (see Greenwood and Levin, 1998; Burns, 2008; Reason and Bradbury, 2008; Coghlan and Brydon-Miller, 2014) (*key value: positive change*).

When reading accounts of research badged as 'participatory', 'inclusive' and 'action' research, it is often impossible to see any material difference. The choice of name may be linked more to home discipline, practice arena, journal title or funding call than to differences in philosophy, methodology or methods. In recent years there has been a mushrooming of types of co-produced research – from collaborative ethnography to community-university action research. What we offer in this book is a similarly broad set of approaches and methodologies, all united by a community development approach that is process-led and focuses on transformative outcomes.

A community development approach to co-producing research

Just as there are many understandings of co-production, so there are multiple and contested meanings of both 'community' and 'community development'. In the original bid for funding for the *Imagine* project we described our basic understanding of communities as 'collectivities of people with some but not necessarily all characteristics in common'. Use of the term 'collectivity' signifies a group of people considered as a body or a whole, while the statement that they may share only certain characteristics in common allows for elements of heterogeneity and diversity. Communities may comprise people sharing a place of residence in common (for example, a village, housing estate or urban neighbourhood), common interests (for example, a football club) or identities (for example, women's group, Muslim religion). The term 'community' has been described as 'essentially contested' (Plant, 1974) in that it has multiple descriptive meanings as listed above and an evaluative meaning, generally with positive connotations linked to care, cohesion, warmth and closeness (Crow and Allan, 1994; Mayo, 2000; Little, 2002; Delanty, 2009; Banks and Butcher, 2013; Somerville, 2016). While 'community' is a very problematic term, its usage is persistent in both everyday language and public policy as a way of promoting social cohesion, inclusivity and emphasising commonality. Yet communities can also be as exclusive and oppressive as they are inclusive and caring – as the sense of belonging, identity, solidarity and being cared about experienced by members of communities can also be experienced as pressure to conform, and relies on members differentiating themselves from others outside their communities. In addition to solidarity with each other, members of communities also need to practise tolerance of non-members, seeing themselves as part of broader society in order to combat stereotyping, marginalisation, hatred and violence based on characteristics such as ethnicity, religion, gender, sexuality, class, age or ability.

Hence the process of 'community development' is neither straightforward nor necessarily positive for all. There are many definitions of community development, most of which entail groups of people coming together to take collective action on issues relevant to their lives (Ledwith, 2011; Gilchrist and Taylor, 2016; Meade et al, 2016). In the UK, the National Occupational Standards for Community Development (2015, p 5) include a statement of purpose developed collaboratively by key organisations and practitioners in the field, which encapsulates the main points of our approach:

> Community development enables people to work collectively to bring about positive social change. This long term process starts from people's own experience and enables communities* to work together to:
>
> • Identify their own needs and actions
> • Take collective action using their strengths and resources
> • Develop their confidence, skills and knowledge
> • Challenge unequal power relationships
> • Promote social justice, equality and inclusion in order to improve the quality of their own lives, the communities in which they live and societies of which they are a part.
>
> * Communities refer to those that can be defined by geography, identity or interest.

The values underpinning community development practice are identified as follows (summarised from National Occupational Standards, 2015, pp 6-7):

• *Social justice and equality:* Working for a more just and equal society that recognises environmental, political, cultural and economic issues.

- *Anti-discrimination:* Respecting, valuing, supporting and promoting difference and diversity while rejecting and challenging any form of oppression, discrimination and sectarianism.
- *Community empowerment:* Enabling communities to develop confidence, capacity, skills and relationships to shape collective action and challenge imbalances of power.
- *Collective action:* Promoting the active participation of people within communities, using the power of a collective voice and goal.
- *Working and learning together:* Creating and encouraging opportunities for collective learning through action and shared reflection.

This purpose and set of values underpins a community development approach to the co-production of research. However, it is important to stress that a community development approach to co-produced research is not the same as community development practice (see the discussion in Chapter 2) – co-produced research has a primary focus on the production of *knowledge* for social change rather than social change *per se*. Nevertheless, it shares the values, and draws on community development purposes, approaches and methods of working with groups. This influence can be seen in much of the literature on community-based participatory research (Banks et al, 2013, Coughlin et al, 2017, van de Sande and Schwartz, 2017; Wallerstein et al, 2017), including the set of ethical principles developed by Durham University's Centre for Social Justice and Community Action (Centre for Social Justice and Community Action and NCCPE, 2012). These principles draw on community development values relevant to a participatory research context, and were used to develop ethical frameworks for some of the *Imagine* projects.

Ethical principles for community-based participatory research (taken from Centre for Social Justice and Community Action and NCCPE, 2012)

1) Mutual respect: developing research relationships based on mutual respect, including a commitment to:

- agreeing what counts as mutual respect in particular contexts;
- everyone involved being prepared to listen to the voices of others;

- accepting that people have diverse perspectives, different forms of expertise and ways of knowing that may be equally valuable in the research process.

2) *Equality and inclusion: encouraging and enabling people from a range of backgrounds and identities (eg, ethnicity, faith, class, education, gender, sexual orientation, [dis]ability, age) to lead, design and take part in the research, including a commitment to:*

- seeking actively to include people whose voices are often ignored;
- challenging discriminatory and oppressive attitudes and behaviours;
- ensuring information, venues and formats for meetings are accessible to all.

3) *Democratic participation: encouraging and enabling all participants to contribute meaningfully to decision-making and other aspects of the research process according to skill, interest and collective need, including a commitment to:*

- acknowledging and discussing differences in the status and power of research participants, and working towards sharing power more equally;
- communicating in language everyone can understand, including arranging translation or interpretation if required;
- using participatory research methods that build on, share and develop different skills and expertise.

4) *Active learning: seeing research collaboration and the process of research as providing opportunities to learn from each other, including a commitment to:*

- ensuring there is time to identify and reflect on learning during the research, and on ways people learn, both together and individually;
- offering all participants the chance to learn from each other and share their learning with wider audiences;
- sharing responsibility for interpreting the research findings and their implications for practice.

5) Making a difference: promoting research that creates positive change for communities of place, interest or identity, including:

- engaging in debates about what counts as 'positive' change, including broader environmental sustainability as well as human needs or spiritual development, and being open to the possibility of not knowing in advance what making a 'positive difference' might mean;
- valuing the learning and other benefits for individuals and groups from the research process as well as the outputs and outcomes of the research;
- building a goal of positive change into every stage of the research.

6) Collective action: individuals and groups working together to achieve change, including a commitment to:

- identifying common and complementary goals that meet partners' differing needs for the research;
- working for agreed visions of how to share knowledge and power more equitably and promote social change and social justice;
- recognizing and working with conflicting rights and interests expressed by different interest groups, communities of practice or place.

7) Personal integrity: participants behaving reliably, honestly and in a transparent and trustworthy fashion, including a commitment to:

- working within the principles of community-based participatory research;
- ensuring accurate and honest analysis and reporting of research;
- being open to challenge and change, being flexible and prepared to work with conflict.

Structure of the book

The chapters in this book give accounts of various elements of the overall *Imagine* project, focusing on different features of the co-production process. We have divided the book into three parts based on three broad themes, while recognising that the section headings do not necessarily capture all features of each chapter: Part I: Forming communities of inquiry and developing shared practices; Part II: Co-creating through and with the arts; and Part III: Co-designing outputs.

Part I: Forming communities of inquiry and developing shared practices. The first theme, from a mainly social science perspective, focuses on the process of the co-creation of knowledge within groups formed of disparate elements, whether this is based on re-revisiting historical community-based knowledge (Chapter 2) or creating individual and community resilience (Chapter 4). Much of this is realised in linguistic-oriented outputs, such as writing together (see Chapter 4 on research retreats), but can include arts activities and outputs as a result of this community-forming process. Constructed spaces, such as community-university partnerships, can also be a way of creating positive working relationships to achieve shared goals, as described in Chapter 3.

Part II: Co-creating through and with the arts. Our argument in this book is that the co-production of research is a cross-disciplinary and complex activity, rooted in a number of different traditions. These chapters describe how literary theory, history and artistic methodologies can be used to co-produce with communities. They explore the contribution of literary texts and films, and include contributions by artists, writers, poets and historians. A community development approach to co-production from an arts and humanities perspective can be led and informed by content that includes oral history, visual art, poetry and reflections on literature. Chapter 5 explores, through a dialogic conversation, the role of the arts in collectively imagining different communities, while Chapter 6 describes the aesthetic experience of co-design and co-creation with reference to the experience of living in the modernist 'concrete utopia' that is Park Hill flats in Sheffield. Chapters in this section also consider how texts can become sites of utopian possibilities when thinking about co-producing – or not, in the much more complex contexts of prisons described in Chapter 7.

Part III: Co-designing outputs. Chapters in this section describe the process of curating or coalescing over shared outputs or endeavours, whether this be re-claiming community histories or co-curating community exhibitions. This process model focuses as much on the texts and the 'stuff' of the work as on the people involved. What is interesting about this work is how a shared output, such as the exhibition in Coventry described in Chapter 8, can become a form of community development. History making and writing is a process that is often colonised by universities, and Chapter 9 uncovers this process for community partners working on Black history. Chapter 10 includes an account of a final workshop, which involved the co-design and co-creation of a booklet representing the work of *Imagine*.

Overview of the chapters

We now briefly introduce the chapters in each of the three parts of the book:

Part I: Forming communities of inquiry and developing shared practices
Chapter 2, Between research and community development: Negotiating a contested space for collaboration and creativity, gives an account of how a community development approach to co-production is experienced through a process of academics and community partners working together to re-imagine better communities. It describes looking back and revisiting previous community development projects in North East England through a process of insider and outsider research. This chapter illustrates how lived experience and community hopes and dreams can infuse research that is carried out on the ground by engaged community activists, university researchers and practitioners, illustrating the importance of reflection and considering a wide spectrum of responses, including artistic responses, to collective action.

Chapter 3, A radical take on co-production? Community partner leadership in research, gives an account of the challenges of working across university and community partnerships. This chapter probes the realities of creating sustainable partnerships in a shared research endeavour between a voluntary sector research organisation and a university that sought to explore how community-university partnerships worked best in practice through a series of interviews. This work was sustained by a vision of equitable and sustainable partnerships. However, real co-production also depends on everyone being treated equally, paid fairly and given enough time to do things, a point that sometimes gets lost in the mire of enthusiasm for such community-university projects. Valuing the strengths of each partner and learning to challenge assumptions and to live with difference prove vital for sustaining these relationships.

Chapter 4, Community-university partnership research retreats: A productive force for developing communities of research practice, discusses the benefits of co-production as an approach in the context of the practice of the 'social' work package holding annual research retreats during the project. A 'communities of practice' approach is identified as a way forward in forming communities that work in this way. Specific aspects of that approach, such as the creation of boundaries and boundary objects that could support healthy and productive growth, together with people who could broker across boundaries, are highlighted. Ways of doing, as well as ways of knowing, are explained in a way that makes such strong partnership work accessible but also valued in a new way.

Part II: Co-creating through and with the arts

Chapter 5, How does arts practice inform a community development approach to the co-production of research?, features a dialogue between four people who came together to begin a reflective discussion about the accessibility of culture for communities, considering at the same time their own experiences of participating in the *Imagine* project. Concerns expressed in this chapter include a focus on whether art can be collaborative and whether hierarchies of exclusion within art can be broken down when the art world continues to be so elitist. The collaborative, conversational nature of the work is highlighted here, and a focus on collective, common and public space as restorative within communities is articulated strongly within the discussion.

Chapter 6, Co-designing for a better future: Re-imagining the modernist dream at Park Hill, Sheffield, explores how the histories of Park Hill (an iconic housing development in Sheffield) are intertwined with the current residents' pre-occupations with future-oriented visions of how they could live. Using the idea of 'making methodologies' from the work of Paul Carter (2004) on material knowledge, through a workshop format, the potential for co-design with communities is explored. Through making models together, residents and architects created a shared space of production. This was community forming as materially informed, held and felt within the space of the flats – an experiment in living. The chapter celebrates space as a site for co-design and experimentation, and listens to the voices of residents who would wish to make their space otherwise. Thinking spatially is another aspect of a community development approach to co-production, through design and a vision of how things 'could be' as well as how they are.

Chapter 7, On not *doing co-produced research: The methodological possibilities and limitations of co-producing research with participants in a prison,* explores the limits of co-production, as well as the possibilities within a confined space. Giving prisoners a chance to script and write their lives differently was a somewhat utopian and emerging finding from the project that Elizabeth Hoult describes. Hoult explores the scripts that prisoners hold and how they could be otherwise through the power of the text. She delineates the limits of co-production in a prison and describes how she encountered barriers to a fully co-productive approach. She argues that hopeful scripts within texts can open up a space of practice from which to be, and to locate future identities.

Part III: Co-designing outputs

Chapter 8, Co-production as a new way of seeing: Using photographic exhibitions to challenge dominant stigmatising discourses, explores the role of a community exhibition in the Hillfields area of Coventry, a co-produced output that illustrated complex community narratives of historic change. This was a type of community forming that focused on visual representations of community that shifted perceptions and created shared visions of the future. By taking photographs of their area, residents created their own sense of community. The process led to the beginnings of a new set of relationships that could be described more loosely as an experimental and iterative process of knowledge creation.

Chapter 9, 'Who controls the past controls the future': Black history and community development, addresses the making and re-making of history within communities with a focus on Black history. The chapter argues that communities need to research their own histories in situations when universities let them down so much through structural discrimination. Black history in the UK is a case whereby exclusion and racism have combined to obliterate the rightful histories of people within places such as Huddersfield in the North of England. Rich and varied local and national histories are surfaced in this chapter, which argues that a community development approach to the co-production of history is vital to redress this balance and provide the power and voice of Black historians inside and outside the academy.

The book ends with *Chapter 10, Conclusion: Imagining different communities and making them happen,* which draws together key messages and learning from previous chapters. It outlines the challenges and rewards of a community development approach to co-producing research, including working with diversity and difference and being prepared to be flexible, creative and patient. It ends by discussing a final writing retreat to encapsulate key achievements and learning from the *Imagine* project, ending with the advice to 'embrace the unexpected'.

Acknowledgements

We are grateful to the Economic and Social Research Council (ESRC) for funding *Imagine – Connecting communities through research* (grant no ES/K002686/2), and to our many co-researchers, collaborators and members of the advisory group (for details of the various organisations and individuals involved, see www.imaginecommunity.org.uk).

References

Banks, S. and Butcher, H. (2013) 'What is community practice?', in S. Banks, H. Butcher, A. Orton and J. Robertson (eds) *Managing community practice: Principles, policies and programmes* (2nd edn), Bristol: Policy Press, 7-30.

Banks, S., Armstrong, A., Carter, K., Graham, H., Hayward, P., Henry, A., et al (2013) 'Everyday ethics in community-based participatory research', *Contemporary Social Science*, 8(3), 263-77.

Bell, D.M. and Pahl, K. (2018) 'Co-production: Towards a utopian approach', *International Journal of Social Research Methodology*, 21(1), 105-17.

Bishop, C. (2012) *Artificial hells: Participatory art and the politics of spectatorship*, London: Verso.

Burns, D. (2008) *Systemic action research*, Bristol: Policy Press.

Campbell, E. and Lassiter, L.E. (2015) *Doing ethnography today: Theories, methods, exercises*, Oxford: Wiley-Blackwell.

Campbell, E., Pahl, K., Pente, E. and Rasool, Z. (2018) *Re-imagining contested communities: Connecting Rotherham through research,* Bristol: Policy Press.

Carter, P. (2004) *Material thinking: The theory and practice of creative research*, Melbourne, VIC: Melbourne University Publishing.

Centre for Social Justice and Community Action and NCCPE (National Coordinating Centre for Public Engagement) (2012) *Community-based participatory research: A guide to ethical principles and practice*, Bristol: NCCPE (www.durham.ac.uk/socialjustice/ethics_consultation).

Coghlan, D. and Brydon-Miller, M. (eds) (2014) *The Sage encyclopedia of action research*, London: Sage.

Coughlin, S., Smith, S. and Fernandez, M. (2017) *Handbook of community-based participatory research*, New York: Oxford University Press.

Crow, C. and Allan, G. (1994) *Community life: An introduction to local social relations*, Hemel Hempstead: Harvester Wheatsheaf.

Delanty, G. (2009) *Community*, London: Routledge.

Facer, K. and Enright, B. (2016) *Creating living knowledge: The Connected Communities programme, community-university relationships and the participatory turn in the production of knowledge*, Bristol: University of Bristol/Arts and Humanities Research Council (AHRC) Connected Communities.

Fals Borda, O. (1987) 'The application of participatory action–research in Latin America', *International Sociology*, 2(4), 329–47.

Gilchrist, A. and Taylor, M. (2016) *The short guide to community development* (2nd edn), Bristol: Policy Press.

Greenwood, D. and Levin, M. (1998) *An introduction to action research: Social research for social change*, Thousand Oaks, CA: Sage.

Hart, A., Davies, C., Aumann, K., Wenger, E., Aranda, K., Heaver, B. and Wolff, D. (2013) 'Mobilising knowledge in community-university partnerships: What does a community of practice approach contribute?', *Contemporary Social Science: Journal of the Academy of Social Sciences*, 8(3), 278–91.

Hart, A., Gagnon, E., Eryigit-Madzwamuse, S., Cameron, J., Aranda, K., Rathbone, A. and Heaver, B. (2016) 'Uniting resilience research and practice with a health inequalities approach', *SAGE Open*, 6(4), 1–15.

Kester, G.H. (2011) *The one and the many: Contemporary collaborative art in a global context*, Durham, NC: Duke University Press.

Kindon, S., Pain, R. and Kesby, M. (eds) (2007) *Participatory action research approaches and methods: Connecting people, participation and place*, Abingdon: Routledge.

Ledwith, M. (2011) *Community development: A critical approach* (2nd edn), Bristol: Policy Press.

Ledwith, M. and Springett, J. (2010) *Participatory practice: Community-based action for transformative change*, Bristol: Policy Press.

Lees, R. (1975) 'The action–research relationship', in R. Lees and G. Smith (eds) *Action-research in community development*, London: Routledge & Kegan Paul, 59–66.

Little, A. (2002) *The politics of community: Theory and practice*, Edinburgh: Edinburgh University Press.

Lloyd, S. and Moore, J. (2015) 'Sedimented histories: Connections, collaborations and co-production in regional history', *History Workshop*, 80, 234–48.

Mayo, M. (2000) *Cultures, communities, identities*, Basingstoke: Palgrave.

McIntyre, A. (2007) *Participatory action research*, Qualitative Research Methods Series 52, Thousand Oaks, CA: Sage.

Meade, R., Shaw, M. and Banks, S. (2016) 'Politics, power and community development: An introductory essay', in R. Meade, M. Shaw and S. Banks (eds) *Politics, power and community development*, Bristol: Policy Press, 1-27.

National Occupational Standards (2015) *Community development National Occupational Standards*, Sheffield: Federation for Community Development Learning (http://cldstandardscouncil.org.uk/wp-content/uploads/CDNOStandards2015.pdf).

Nind, M. (2014) *What is inclusive research?*, London: Bloomsbury.

Pahl, K., Escott, H., Graham, H., Marwood, K., Pool, S. and Ravetz, A. (2017) 'What is the role of artists in interdisciplinary collaborative projects with universities and communities?', in K. Facer and K. Pahl (eds) *Valuing interdisciplinary collaborative research: Beyond impact*, Bristol: Policy Press, 131-52.

Pente, E., Ward, P., Brown, M. and Sahota, H. (2015) 'The co-production of historical knowledge: Implications for the history of identities', *Identity Papers: A Journal of British and Irish Studies*, 1(1), 32-53.

Plant, R. (1974) *Community and ideology*, London: Routledge & Kegan Paul.

Reason, P. (1998) 'A participatory world', *Resurgence*, 168, 42-4.

Reason, P. and Bradbury, H. (2008) *The Sage handbook of action research: Participative inquiry and practice*, London: Sage.

Somerville, P. (2016) *Understanding community: Politics, policy and practice* (2nd edn), Bristol: Policy Press.

van de Sande, A. and Schwartz, K. (2017) *Research for social justice: A community-based participatory approach* (2nd edn), Winnipeg, MB: Fernwood Publishing.

Wallerstein, N., Duran, B., Oetzel, J. and Minkler, M. (eds) (2017) *Community-based participatory research for health: Advancing social and health equity* (3rd edn), San Francisco, CA: Jossey-Bass.

Walmsley, J. (2008) *Inclusive research with people with learning disabilities: Past, present and futures*, London: Jessica Kingsley Publishers.

Ward, P. and Pente, E. (2017) 'Let's change history! Community histories and the co-production of historical knowledge', in K. Pickles, L. Fraser, M. Hill, S. Murray and G. Ryan (eds) *History making a difference: New approaches from Aotearoa*, Cambridge: Scholars Press, 94-112.

Wenger, E. (1998) *Communities of practice: Learning, meaning and identity*, Cambridge: Cambridge University Press.

Part I
Forming communities of inquiry and developing shared practices

---

Between research and community development: Negotiating a contested space for collaboration and creativity

Sarah Banks, Andrea Armstrong, Anne Bonner, Yvonne Hall,
Patrick Harman, Luke Johnston, Clare Levi, Kath Smith
and Ruth Taylor

Introduction

This chapter explores the interface between co-produced research and community development, drawing on work undertaken in North East England as part of the *Imagine* project. Discussion of the process and outcomes of *Imagine North East* provides fruitful material for contributing to perennial debates about whether certain forms of co-produced research (especially participatory action research) are, in fact, indistinguishable from community development. In this chapter we offer a brief overview of the work of *Imagine North East* before outlining the debates about the relationship between co-production and community development. We then examine three elements of *Imagine North East*: (1) an academic-led study of community development from the 1970s to the present; (2) a series of community development projects undertaken by local community-based organisations; and (3) a joint process of reflection and co-inquiry. We consider the role of co-produced research in challenging stigma, celebrating place and developing skills and community networks, and also the challenges of a co-inquiry approach.

Exploring community development from the outside and inside: The work of *Imagine North East*

Imagine North East was a partnership between 12 community-based organisations in Tyneside (including a local museum) and Durham

University, officially running during 2014 and 2015, with dissemination and reflection work continuing in 2016. Community development featured in several ways. Not only did community-based sub-projects use processes of community development (mobilising people to work together) and generate community development outcomes (for example, strengthened communities, improved facilities) in their work for *Imagine North East*, but our study also had community development as its main focus. We adopted three approaches to the study of community development, as outlined below:

1. *Studying community development from the outside:* The starting point of the research was the community development projects of the 1970s in Benwell (Newcastle-upon-Tyne) and North Shields. These were part of Britain's first anti-poverty programme, combining community development work and research with a view to diagnosing and alleviating poverty locally (Loney, 1983; Banks and Carpenter, 2017). We also looked at community development processes over time (from the 1970s to the present) as these areas were subject to numerous regeneration schemes in which local people were more or less engaged. This research was largely done by academic researchers and then shared in the wider group.

2. *Doing community development projects and then reflecting on the learning from the inside:* At the same time, each community partner organisation undertook a project linked to the theme of *Imagine*, exploring aspects of the past, present and future of the areas in which they were based. These projects were designed to fit into the everyday practice of the community organisations involved, engaging existing and new 'service users' and/or residents. Hence they were, in effect, community development projects, involving local people in undertaking oral history, filmmaking and other creative projects. In many cases, the activities undertaken were not necessarily regarded by the people participating in them as research projects or as part of a larger research project.

3. *Co-inquiry, bringing the outside and inside together and creating new knowledge:* The drawing together of all elements of *Imagine North East* happened in quarterly meetings of academic and community partners, and also in the preparation for and participation in local exhibitions and workshops and national *Imagine* events. The meetings were originally designed as 'co-inquiry' groups (Heron, 1996), with the aim of sharing experiences and reflecting on learning. In practice, these meetings often had as much of a focus on business items (for example, reviewing progress with projects,

planning exhibitions) as they did on co-inquiry (reflecting together on learning). A smaller Writing and Reflection Group, convened after *Imagine North East* officially ended, effectively functioned as a co-inquiry group, and members of that group pulled together and developed material for this chapter.

Debates about co-produced research and community development

Research is often carried out in teams (especially in the natural sciences) and partnerships (for example, between companies, universities and government agencies). However, the term 'co-produced' tends to be used when the research team, partnership or group involves people who have a direct experience of, or interest in, the research topic (for example, young people, local residents) working as 'co-researchers' alongside academic or other 'professional' researchers (people who do research for a living). Hence co-produced research, as described in Chapter 1 of this book, is an umbrella term covering a variety of types of research, entailing diverse groups of people creating knowledge together.

This type of research is often undertaken as a way of bringing to the surface the existing experiential knowledge of people who may otherwise be marginalised or ignored, enabling them to create new knowledge and evidence that can contribute towards positive changes in their communities and in society. Described in this way, co-produced research almost inevitably entails both a process of community development (facilitating shared learning and engendering respect for diversity among a group of people with something in common) and community development outcomes (people feeling increased power and agency, development of new services/facilities). This helps explain why some critics question whether co-produced research is actually research at all – because it often looks and feels like community development.

What we call 'co-produced research' draws on a long tradition of participatory and action-oriented research, inspired by radical social movements concerned to democratise knowledge production (see, for example, Freire, 1972; Fals Borda, 1988; Smith, 1999) and counter what has come to be called 'epistemic injustice' (privileging powerful people's knowledge; see Fricker, 2007). These approaches to research may be more or less radical in practice, but what unites them is a commitment to an 'extended epistemology' (valuing experiential as well as theoretical knowledge) and a 'participatory worldview' (valuing inter-connectedness) (Heron, 1996; Reason, 1998; Heron and Reason, 2000). This means that co-produced research as we understand it is essentially a value-based practice, drawing extensively on theoretical and methodological traditions of participatory action research (Kindon et al, 2007; McIntyre, 2007; Kemmis et al, 2014).

The link between participatory action research (PAR) and community development is long established, and there have been some debates about whether PAR is just a particular approach to community development. As Grant et al (2008, p 298) comment: 'Some question whether PAR confuses community development with research.' Indeed, according to Krimerman (2001, p 63):

> ... there appears to be no way for PAR practitioners to distinguish good scientific research carried out according to their precepts from good community or social change organising.

This argument may have some justification, as it is difficult to separate the 'research' element from the community development process and outcomes in a PAR project. PAR is traditionally seen as comprising a recursive (continuous) cyclical process of moving from reflection to research to action to reflection and back again. There is not necessarily a point when it can be said 'this is research' or 'this is community development'; the processes are interwoven. Arguably what distinguishes PAR from community development is the intention of its practitioners. As Wadsworth (1998, p 7) comments: 'PAR sets out to *explicitly study* something in order to change and improve it' (emphasis added). This is how PAR differs from community development on its own:

- *PAR* is an approach to research that uses a community development process and leads to community development outcomes.
- *Community development* is a process of bringing people together in an egalitarian way to create social change. Sometimes it uses research, informally and formally, to provide evidence.

If a co-produced research project is a partnership between a research-focused organisation and a community development-focused organisation, each party may view what they are doing through different lenses. The research-focused organisation may regard their activities as research that takes a community development approach while the community organisation may regard their activities as community development with a research focus (see Banks, 2015). Some aspects of the organisation of *Imagine North East* tended to exacerbate these differences, as there were two substantive strands to the project: a university-led element studying community development practice from the 1970s to the present using fairly traditional methods (interviews, archival and statistical research), and a community organisation-led element that involved doing community development projects and reflecting on them. The third element, a co-inquiry group, was where the co-production was most explicitly built in. However, the creation of a 'co-inquiry space' – a space for co-production of new knowledge – was challenging to achieve, as the first two elements were happening in parallel, making attempts to interweave them quite difficult.

We now discuss each element of *Imagine North East* in turn, culminating with a discussion of co-inquiry and how this group of co-authors finally managed to reflect together on our learning and engage in collaborative reflexivity (critical reflection on how we, ourselves, worked as a group).

Element 1: Studying community development from the outside – Creating the context for *Imagine North East*

The starting point of *Imagine North East* was the community development projects (CDPs) that happened in Benwell and North Shields during 1973-78. These areas were selected as two of the 12 sites that comprised the Home Office's experimental National Community Development Project in the 1970s, as they were relatively 'deprived', suffering the effects of de-industrialisation, reducing employment opportunities, poor housing and other services and facilities. In *Imagine North East* our aim was to re-examine the North East CDPs of the 1970s, considering what happened and what the lessons and legacies were, as well as tracing the subsequent history of regeneration and community development in these areas, which still remain relatively 'deprived' today. This part of *Imagine North East* was essentially the context, or backdrop, against which the community-based projects were designed to be conducted and interpreted. Or, from another perspective, the community-based projects were designed to add contemporary texture and grassroots voices to the historical and policy backdrop.

The findings of this part of the *Imagine North East* project are published elsewhere (see Robinson and Townsend, 2016a, b; Armstrong and Banks, 2017; Banks and Carpenter, 2017; Green, 2017). Here we summarise some of the key points relevant to the theme of this chapter, in particular, the action–research focus of the CDPs and some of the reflections of local residents, current and past activists, community workers and policy-makers on past and contemporary community development processes and outcomes. This short section essentially provides the background for the following two sections, as it outlines the context for the study and the bigger picture into which the community projects described in the next section were deigned to fit.

The CDPs were described as 'action–research' projects (Lees, 1975), employing community development workers and researchers, with the aim that community development work would generate issues for research that would then inform community development practice and policy recommendations. The use of the hyphen in 'action–research' was, apparently, fought for by the CDP workers 'to demonstrate the linking of action and research in real time – not post-hoc evaluation of the action by detached researchers' (Banks and Carpenter, 2017, p 231). In many CDP teams, the researchers were based physically alongside the community development workers and there was some interchangeability of roles. They worked very closely with groups of local residents, collecting data for local campaigns and actions and producing pamphlets, leaflets and videos on topics such as social and housing conditions, changing employment patterns and property ownership. They also produced very detailed reports based on the collation of social and economic facts and figures, and statistical and political analyses of the global and structural causes of local economic and social problems (see, for example, North Tyneside CDP, 1978a, b; Benwell Community Project, 1978, 1979). These reports informed actions taken on the ground alongside local people, as well as contributing to bigger national campaigns and alliances with other CDPs and social movements of the time (CDP Inter-Project Editorial Team, 1977; CDPPEC, 1979).

One of the criticisms of the CDPs was that they focused excessively on politicised research and campaigning at the expense of community development processes on the ground (Thomas, 1983, p 34). However, the argument of the CDP workers was that unless they understood the broader political and policy context, they would be colluding with the original Home Office understanding that the solutions to the problems in these areas lay solely in mobilising local people to develop self-help schemes and creating better communication between social services. At the time the analysis produced by the CDPs was new, challenging and unwelcome to many in both central and local government. The CDPs argued that the problems in the CDP areas were not the fault of the people who lived there, but were caused by processes of de-industrialisation and the movement of capital to other parts of the world (National CDP, 1977), one facet of what is now widely described as 'globalisation'.

Following the CDPs, North Shields and the West End of Newcastle were subject to numerous regeneration schemes, including the development of the riverside area in North Shields and the demolition of large swathes of houses (especially in the West End of Newcastle) (Robinson and Townsend, 2016a, b). These regeneration programmes began to include increasing community consultation, involvement, engagement, participation and control over aspects of the agenda, and many of the community organisations involved in *Imagine* played significant roles in these processes. However, the overwhelming feeling of residents and CDP workers interviewed for *Imagine North East* during 2014-15 was that they were still marginal in the face of the juggernaut of major redevelopment schemes, as this interviewee commented:

> 'I feel like they ask you and then don't take any notice. They go ahead regardless of what you say.' (member of Riverside Women's Group, interview, Benwell, 2015)

Since the economic recession and impact of austerity measures on government spending, which gained momentum from 2010, large-scale regeneration schemes have waned (Wilks-Heeg, 2016). Many local groups are struggling while at the same time being encouraged to take over facilities and services formerly run by local authorities. For example, one of the *Imagine North East* community partners, Cedarwood Trust in North Shields, recently took over a much larger building from the local authority, expanding its range of activities to meet growing local needs.

This was the context in which the *Imagine North East* community partner organisations embarked on their own small community development projects, as discussed in the next section.

Element 2: Doing community development projects and reflecting on them from the inside

Twelve community-based organisations (four from North Shields, seven from Benwell and the Discovery Museum in Newcastle) participated in *Imagine North East*. Each planned a small project that could be delivered as part of their everyday work. The projects were coordinated and supported by Judith Green through St James' Centre for Heritage and Culture in Benwell. The projects involved workers and volunteers in each organisation engaging with residents and service users to explore aspects of the past, present and future of their neighbourhoods, using a variety of oral history, archival and creative methods. Judith also supported the projects to evaluate their work in the light of the *Imagine North East* themes, and to reflect on the outcomes achieved and learning gained. The projects are outlined in Tables 2.1, 2.2 and 2.3, grouped under the headings of: (1) Exploring community history and change over time; (2) Using arts-based activities to engage communities; and (3) Providing support and training for participants.

Table 2.1: Exploring community history and change over time

Organisation and project title	Description of project
Cedarwood Trust, North Shields *Imagining community at Cedarwood*	A family and community history project that built confidence and pride among participants, producing films, booklets, skills in oral history and further projects
Meadow Well Connected, North Shields *Bridging the history*	A community-led oral history project designed to create a positive image of the Meadow Well Estate, producing a timeline display, handling book, Facebook page and a short film of the streets of Meadow Well
Pendower Good Neighbour Project, Benwell *Time traveller*	Two inter-generational history projects involving local children: *Illuminating lives*, a performance and a lantern event in a local graveyard, and *Today's news, yesterday's history*, involving archive research, creating characters, arts-based activities, writing scripts, and promenade performance
Search, Benwell *Growing old in West Newcastle*	Engaging 300 older people in a series of events/trips to explore their lived experiences of change over time
St James' Heritage and Environment Group, Benwell *Filming change*	Creating a film of the historic graveyard in Benwell; participants learned filmmaking skills and a greater understanding of local history and the wider historical context
Discovery Museum (Tyne and Wear Archives and Museums), Newcastle *West End Stories*	Creating a website called West End Stories, exploring connections between personal experiences and wider historical events. This enabled the Museum to strengthen connections with community organisations

Drawing on the evaluations of each project (which involved interviews with some participants), case studies prepared for the Writing and Reflection Group (WRG) and discussions in the WRG, two broad themes emerged about the processes and outcomes of the projects. First, significant learning took place during and after the projects for the organisations, workers and service users/participants involved, through the development of new skills, networks and ideas. Second, a key theme stressed during the WRG was the importance of challenging the stigma attached to the places and people in Benwell and North Shields. We now examine each of these themes in turn.

Table 2.2: Using arts-based activities to engage people

Organisation and project title	Description of project
Phoenix Detached Youth Project, North Shields *A journey through time*	An inter-generational graffiti art project that produced a graffiti wall, film and inter-generational conversations
St James' Centre for Heritage and Culture, Benwell *Benwell in felt*	A felting art project involving 350 people reflecting on the area's past, present and future; they learned new skills, producing 27 pictures in felt, a book and an exhibition
Riverside Community Health Project, Benwell *Playing with change and ideas*	Creating a prototype mobile interactive toy made from recycled materials through a series of activities with local families
West Newcastle Picture History Collection, Newcastle *Remembering Benwell*	Using historical photos and maps to engage residents through a series of slide and film shows, themed ring-binders, framed photos, an exhibition, collecting and sharing new photos
Patchwork Project, Benwell *Hopes and fears*	A filmmaking project with young people, producing a film called *Hopes and Fears* with about 50 young people involved in filming and 12 in editing, from different ethnic backgrounds

Table 2.3: Providing support and training for participants

Organisation and project title	Description of project
Remembering the Past, Resourcing the Future (RPRF), North Shields *Training and support in oral history skills*	Providing support to North Shields projects through oral history and reminiscence training; acting as a 'buddy' during the process; support for exhibitions
St James' Centre for Heritage and Culture, Benwell *Coordination of all community projects*	Providing support and coordination of all community projects, producing final evaluation reports and coordinating exhibitions

Learning, developing and connecting

Based on interviews conducted by the community coordinator (Judith Green) with the lead person from each community organisation, and reflections and comments during events and the WRG, the development of new knowledge, understandings, skills and community capacity was significant, and was identified as follows:

Creating material knowledge

Many of the projects created artistic 'products' (such as felt pictures, films, graffiti art, booklets or photo displays), which could be regarded as 'material knowledge' in their own right (Carter, 2004). For example, Image 2.1 is a photograph of a picture in felt created by the children at Hadrian School, showing a play bus going down to the river, which is 'one of the things they would like to see happen in their area in the future' (St James' Heritage and Environment Group, 2015, p 39). Thus knowledge of the children's hopes is embodied in the picture. The graffiti art project organised by Phoenix Detached Youth Project in North Shields resulted in a very strong and striking visual statement, as shown in Image 2.2.

Image 2.1: Benwell in felt, 'The wheels on the bus', by Hadrian School

Photo: Judith Green

Developing creative and practical skills

Across the projects, participants consolidated existing skills and learned new ones in interviewing, archiving, filmmaking, arts and crafts, internet use and writing scripts. For example, one of the projects led by Pendower Good Neighbour Project, *Illuminating lives*, explored notable people buried in St James' Graveyard, Benwell. The children each chose a grave from the graveyard guide and imagined what the life of the person buried there would have been like. They conducted library research and participated in an historical tour around Grainger Town in Newcastle. They decided to present their findings at a lantern event in the graveyard:

> The children then agreed what kind of light or lantern would be best for each grave and then made them. We made lanterns from willow and tissue paper, lampshades, recycled cartons and lit the carriage drive with flaming cans. It all looked very spectacular. The children then led small groups around the installations and read a script about each grave. (Ruth Taylor, written case study for WRG, 2016)

Image 2.2: Graffiti art, North Shields, Phoenix Detached Youth Project

Photo: Phoenix Detached Youth Project

Building and extending relationships (especially intergenerational) through group work

Some projects involved people working in groups with people they did not know. Several projects also had inter-generational components. For example, the Phoenix project partnered well-known graffiti artists with young people and involved a "sharing of ideas and a crossing of cultures" (Luke Johnston, evaluation interview, 2014).

Developing understandings of the past and reclaiming community identity

Examining the past was an opportunity for the different community groups to reconnect with the history of their neighbourhoods and claim that "they mattered and still do". Yvonne Hall (Cedarwood Trust) commented during the WRG about their history project in North Shields:

> 'This project was an opportunity to honour the area they [residents] and their families had lived in, died in, had heartache and celebration in through listening, discussing, researching, learning, collating and producing, all collaboratively.'

Creating impacts and legacies

These projects benefited individuals, organisations and communities in numerous ways and were often part of an ongoing process of community development. Here is one example, from the Riverside Project in Benwell:

> We have decided to evaluate our women's work using a similar method to the *Imagine* work we undertook. An artist is working with the group to help them to reflect on their experiences at Riverside. Each woman is making a short book. (Anne Bonner, written case study for WRG, 2016)

Challenging stigma and celebrating place

A significant theme emerging strongly during the WRG was 'stigmatised neighbourhoods', including how residents can change the reputations of places where they live. We noted commonalities between Benwell and North Shields in the 1970s and how this continued into the present. For example, CDP areas were chosen because they were classified as 'deprived' in the late 1960s (Corkey, 1975). Both Benwell and North Shields experienced riots in the early 1990s (Campbell, 1993), contributing further to what Wacquant (2007) describes as 'territorial stigmatisation', and have been subject to numerous regeneration initiatives (Armstrong, 2010; Robinson and Townsend, 2016a, b). More recently, although housing and environmental conditions have improved, both areas are still relatively deprived within their local authorities, as illustrated by the Census statistics prepared for *Imagine North East* showing change between 1971 and 2011 (see www.durham.ac.uk/socialjustice/imagine).

Patrick Harman, visiting from the USA and working with the WRG during early 2016, commented that the discussions about stigma resonated very strongly with his work in High Point, North Carolina: "The baggage of an area is like a weight. It is hard to overcome a neighbourhood's reputation even when things have changed." One of the challenges facing 'notorious areas' is that print media (particularly local newspapers) publish sensationalist stories, reinforcing negative images and contributing to poor reputations and stigmatisation (Kearns et al, 2013). An example occurred in North Shields when a local newspaper ran a story about the Meadow Well riots because it was the 25th anniversary (Sharma, 2016). It is unsurprising, therefore, that challenging stigma and celebrating place was both an explicit and implicit theme of a number of *Imagine North East* projects. One example is *Bridging the history*, facilitated by Meadow Well Connected, a community organisation on the Meadow Well Estate in North Shields. A negative media portrayal, in this case a television programme, instigated local action, with social media playing a role in bringing the community together. A case study of this project is given below, drawn from the final evaluation report on the project and interviews with participants, community workers and visitors to an exhibition.

Case study 1: Bridging the history – Challenging stigma on the Meadow Well Estate

The *Bridging the history* project came about after a BBC television programme called *Living with Poverty: The Queen of North Shields* in 2013.[1] The 'Queen of North Shields' was a refugee from Africa, living with her husband on the Meadow Well Estate. According to the Chief Executive of Meadow Well Connected, many residents were unhappy about the programme because "it made lots of stereotypical accusations about people's lives on Meadow Well" (interview, Timeline launch, May 2014). According to a member of the *Bridging the history* group, the programme reinforced stereotypes such as:

> '… everyone's out of work, no one wants to work, everybody lives on the borderline…. It was awful the way it was portrayed.'

A few people who felt the same got together and made a post on Facebook asking if people wanted to meet, discuss the TV programme and decide what they could do to challenge perceptions. They were aware that if anyone did an internet search for Meadow Well or The Ridges (the former name of the estate):

'The first thing that comes up is the riots. The first and foremost. And it's wrong. Because there is other stuff, and there's good stuff.' (interview with member of *Bridging the history*, Timeline launch, May 2014)

To counter the stigma they embarked on their project to reclaim the history of the estate by creating an illustrated timeline of events and developments they thought were significant. Starting in January 2014, a small group of people, facilitated by Philippa Southall (a worker at Meadow Well Connected) met weekly at The Meadows community centre in North Shields. It was the first *Imagine North East* project to finish, and the timeline was launched in May 2014. Several visitors at the launch commented on how important it was to challenge negative perceptions and celebrate place:

'I think it's a going forward thing, and it's moving away from the riots, and having a more positive spin on the place. It has a better history than that.' (interview, Timeline launch, May 2014)

The event was opened by Norma Redfearn, elected mayor of North Tyneside, who commented:

'I really think this is a wonderful project, because what it does is give everyone in this particular community a purpose, because they all want to tell a story about what happened to them, their families, and keeping them together. They've got so much to celebrate really, because they've had a lot of issues to deal with in this community, but the strength of the community has kept them going.' (interview, Timeline launch, May 2014)

As this case study shows, the Meadow Well Estate suffers from a persisting poor reputation, not just locally, but also nationally and internationally. The sociologist Wacquant (2007, p 68) even mentions Meadow Well by name, alongside the Bronx (New York) and Cabrini Green (Chicago) as experiencing 'territorial stigmatization linked to zones reserved for the urban outcasts'. He describes these areas of 'advanced marginality' as:

... increasingly perceived by both outsiders and insiders as social purgatories, leprous Badlands at the heart of the postindustrial metropolis where only the refuse of society would accept to dwell. (Wacquant, 2007, p 67)

It is precisely this kind of unfounded reputation that the Meadow Well residents were keen to dispel. It is not clear whether Wacquant ever visited Meadow Well (he mistakenly locates it in Newcastle), but he makes the point that:

> Whether or not these areas are in fact dilapidated and dangerous, and their population composed essentially of poor people, minorities and foreigners, matters little in the end: the prejudicial belief that they are suffices to set off socially noxious consequences. (Wacquant, 2007, p 68)

Benwell in the West End of Newcastle has similar reputational problems, although not named in Wacquant's international roll call of 'neighbourhoods of relegation'. The second case study is of the *Benwell in felt* project, the starting point of which was the celebration of place, which also served as a counter-story to an out-dated negative reputation linked with riots, poor housing and environment.

Case study 2: Benwell in felt – Celebrating place

Benwell in felt was coordinated by St James' Centre for Heritage and Culture Partnership, a voluntary group based in Benwell. Designed as an intergenerational cross-community initiative, it brought together groups of people of different ages, abilities, ethnic backgrounds and neighbourhoods to create an exhibition of felt pictures, depicting what people thought was significant and valuable about their area. The craft of felting was chosen as it is easy with the right materials and training, can be accomplished by a group working together, and produces attractive and colourful finished products, even if people have limited experience, skills and abilities.

An estimated 350 people participated from 19 different local groups and organisations, producing 27 felt pictures, examples of which are shown in Images 2.1 and 2.3. The completed pictures were launched in September 2014 at St James' Church at the opening of the Benwell and Scotswood Community Arts Festival. The exhibition was met with such enthusiasm that the group was invited to exhibit it at Newcastle's main library in the city centre, where it was officially opened at an event attended by the local MP, councillors and other interested people as well as some of those who had participated in the felting. The exhibition was on show during April 2015, thus reaching a larger audience.

The pictures are now permanently displayed in the Carnegie Centre (the former Benwell Library building adjacent to St James' Church, which has been developed by the Riverside Project as a community facility). This secured the long-term future for the pictures in a location where they can be seen by residents and may stimulate future discussions about the changing area. A book was created called *Never felt so good* (St James' Heritage and Environment Group, 2015), featuring photographs of each felting picture accompanied by descriptions of what they depict and relevant photographs of the area showing the process of change. These pictures were described as helping to:

> ... put the area on the map as a place of interest for reasons of culture and heritage rather than for its history of poverty, disadvantage and social unrest.... The individual images produced have shown in very different ways how much people value aspects of their physical environment and their community. In light of the dramatic changes experienced in the past decade, which have left large areas of former residential land as empty patches of mud, and the failed promises of large scale regeneration, we had expected some of the felting pictures to show negative images. This did not happen. Instead there was a clear emphasis on the positive. Nevertheless, there was a distinct sense of loss embodied in several of the pictures representing valued places and organisations that had disappeared or declined. (St James' Heritage and Environment Group, 2015)

Image 2.3: Benwell in felt, 'Working with young people' by Patchwork Youth project

Photo: Judith Green

These two case studies illustrate the important role of local community organisations in bringing together different groups of residents to take action together, not just to preserve and develop community facilities and support networks, but also to develop the social and cultural capital of an area through changing perceptions and attitudes and developing pride and a sense of belonging. Taking the long view through exploring the histories of places and their location in bigger political and economic changes helps us understand and appreciate the present and look forward to the future. We now look in a little more detail at how the learning from each of the separate community-based projects was drawn together.

Element 3: Co-inquiry – Bringing the outside and inside together, creating connections and new knowledge

In order to hold the project together, make sense of complexity and co-produce new knowledge and learning, the original conception of *Imagine North East*, as outlined in the research bid, had at its heart a co-inquiry action research (CAR) group that would meet quarterly. This collaborative approach to research had been developed and used successfully by the academic partners in previous projects (Banks and Armstrong et al, 2014), drawing on a co-inquiry model. Co-inquiry entails bringing people together in a facilitated group to study a topic of interest to them, drawing particularly on their own experiential knowledge. There are many examples of co-inquiry groups that comprise peers (people at the same level or with similar experience) in workplaces and community organisations, and some that include people from diverse backgrounds with different statuses and access to power, such as academics, students, residents and community workers (see Reason and Rowan, 1981).

Whole group meetings: The challenges of creating connections

The collaborators in *Imagine North East* included academics, voluntary and paid workers from community organisations and a museum. Each participant/organisation brought their own experiences of research collaborations, varying from no experience of research to being heavily involved, with some describing past negative experiences. There was resistance to the idea of 'co-inquiry' meetings by some members of community organisations on two counts. First, the prospect of quarterly meetings was questioned, as people were busy and wanted to contain the amount of time spent on the *Imagine* project. Second, both the terminology and concept of 'co-inquiry' were questioned by the community coordinator and some community partners, who wanted to know what they had to do to complete their projects, rather than spending time getting to know each other and undertaking group exercises. As a result, attendance at quarterly gatherings of representatives of the community organisations and key academics was made voluntary and they were simply called 'meetings', with agenda items for report and discussion and some spaces created for sharing and reflecting. Even this was too much for some members of community organisations, who felt the meetings were too long and unfocused. The academics, on the other hand, were concerned to create sufficient space for sharing and creating knowledge together, on which the project was premised. For each person, experience of the group was different – some were (or became) more positive about its value than others. As Kath Smith commented, when reflecting later in the WRG: "The meeting schedule was heavy, but over the period there was a process of unconscious learning and development."

The Writing and Reflection Group: Connecting and creating new knowledge

The WRG, which was set up after the project officially ended, ran more smoothly and functioned, in effect, as a co-inquiry group. It comprised academics and representatives of community organisations who volunteered to participate. By this time we knew each other quite well, had built up mutual trust and were better able to process the learning from the project.

The WRG met three times to review learning from *Imagine North East* and develop material for this chapter. Six community partners volunteered with three academics during February–April 2016. Working in pairs or small groups and then feeding back to the whole group, the aim was to facilitate critical reflection, share ideas and identify key themes for the chapter. Each person wrote a case study from their perspective, reflecting on the process, successes and challenges encountered. We also drew on the numerous interviews, reports and statistical analyses already conducted as part of *Imagine North East*. At the final meeting a skeleton draft chapter was agreed. This was developed further by Sarah Banks and Andrea Armstrong, shared with all co-authors of the chapter and editors of this book, substantially revised and then sent to all project partners in *Imagine North East* for additional comments. We were not able to incorporate all comments in the final version, due both to space constraints and a desire not to overwhelm readers with too much complexity.

In this chapter, therefore, we consider just two key themes generated by WRG members in their reflections on *Imagine North East*. The first is how working together enabled people to gradually see more of the bigger picture of which they were a part – historically, regionally and internationally. This could be described as one of the outcomes of the project. The second theme relates to the process of working together and making connections: how this changed over time, what we learned from studying the process and how we engaged in a kind of 'collaborative reflexivity' (Finlay, 2002, p 220; Banks and Armstrong et al, 2014, p 45) as we reflected on the workings of our own group.

'Seeing the bigger picture': Connecting through reflecting, remembering, re-thinking and re-imagining

Reflections generated as part of the WRG revealed that participation in *Imagine North East* led to being able to 'see the bigger picture' through making connections in several ways:

1. Beyond the everyday and local – through regional, national and international networks.
2. Beyond the 'here' and 'now' – through exploring history and imagining the future.
3. Beyond talking and writing – through visual and audio materials and exhibitions.

We briefly elaborate now on each of these points.

1. Beyond the everyday and local: Connecting through wider networks

For some partners, being part of *Imagine North East* provided time, space and encouragement for reflection on the wider context in which they operated – offering a critical distance from everyday work:

> 'This project encouraged us to *reflect*. We never have any time these days for reflection.' (Ruth Taylor, discussion during WRG, 2016)

> 'It gave us *the breathing space to reflect* on the role of youth projects in developing graffiti art, and re-address the riots

and developments since the 1980s and what has or hasn't changed.' (Luke Johnston, discussion during WRG, 2016)

This reflective space for engaging with others from different organisations and with different experiences – reminiscent of what Torre and Fine et al (2008) talk about as 'contact zones' – enabled the work of re-thinking priorities, raising consciousness about the bigger picture and making connections beyond the everyday and local:

> This project was useful in *re-focusing us on wider and longer-term issues* rather than focusing just on how to tackle presenting immediate issues. (Anne Bonner, written case study for WRG, 2016)

> 'Looking at the *bigger picture* of the Meadow Well Estate and how people moved there, it shows there is a huge diversity of backgrounds on The Ridges [as it was called].' (Yvonne Hall, discussion during WRG, 2016)

The benefits of engaging with people working in different parts of the *Imagine* project, including collaborators from the USA, Crete and Germany, was also enormously valuable in placing the problems and issues of North East England in a global context.

2. Beyond the 'here' and 'now': Connecting through history

A focus on history helped situate people and places throughout time and in the future, stimulating a process of remembering and re-imagining:

> It was useful to understand the history of the area better and also the subculture as this helped us to better understand why the attitudes that are around now may have been formed. It also allowed us to look at what the issues were in the 1980s and what has or hasn't been done to address them. (Luke Johnston, written case study for WRG, 2016)

> By imagining the past this made us think about what our community is like now which in turn may help us to imagine the future. (Ruth Taylor, written case study for WRG, 2016)

3. Beyond 'talking' and 'writing': Connecting through materials and exhibitions

The locally produced materials from the *Imagine North East* projects also mobilised connections and generated wider interest outside the area, especially those of a heritage and arts-based nature, demonstrated by the various exhibitions held in Newcastle and North Shields (Armstrong et al, 2016a, b) and the collection of digital West End stories at the Discovery Museum in Newcastle. Some pieces were displayed outside the region, including one of the *Benwell in felt* pictures by The Co-op Guild (a long-standing local group linked with the cooperative movement), which was displayed at a national Co-op conference. These materials communicated with people at an emotional level, generating responses and memories (for example, West Newcastle Picture History Collection's framed photographs and an exhibition of maps of Benwell through the ages).

There is no doubt that for many people 'seeing the bigger picture' was very important in terms of developing a greater understanding of other organisations, becoming less insular, widening horizons and making connections. Indeed, involvement in *Imagine North East* was seen as a valuable, if not unique, networking opportunity, laying the basis for possible joint work, new ideas and other benefits in the future:

> 'It's about investing. So, if you decide to do a project, like something similar to the timeline at Meadow Well, you might be able to go and have a look at their things and know the people that are there, and – you know – get some ideas. That's all. Nothing complex or completely solid. It's just about knowing different organisations.' (Clare Levi, evaluation interview, Search project, 2015)

It takes time to connect

We have already mentioned the difficulties of the whole project quarterly gatherings. These in themselves constituted a process of community development, as a diverse group of people came together to work on a shared project. While those people working in the same area already knew each other, Benwell and North Shields are 12 miles apart and participants from the two areas were not familiar with each other. Like all groups, it went through various stages of development (Heron, 1999, pp 51–68; Doel, 2006), with some similarities to the 'community of practice' described in Chapter 4 on research retreats.

Andrea Armstrong, Durham University Research Associate, felt that the co-inquiry aspect of the project was the most challenging:

> Calling them [whole project gatherings] "meetings" meant they became just that – with Durham University chairing each of the eight meetings held over two years. We anticipated that community partners would lead meetings too. We did not want the "University" to be seen as the sole "experts" and decisions and control of the research process were meant to be shared. (Andrea Armstrong, written case study for WRG, 2016)

Sarah Banks (Durham University, Coordinator of *Imagine North East*) reported being greatly exercised about how best to facilitate the meetings, reflecting in the WRG (2016) that she "struggled to maintain everyone's interest and hold the group together". For the last meeting of the WRG she prepared Table 2.4, illustrating the phases of the group as she saw them.

One of the main messages from the discussions in the WRG was that it takes time to build a community-university partnership. The complexities of the project and different agendas of different individuals

Table 2.4: The *Imagine North East* journey

Time period	Theme identified	Description
1. Early phase Spring/summer 2014	Confusion and separateness	*Confusion:* 'What is this about, what is required?' Each organisation was separately doing their own projects to meet 'outcomes', wondering how much time to give to *Imagine North East* meetings when busy with everyday work
2. Middle phase Autumn 2014 to autumn 2015	Some dissatisfaction and some celebration of success	*Mixed feelings:* Some people felt meetings were too long and unfocused: 'Is this really relevant to us?' Some celebration of successes and outputs (eg, *Benwell in felt*, Phoenix graffiti art, Meadow Well timeline) and making displays for conferences and exhibitions that focused on each project's achievements in the context of all projects and *Imagine North East*
3. Last phase Winter 2015 to spring 2016, extending to autumn 2016	Deeper dialogue and understanding	*Gelling as a group:* Digging deeper, more dialogue with each other. Preparing for Benwell and North Shields exhibitions and workshops. Smaller and more focused WRG and preparation for *Imagine* national exhibition, Sheffield

and organisations meant it took longer and was more challenging than expected. Some of the challenges and lessons we identified for building a co-inquiry group over time are shown in Table 2.5, which are relevant to all co-produced research. Although listed separately, there is overlap between them.

Table 2.5: Challenges and lessons for building a co-inquiry group over time

Challenge	Lesson learned
A variety of understandings and experiences of research in general and confusion about structures and aims of the specific research project	A shared aim, purpose and vision takes time to develop and cannot be assumed at the start of a project. The focus of the WRG was much clearer as it had a defined purpose
A lack of enthusiasm for attending co-inquiry meetings	Reaching an agreement on all aspects of involvement (including meetings) at the start of the project is vital to ensure a commitment to a shared vision. The WRG was well attended
Feelings of mistrust towards universities and research projects	Time is needed for people to get to know each other and their organisations, and to develop trusting relationships, where concerns can be expressed and disagreements openly acknowledged
Working with commonalities and differences	It is important to listen to each other and appreciate differences. Not everyone was comfortable with small group work, experiential exercises and reflecting collaboratively in the *Imagine North East* group. Group work can be introduced gradually and its purpose needs to be explained
Variable skills in collaborative and reflexive working	For some people, collaborative working and reflecting on learning comes naturally, and for others it does not. These skills can be developed slowly through practice. They were very evident in the WRG
The complexity of facilitation – maintaining everyone's interest and holding the group together	The role of a group facilitator is complex, and is not the same as chairing a meeting. It involves planning ways to engage people, drawing out experiences and creating spaces for dialogue. While the whole group meetings tended to be chaired, interspersed with small facilitated exercises, the WRG was carefully facilitated both by the Durham University Coordinator and by members of the group themselves, who started to take on roles of responsibility for ensuring its smooth running

Conclusions and lessons learned

In this chapter we have attempted to draw together some of the learning from a complex co-produced research project, *Imagine North East*.

The project had a substantive focus on community development as a topic of study; entailed elements of doing community development in local neighbourhoods; and involved reflecting on the learning through co-inquiry (which was itself a community development process). Most co-produced projects do not have such an intense focus on community development. However, in much co-produced research the co-researchers are from community-based organisations and collaborative projects tend to involve some kind of project group, research team or community of practice, which develops over time. So community development processes and outcomes might be expected, even if they are not consciously designed into a research project or identified and examined by the partners.

In the case of *Imagine North East*, the explicit community development focus and relevant experience of the community partners and academics meant we were readily able to identify what we were doing as community development. Indeed, the focus was so much on community development, especially in the community-based projects, that at times the research element was relegated to the background and more than once representatives of community organisations asked: "How is what we are doing research?" One answer relates to the intentionality of the people asking the question: whether they conceive of themselves as practitioner-researchers (with a hyphen) and think they are creating new knowledge and reflecting on the practice of community development. Identities develop and change over time, and to see community development activities also as research, and ourselves as practitioner-researchers, emerges in the context of a group of co-researchers/practitioners undergoing a journey of discovery together, and coming to see their work as 'community development-research'.

Some of the lessons learned from our experience with *Imagine North East* include:

- The value of taking an historical lens to understand the present and imagine the future, especially in post-industrial neighbourhoods affected by territorial stigmatisation.
- When working with diverse groups and organisations with different priorities and understandings, it takes time and commitment to create together a shared learning space that facilitates co-existence, cross-fertilisation and eventually collective action.

Acknowledgements

We are grateful to all the representatives of the *Imagine North East* partner organisations who contributed to the work described in this chapter, particularly Judith Green who coordinated the community projects, undertook interviews and evaluations and commented on this chapter. We are grateful to those who agreed to be interviewed and supplied information, the Economic and Social Research Council (ESRC) for funding the research, and Durham University's Research Impact Fund for contributing to the WRG expenses.

Note

[1] See www.open.edu/openlearn/whats-on/tv/ou-on-the-bbc-living-poverty

References

Armstrong, A. (2010) 'Creating sustainable communities in Newcastle, Gateshead', Unpublished PhD thesis, Durham: Department of Geography, Durham University.

Armstrong, A. and Banks, S. (2017) 'Organizing for change: North Tyneside Community Development Project and its legacy', *Community Development Journal*, 52(2), 290-312.

Armstrong, A., Banks, S. and Harman, P. (2016a) *Report: Imagining Benwell Workshop and Exhibition – Community Development in Benwell and the West End of Newcastle: From the National Community Development Project to 'Our Place' and beyond,* Durham: Centre for Social Justice and Community Action, Durham University (www.dur.ac.uk/socialjustice/imagine).

Armstrong, A., Banks, S. and Harman, P. (2016b) *Report: Imagining North Shields Workshop and Exhibition – Community development and engagement in North Shields: From the National Community Development Project to 'My Community',* Durham: Centre for Social Justice and Community Action, Durham University (www.dur.ac.uk/socialjustice/imagine).

Banks, S. (2015) 'Action research for social justice: Researching and organising on household debt', in L. Hardwick, R. Smith and A. Worsley (eds) *Innovations in social work research: Using methods creatively*, London: Jessica Kingsley Publishers, 18-39.

Banks, S. and Armstrong, A., with Booth, M., Brown, G., Carter, K., Clarkson, M., Corner, L., Genus, A., et al (2014) 'Using co-inquiry to study co-inquiry: Community-university perspectives on research collaboration', *Journal of Community Engagement and Scholarship*, 7(1), 37-47.

Banks, S. and Carpenter, M. (2017) 'Researching the local politics and practices of radical community development projects in 1970s Britain', *Community Development Journal*, 52(2), 226-46 (https://doi.org/10.1093/cdj/bsx001).

Benwell Community Project (1978) *Permanent unemployment, Benwell Community Project, Final report, series no 2*, Newcastle-upon-Tyne: Benwell Community Project.

Benwell Community Project (1979) *The making of the ruling class, Final report, series no 6*, Newcastle-upon-Tyne: Benwell Community Project.

Campbell, B. (1993) *Goliath: Britain's dangerous places,* London: Methuen.

Carter, P. (2004) *Material thinking: The theory and practice of creative research*, Melbourne, VIC: Melbourne University Publishing.

CDP (Community Development Project) Inter-Project Editorial Team (1977) *Gilding the ghetto: The state and the poverty experiments*, London: CDP Inter-Project Editorial Team.

CDPPEC (Community Development Project Political Economy Collective) (1979) *The state and the local economy*, Newcastle: CDPPEC.

Corkey, D. (1975) 'Early stages in North Tyneside CDP', in R. Lees and G. Smith (eds) *Action-research in community development*, London: Routledge & Kegan Paul, 47-50.

Doel, M. (2006) *Using groupwork*, London: Routledge.

Fals Borda, O. (1988) *Knowledge and people's power: Lessons with peasants in Nicaragua, Mexico and Colombia*, New Delhi: Indian Social Institute.

Finlay, L. (2002) 'Negotiating the swamp: The opportunity and challenge of reflexivity in research practice', *Qualitative Research*, 2(2), 209-30.

Freire, P. (1972) *The pedagogy of the oppressed*, London: Penguin.

Fricker, M. (2007) *Epistemic injustice: Power and the ethics of knowing*, Oxford: Oxford University Press.

Grant, J., Nelson, G. and Mitchell, T. (2008) 'Negotiating the challenges of participatory action research: Relationships, power, participation, change and credibility', in P. Reason and H. Bradbury (eds) *The Sage handbook of action research: Participative inquiry and practice* (2nd edn), London: Sage, 589-601.

Green, J. (2017) 'Action-research in context: Revisiting the 1970s Benwell Community Development Project', *Community Development Journal*, 52(2), 269-89.

Heron, J. (1996) *Co-operative inquiry: Research into the human condition*, London: Sage.

Heron, J. (1999) *The complete facilitator's handbook*, London: Kogan Page.

Heron, J. and Reason, P. (2000) 'The practice of cooperative inquiry: Research "with" rather than "on" people', in P. Reason and H. Bradbury (eds) *Handbook of action research*, London: Sage, 179-88.

Kearns, A., Kearns, O.and Lawson, L. (2013) 'Notorious places: Image, reputation and stigma. The role of newspapers in area reputations for social housing estates', *Housing Studies*, 28(4), 579-98.

Kemmis, S., McTaggart, R. and Nixon, R. (2014) *The action research planner: Doing critical participatory action research*, Singapore: Springer.

Kindon, S., Pain, R. and Kesby, M. (eds) (2007) *Participatory action research approaches and methods: Connecting people, participation and place*, Abingdon: Routledge.

Krimerman, L. (2001) 'Participatory action research: Should social inquiry be conducted democratically?', *Philosophy of the Social Sciences*, 31(1), 60-82.

Lees, R. (1975) 'The action-research relationship', in R. Lees and G. Smith (eds) *Action-research in community development*, London: Routledge & Kegan Paul, 59-66.

Loney, M. (1983) *Community against government: The British Community Development Project 1968-78*, London: Heinemann Educational Books.

McIntyre, A. (2007) *Participatory action research*, Qualitative Research Methods Series 52, Thousand Oaks, CA: Sage.

National CDP (Community Development Project) (1977) *The costs of industrial change: Industry, the state and the older urban areas*, London: CDP Information and Intelligence Unit.

North Tyneside CDP (Community Development Project) (1978a) *North Shields: Organising for change in a working class area, North Tyneside CDP final report, vol 3*, Newcastle: Newcastle-upon-Tyne Polytechnic.

North Tyneside CDP (Community Development Project) (1978b) *North Shields: Working class politics and housing, 1900-1977, Final report, series no 1*, North Shields: North Tyneside CDP.

Reason, P. (1998) 'A participatory world', *Resurgence*, 168, 42-4.

Reason, P.and Rowan, J. (1981) *Human Inquiry. A sourcebook of new paradigm research*, Chichester: John Wiley.

Robinson, F. and Townsend, A. (2016a) *Forty years on: Policy and change in Benwell after the community development project*, Durham: Centre for Social Justice and Community Action, Durham University (www. dur.ac.uk/socialjustice/imagine).

Robinson, F. and Townsend, A. (2016b) *Forty years on: Policy and change in North Shields after the community development project*, Durham: Centre for Social Justice and Community Action, Durham University (www. dur.ac.uk/socialjustice/imagine).

Sharma, S. (2016) 'Meadow Well riots 25 years on: An estate ravaged by violence shows little sign of its scars', *Chronicle Live*, 8 September (www.chroniclelive.co.uk/news/north-east-news/meadow-well-riots-25-years-11848759).

Smith, L. (1999) *Decolonizing methodologies: Research and indigenous peoples*, London: Zed Books.

St James' Heritage and Environment Group (2015) *Never felt so good: Benwell and Scotswood in felt*, Newcastle: St James' Heritage and Environment Group (https://stjameschurchnewcastle.files.wordpress.com/2015/05/feltbook_lores.pdf).

Thomas, D. (1983) *The making of community work*, London: Allen & Unwin.

Torre, M.E. and Fine, M., with Alexander, N., Bilal Billups, A., Blanding, Y., Genao, E., Marboe, E., Salah, T. and Urdang, K. (2008) 'Participatory action research in the contact zone', in J. Cammarota and M. Fine (eds) *Revolutionising education: Youth participatory action research in motion*, New York: Routledge, 23-44.

Wacquant, L. (2007) 'Territorial stigmatization in the age of advanced marginality', *Thesis Eleven*, 91, 66-77.

Wadsworth, Y. (1998) *What is participatory action research?*, Action Research International, Paper 2 (www.aral.com.au/ari/p-ywadsworth98.html).

Wilks-Heeg, S. (2016) 'Urban policy and communities', in D. O'Brien and P. Matthews (eds) *After urban regeneration: Communities, policy and place*, Bristol: Policy Press, 9-26.

THREE

A radical take on co-production? Community partner leadership in research

Susanne Martikke, Andrew Church and Angie Hart

Introduction

In this chapter, we examine a research collaboration between Susanne Martikke, Research Officer at the Greater Manchester Centre for Voluntary Organisation (GMCVO), and two academics from the University of Brighton, Andrew Church and Angie Hart. Because all of the partners were professional researchers, the research collaboration has to be seen as a very specific case. It would have been more challenging for someone who was not a professional researcher to play the role Susanne played on the project. However, it must also be acknowledged that being a researcher in a voluntary and community sector (VCS) organisation like GMCVO differs from being a researcher at the university in several ways:

- The operating context and expectations placed on research are different.
- The nature of research undertaken differs.
- The nature of publications does not follow the same conventions.
- Although Susanne had 10 years' practical experience of researching the VCS, she did not have an academic qualification in social research or a PhD. Therefore, from a traditional academic perspective, her credibility as a researcher was constrained.

Initially Susanne's lack of traditional academic credibility automatically placed her into a subordinate position in the hierarchy of project partners. As a result, despite its differences, this community–university partnership (CUP) still had some of the same power dynamics as other CUPs. It was necessary for those involved to overcome these unequal power relations.

The project was part of the larger *Imagine* study. This collaboration was a CUP, and the subject of the research was also CUPs. Therefore, this project afforded us the opportunity to study 23 cases of CUP working across England and Scotland while also reflecting on our own partnership research practice.

Public engagement through CUPs can take various shapes, with research collaborations being one of many possibilities. In this chapter we are interested in exploring the research aspects specifically. The majority of our case studies also contained a research dimension.

In recent years there has been an increase in partnership working between sectors internationally, for example, between the VCS, and the public and private sectors (NCCPE, 2011). In the UK specifically, since the election of Tony Blair's New Labour government in 1997 the voluntary sector had increasingly been perceived as an attractive partner in the delivery of public services (O'Brien and Matthews, 2015). The main driver for this was the intention to reform public services by making them more responsive to existing needs in the community. However, the recent reductions in support for VCS organisations have often limited their capacity to play this role. VCS organisations have been touted as perfectly positioned to connect to segments of the population considered 'hard to reach', and being knowledgeable about the types of needs these potential service users have. An iteration of this trend that is explored in this chapter is the involvement of voluntary organisations (alongside statutory agencies and other community partners), in CUPs. These are increasingly common entities in many different countries. CUPs are typically defined as a relationship in which anyone from the community who is not at the university collaborates in some shape or form with someone from the university who acts as a member of the university and not as a citizen in some other capacity (Facer and Enright, 2016).

In many ways, community involvement in research as part of a VCS organisation's community development role is slightly less intuitive to most people than other forms of community engagement by universities. Examples of this include student placements or community access to university resources, such as museums and art galleries (Laing and Maddison, 2007). With regard to research partnerships, the community partner is often relegated to the role of the recipient of knowledge. If knowledge exchange is the intention, they are understood to be the provider of very limited practical knowledge, such as access to research participants and, when it comes to dissemination, policy-makers and other potential research users (Beebeejaun et al, 2015). There is acknowledgement of the VCS in specific forms of research, such as community-based participatory research (CBPR) or action research. This research can take the form of working with communities to support community development rather than doing research about them (Kindon et al, 2007). However, research collaborations that are not specifically indebted to such models are still often conceptualised in terms of knowledge transfer or knowledge exchange. In this model knowledge is situated in the university, and is made available to entities outside of the university, similar to a consultancy service (Facer et al, 2012).

This dynamic may be explained by the fact that, traditionally knowledge exchange or transfer activities had focused on collaborations between universities and commercial businesses in the private sector. In this case the extent of the collaboration was perhaps limited by necessity because of the need for research to be seen as neutral from mercantile interests. However, in 2006 the Higher Education Funding Council for England (HEFCE) stated in its 2006 strategic plan that academics needed to pursue partnerships with sectors of society other than private business, and stressed that 'innovation in public services and the not-for-profit sector will be equally important to the nation as business innovation' (HEFCE, 2006, p 13).

The way academic work is assessed has also changed (Manners and Duncan, 2017). Introduced in 1986, Research Assessment Exercises (RAE) were the main instrument for accountability of higher education research until 2008. RAEs recurred every five to six years. These were found internationally and produced league tables of universities that influenced the distribution of research funding based on the quality of university research and the environment that supports research (Manners and Duncan, 2017). In 2014 this activity changed slightly, when the Research Excellence Framework (REF) was introduced. Alongside assessing the quality of university research in terms of what is produced and the supporting environment, the REF also places a certain emphasis on the impact of research on the wider economy and society (NCCPE, 2017). This encourages collaborative approaches to research, and for some types of research community partner organisations are often seen as appropriately positioned to ensure that research findings reach the right audiences to make an impact in society.

These developments have prompted academics to collaborate with community partners, including voluntary organisations, on research. However, from the community perspective there are a number of concerns about the equity of these partnerships and the applicability of existing models of research collaborations for non-profit-making entities. This is often due to the large power differential between universities and community-based groups. Another challenge is the fact that 'There is an absence of established models for how to do this kind of work with the public and particularly the community and voluntary sectors' (Laing and Maddison, 2007, p 14).

In summary, community partners, including voluntary organisations, are more likely to be approached by academics for joint work. It is useful to reflect, as we do in this chapter, on how our partnership worked (within the context of our findings about other CUPs) and to extract the lessons relevant for community partners based in the voluntary sector.

The partnership and the project

Our partnership was situated in a research project that collected data about other, similar, partnerships. The study used interviews, focus groups, memory stories, analysis of data from existing consultation and engagement processes. This approach was taken to give a maximum number of CUPs the opportunity to be included in the study. The interviews were conducted with both partners involved in a given CUP. Depending on the preferences of the participants and on scheduling constraints, interviews were either conducted as joint interviews or with each partner separately.

Different aspects we explored as part of our research were: what characterises such partnerships, how they benefit partners, the challenges they face and what the future might hold for this type of partnership work. Although we were interested in a diverse range of partnerships, we also wanted to feature case studies that seemed to present the most potential for yielding principles of successful partnership working, as well as provide inspiration for others working in this field.

Table 3.1 gives an overview of the characteristics of the CUPs that were included in our study. As Table 3.1 shows, we included as diverse a range of CUPs as possible in terms of partnership age. We wanted to include a sizeable number of partnerships that had been in existence for a relatively long period of time in order to draw out some learning from these. However, it also seemed important to capture CUPs that were younger and had just been formed, in order to understand what factors played a role in influencing the different stages of partnership working.

Table 3.1: Partnership demographics

Characteristic	Number of partnerships in study
Age of CUP	
Less than one year	3
Just over a year	3
Several years	7
Ongoing[a] and more than several years	9
Not applicable (project completed)	1
Subject domain	
Arts and humanities	4
Criminal justice	3
Education	3
Health and social care	6
International development	1
Urban planning/regeneration	2
Miscellaneous (CUP does not have one specific subject)	4
Main engagement mechanism	
Community development	3
Staff volunteering	2
Networks	2
Research	7
Linked to a research centre	3
Student placements	3
Training	1
Miscellaneous (CUP uses various engagement mechanisms)	2

Note: [a] This category is also used where CUPs have been around for so long that it was difficult to pin down where the CUP began and when, if ever, it would end. It appears that these have just become an integral part of the fabric of how work is done for all partners involved.

The subject domains of the cases reflect areas in which community partner organisations make an important contribution in their own right, such as criminal justice, health and social care, urban planning/ regeneration and education. In light of the arts and humanities focus of the overall *Imagine* study, we also included partnerships that worked in the arts and humanities.

The sample also contains four CUPs in the miscellaneous category. These include CUPs that use student placements where the focus of activity differs depending on the host organisation and one CUP that uses a consultancy approach to respond to a wide range of community partners' needs.

There is a strong research component in the sample, but CUP activity involving networks, student placements and staff volunteering were also included. CUPs in various locations in the UK were included, but given the base of the lead researcher, there is an emphasis on the North West.

Our own CUP was similar to or different from most of the CUPs we studied in the following ways:

- It was very new.
- Its main engagement mechanism was research, as with seven others in our overall sample.
- As a CUP that studied CUPs we were researching ourselves; in that sense we 'walked the walk but also talked the talk'.
- Aligning the subject of the study with the method of delivery meant that we could be seen as peers by participants.
- We did have a social justice agenda, in that we hoped the research findings would make an impact in the real world by raising awareness of CUPs and outlining how co-production could be achieved and what its benefits would be.

The following section outlines other ways in which our partnership was similar to the ones we studied.

The beginning of our research partnership

Our collaboration started in the same way as most of those in our sample – through personal relationships facilitating the realisation of a shared passion after being introduced to each other by personal contacts. Partnering on this research study was motivated by a shared concern about the role that is often assigned to community partners in CUPs. All of us had personal experience of this problem. Angie and Andrew have been involved with the Community University Partnership Programme (CUPP) at the University of Brighton since its inception in 2003. The CUPP is one of the pioneers in community engagement in the UK. In her role as researcher at GMCVO, Susanne had been collaborating with academics in a variety of forms, often to support community development. GMCVO is also an organisation that has had a strong stance about voluntary sector collaborators in CUPs being valued properly.

It was clear that we would have to consider how our collaboration might be a partnership in the true sense of the word. We were more interested in finding inspiring examples of CUP working than focusing on the cliché problems and challenges; even inspiring CUPs that start out with the best intentions for co-production face challenges. The difference is that they find ways around these challenges that sustain partnership working or make CUPs more resilient, and thus make a contribution to certain aspects of community development. There is evidence in our data that it is precisely working through challenges together that makes partnerships particularly strong, and we consider this later on in this chapter.

Leadership and organisational support

Personal leadership by individual academics and community partners is essential to ensure that opportunities and mutual benefits that make CUP working possible are identified. Our CUP was only viable because Angie and Andrew had secured funding by applying for a grant from the Economic and Social Research Council (ESRC) to pay for community partner input. Furthermore, the project was mutually beneficial; Angie and Andrew were interested in obtaining new insights on the community partner perspective on CUP working, which is something that is largely absent from the literature, whereas GMCVO was interested in exploring the feasibility of CUP working as a potential opportunity for the voluntary sector it supports.

In our study of CUPs, leadership was often an important prerequisite for either generating organisational support of the partners involved in a CUP, or alternatively, compensating for a lack of organisational support and buy-in. At a very basic level, a CUP is a partnership between individuals and is very dependent on good personal relations between the people involved. However, where there is also organisational ownership, this is a source of strength, legitimacy and continuity for the CUP, and means that its benefits can be shared across the organisation and beyond.

In our case, our CUP was strengthened by the fact that both the University of Brighton and GMCVO supported our work. As mentioned, the CUPP at the University of Brighton is a pioneer of finding approaches to enable CUP work in the UK (Hart et al, 2013). Consequently the university had mechanisms in place that enabled Susanne to benefit from access to the university library and software resources as an Honorary Community Fellow. GMCVO as an organisation was confident enough to enter formal contract negotiations and stood firmly behind Susanne as she undertook quite a challenging brief.

However, there are still some systemic constraints that even the most committed organisations find hard to overcome. On the university side one of the main constraints was slow processing time for payments to community partners. On the community side the largest constraint was time and capacity. Once again personal leadership played a role in overcoming these constraints. Angie and Andrew recognised the need for an organisation like GMCVO to be paid promptly due to an absence of extensive reserves, so they both worked hard to get this issue resolved quickly. Within GMCVO, personal leadership by Susanne and the research manager John Hannen was necessary to lobby for additional time to complete the project. In order to achieve this they clearly articulated the potential benefits for GMCVO, while simultaneously emphasising the concomitant damage of leaving the project unfinished. Most crucial for making their lobbying successful was GMCVO's identity as an organisation whose reputation is partly dependent on research activity, which meant that investing additional time and resources beyond what was initially available made some sense. Working through these various challenges regarding the relationships between the two organisations allowed us to build an effective CUP, but addressing these challenges took time and involved dealing with the topic of the next section, which is unpredictability.

Unpredictability and expectations

One of the truisms about CUP work is its unpredictability – a theme that came across strongly in our interviews. Susanne and GMCVO have a strong track record in conducting qualitative research but were unfamiliar with the protocols for rigour and auditability that constrains research within a university context. As a result, they underestimated the time that a project like this needed. This illustrates two of the findings of our research, that organisations have to be flexible about resourcing and supporting CUPs, and that the funding allocated for GMCVO's contribution was insufficient for what was delivered. This may be linked to the fact that Andrew and Angie, while being aware of community partners' needs to be funded, did not anticipate the level and depth of professionalism with which the research would be conducted. Therefore, they did not fully appreciate the resource implications for engaging a professional community-based researcher in the project.

With hindsight, the increasing pressure to finish the research, combined with the weakening of organisational commitment, could have led to a crisis in the CUP. This was managed through ongoing, transparent communication about the challenges. The other consortium leaders were themselves engaged in CUPs, and were very understanding of the situation.

Ultimately, it was both sides' willingness to see the experience as a learning process that created a context where failure to adhere to deadlines was not seen as a personal shortcoming, but as a consequence of the system we were working within. Rigorous academic research takes tools such as transcription, and computer-assisted qualitative data analysis, which speed up the research process. These resources are often inaccessible within a voluntary sector context that slows the research process, ultimately making deadlines trickier to meet. With empathy and resilience, the CUP continued despite these difficulties.

Different interpretations of the term 'research' also posed a challenge. Because we were all professional researchers, we assumed that we were talking about the same thing when using the term 'research'. Susanne's working definition of research was slightly different to that of Angie and Andrew, as her concept of research was adapted to the operational constraints of a voluntary sector organisation. This meant that Susanne usually interviewed participants without recording the interview, and simply took notes during the interview. These notes were given to the participant at the end of the interview to check accuracy, and then used as data. Although it was clear to her that transcription would add time in terms of getting the data ready for analysis, she did not anticipate just how long it takes to transcribe interviews, nor how much time would be consumed analysing the higher volume of data that the interviews generated. It was only when deadlines started to look unreasonable that we began to recognise that our perceptions of the term 'research' differed.

Conversely, Angie and Andrew's expectations of the quality of the work also turned out to be different from Susanne's. They did not anticipate that a community-based researcher in a resource-constrained organisation would be able to be as thorough as Susanne, and be able to lead on the production of a substantial report from the data. However, GMCVO is an organisation that prides itself on being research-minded and whose main audiences include funders and statutory agencies, which in turn gives rise to a more traditional view of what research is. Underpinning this pride is the commitment to produce research outputs that could be seen as robust by these audiences. The fact of having been asked by the University of Brighton to collaborate on a research project meant that GMCVO set the bar high, in order to meet the high expectations of Angie and Andrew, with regard to rigour. Angie and Andrew had a different, less traditional, but possibly also less sophisticated, output in mind to the one that Susanne was working towards.

This once again illustrates a point that emerged from our interviews with colleagues in the CUP realm: good CUPs are an active learning experience and challenge partners' assumptions about each other's, and their own, capabilities.

Co-production

The standard core aspiration for CUP working is to enable co-production to happen. Chapter 1 of this book contains a wider discussion of co-production and a number of studies consider the challenges this creates for CUPs (Banks et al, 2014). Among the case study's CUPs, co-production had the following effects:

- mutual benefit;
- enhancing the impact and quality of research;
- generating appropriate and ethically sensitive research approaches;
- enabling practice-relevant outputs;
- securing buy-in and ownership from research participants and partners.

Co-production is a process whereby people from different settings and backgrounds work together. In co-production different skill sets and levels of expertise are valued equally (Hart et al, 2013). While co-production is both a perennial aspiration and persistent claim among those advocating CUPs, in practice it is difficult to achieve given the pressures of time and money that CUP working is subject to, similar to all other areas of the British economy. Where CUP working is usually funded by universities or funding bodies such as the research councils, there is a recurrent problem in that time horizons are either too long or too short in the research process to make co-production feasible from the beginning. On the one hand, there are cases where bids for funding have to be submitted too quickly to allow academics to bring in community partners at this bidding stage. In other cases, the period from submission of the bid to hearing the bid's outcome is too long to make the involvement of community partners, which has resource implications, feasible.

This means that co-production typically occurs during implementation rather than during the design and idea generation phase of the research process. In our data set this problem of co-production only occurring in the implementation phase was particularly prevalent where partners were fairly new to each other, and this issue also applied to our own CUP.

In our case, Angie contacted Susanne in February 2014 with the suggestion of getting involved in *Imagine* in September. Although this meant that Susanne had not been involved in the overall *Imagine* bid, the work package Angie wanted to partner with her on was generic enough to still allow for personalisation. Initial co-production was mainly by email and phone, but Andrew, Angie and Susanne also utilised opportunities for meeting in person – which were an important factor to making joint work more tangible. GMCVO appraised the project in a similar way to other pieces of work that it might get involved in, by trying to estimate how much staff time would have to be allocated to the project and if the funding was sufficient to cover that time.

Co-production on basic issues such as the definition of CUP and the geographical scope of the research were already in full swing by the time a contract was signed in July. This correlates with our interviews with colleagues from other CUPs. Interviewees stated that it is often beneficial to get stuck in with practical work before the formalities of contracts have been completed, which can take several months. If we had waited for them to be complete before starting our work, we would have lost valuable time for understanding our respective points of view and requirements. Additionally, there is some momentum at the beginning of a partnership that can easily dissipate if it is not reinforced. That said, all of this demands a great deal of trust between the partners.

Utilising a contract based on a template used by GMCVO for consultancy work meant contract negotiations went relatively smoothly. The contract was between GMCVO and Boingboing, the social enterprise partner, which was also working on the *Imagine* project. The use of the basic GMCVO contract ensured that GMCVO's perspective was already taken into account. This was then supplemented by some clauses on intellectual property that were more typical in university research. Part of the contract negotiations was also to ensure that GMCVO would have access to the qualitative analysis software NVivo, with the relevant training to use this software, without GMCVO incurring further costs.

A specific goal in the *Imagine* project was to undertake this study of CUPs as a collaborative enquiry between a community researcher and academic researchers, to ensure different views and ways of working were integrated into the study. All authors contributed at all stages as follows, with different people taking the lead on different aspects:

- All authors were involved in scoping the project, preparing interview schedules, information sheets and other data collection methods.
- Angie and Susanne liaised with related projects, the findings of which have also been incorporated into this project.
- Susanne undertook the data collection and data analysis.
- Angie was interviewed as part of the study.
- Andrew led on the ethics approval process.
- Angie led on liaising between this project and the wider *Imagine* project.
- All authors contributed to writing the report, with Susanne taking the lead.
- All authors contributed to disseminating the results of this study as wide as possible.
- Susanne had suggested that we write a paper about the process of collaborating on this research project, so that other VCS organisations could learn from it. This was the motivation for this chapter. Accordingly, she drafted the first iteration of this chapter.

We all made a significant collaborative investment in the scoping phase of the project, but once the study was on track and data collection had begun, Angie and Andrew took a back seat and Susanne drove the process. During the analysis and reporting stage co-production took on a larger role once again, and it is planned that co-production will maintain its sizeable role throughout the dissemination of our findings.

Sample design and recruitment

In sample design, co-production meant that the research included more cases that would be relevant from a GMCVO perspective than it otherwise would have. Because GMCVO was the selected community partner, the geographical focus of the study was the North West, although CUPs in all other major regions of England were also included. GMCVO's involvement also shaped the sample to include more CUPs that involved voluntary organisations rather than those simply involving individual members from the community. Additionally, Angie and Andrew's input ensured that the sample included a sufficient number of CUPs within the subject area of the arts and humanities, as well as a good mix of different types of universities, which is aligned with the aims of the *Imagine* project.

As a group, we pooled our expertise and access to networks to identify participants. GMCVO was instrumental in publishing a call for participants on the GMCVO website, which received a record response. Susanne took the lead in compiling a list of cases and evidenced why they would be interesting to include. Angie and Andrew then commented on the list and supplemented it with their own suggestions. This produced a list of 37 potential CUP cases.

Research questions

There was also an ongoing discussion about the types of partnerships that the research should focus on in order to explore topics that were relevant to the academic partners' wider research interests, which were heavily reflected in the original project brief. This envisaged a comparison of three approaches to CUPs: a social enterprise approach, a community of practice (CoP) approach and a place-based approach. Details on these approaches are as follows:

- A *social enterprise approach* entails that partners start their own social enterprise in order to facilitate their partnership work.
- A *CoP approach* emphasises developing a learning process within a group that comprises members from different backgrounds, who have different skill levels, expertise and who occupy different roles in the hierarchy.
- A *place-based approach* brings together partners who take an interest in a geographical place and who work together to address issues that are particular to the place.

Rather than using this typology, we collaborated to develop a more pragmatic approach. In the process of developing this method, the social enterprise and place-based categories were not dismissed entirely, but were supplemented by a fuller range of different approaches to developing CUPs. The one element that informed the study overall was the idea of CUPs as CoPs that are ongoing, voluntary learning communities.

This concept was useful for capturing characteristics we were looking for, and for identifying genuine partnership approaches as opposed to finding singular transactions between universities and community partners. The CoP as a concept was developed by Wenger to promote social learning (Wenger, 1998), and included three distinct dimensions or characteristics:

- The voluntary dimension, which underpins the voluntary nature of partnership work.
- The time dimension, which is characterised as continuing on an ongoing basis until members decide to stop.
- The learning dimension, which is the ability to learn from each other and appreciate different levels of knowledge.

Angie and others at the University of Brighton had successfully used the CoP approach for developing CUPs in the past (Hart and Wolff, 2006; Hart et al, 2013). The team decided that to be eligible for the study, participant CUPs had to display characteristics of a CoP, so Susanne had to be brought up to speed on the concept of CoP and how to explain it to potential participants. She initially found the concept of a CoP difficult to grasp, especially when trying to differentiate between a CoP and a network, with networks being commonplace in the VCS context. Ongoing dialogue between Susanne and Angie increasingly clarified her understanding, as did attending an *Imagine* conference where Etienne and Beverly Wenger-Trayner conducted a workshop about CoPs. Eventually Susanne was in a position to explain this concept to the potential participants, and particularly those in the VCS.

Two of the project's research questions reflected the centrality of the CoP concept. These were:

- Examine the key features of CUPs.
- Identify the degree to which they have developed into CoPs.
- Identify how the partners learn from each other in CUPs.

A second aspect that Angie wanted to include in the research, as a sensitising concept, was resilience, reflecting her own interest and past work about the topic (Hart et al, 2007). Susanne was not fond of the concept, in light of its overuse in the public discourse around public sector cuts in the UK, which always made reference to a need for communities to become more resilient. She was also unsure about how resilience related to the topic of the study. It transpired that the primary relevance of resilience in the context of this research related to how people involved in CUPs maintained their resilience, how they continued to work and sustain the CUP despite the presence of adverse conditions. Resilience was connected to navigating practical problems in partnership working, as well as about the future sustainability of CUPs.

All written materials, from the 'Call for participants' to the qualitative interview schedule through to the final report, were drafted by Susanne. Susanne then incorporated comments by Angie and Andrew to ensure that resilience and CoP thinking was reflected throughout the documents she created. By employing this approach Susanne could lead the process, drawing on previous experience of research on partnership working. She was also able to re-use existing GMCVO resources – some existing interview questions from a research project about the experiences of VCS organisations in partnerships with the public sector.

Limits of co-production

In our experience, co-production is time-intensive on the one hand, but it does lead to better research design on the other. This was borne out in interviews with academics and community partners. For Susanne, collaborating with Angie and Andrew was a pleasant change from working as a lone researcher. However, the fact that we had never worked together as a team before also meant that we spent much time figuring out how we would co-produce the work. This is time that was not spent thinking about how research participants could be involved in co-production. Therefore, rather ironically, the research methodology itself, as far as the research participants are concerned, was quite traditional. While the approach to our own partnership broke the mould in many respects, it also showed how co-production can be limited, but can also occur in unexpected ways.

Susanne incorporated the elements of co-production that she usually employs in her research for GMCVO. This included regular updates on the research process, and giving participants opportunities to comment on the report. However, as mentioned earlier, one of her routine ways of involving participants was rendered impossible by the fact that interviews had to be recorded and transcribed. Susanne usually drafted interview notes rather than using interview transcripts, which allowed participants to read the notes and comment on them without placing a great toll on their time. However, the sheer length and detail of the interview transcripts exceeded participants' capacity and willingness to do this. This is interesting, since qualitative research often seeks to validate interview data by asking respondents to comment on notes, but in this case this was not possible.

Despite this, many of the interviews, especially the ones in which both partners from the CUP participated, felt like a genuine co-production of meaning because participants do not often get the opportunity to reflect on their partnerships. For many of them it was the first time they could sit down with their partner to think about the reason behind their CUP, what they were doing together and for what result. Although new insights did not always occur for interviewees, there were definitely interviews that generated surprising thoughts and ideas for the partners in the CUP and that might have changed the course of the partnership in future.

Benefits and impact

Community partners appreciated the reflective element that is usually introduced by the research process and that is integral to being part of a CUP.

For Susanne, too, the CUP with Angie and Andrew combined with the opportunity to follow properly academic methods provided a reflective space where she was able to learn and re-evaluate her research practice. Because of this, she has become more aware of the constraints, but also of the opportunities that her role as a researcher based in the community presents.

For GMCVO as an organisation with a research identity, the project provided valuable learning about the implications of getting involved in an academic research project that aspires to meet academic expectations for rigour. GMCVO will enter future projects with more awareness about the resource implications that certain methods bring with them. GMCVO has also benefited from the professional development Susanne gained through her participation in the project. The project afforded numerous opportunities to present her work to different audiences including academics, as well as formal and informal training, especially in NVivo, which will enhance GMCVO's overall skillset.

Ultimately, this has inspired Susanne and GMCVO to embark on a collaborative doctoral studentship, which is going to lead to her getting a PhD and the organisation having even more internal research expertise. This will hopefully lead to new business opportunities and greater sustainability in the long run that will support GMCVO's role in community development more broadly.

Similarly to Susanne, interviewees in our sample predominantly saw the personal and organisational benefits of CUP working. Conversely, respondents also argued that cases in which service users or the wider community had benefited from an organisation's involvement in CUP work were rarer. However, this is linked to the general difficulty of proving impact, as well as the long-term nature of impact creation.

For GMCVO, the advantages for the members of the voluntary sector that the organisation serves will mainly arise from GMCVO's awareness of CUPs at the theoretical and practical level, and its ability to advise the sector on the opportunities of CUPs while being a credible player in this arena. In collaboration with the UK Community Partner Network, that GMCVO is a founding member of, it is hoped that some of the findings of this research will have an influence beyond Greater Manchester, and will inform training content and resources for community partners.

Conclusions and lessons learned

In this chapter we have examined our own CUP in the wider context of our collaborative research study on CUP working in general. We consider it important to share our experience more widely owing to an external environment in which community partners, including VCS organisations, are increasingly likely to be approached by academics who want to work jointly with them. Our study has also found that wider sharing of collaborative experiences, and reflection on them, is not currently happening as often as it should.

It appears that our experience of collaborating was typical of other CUPs' experiences in several ways:

- Our CUP started through personal relationships and was founded on a shared passion.
- There were practical reasons why embarking on this CUP seemed advantageous for all involved.
- It is this advantage that helped to keep the CUP going, despite difficulties that arose from the unpredictability of CUP working.
- The CUP remained resilient through leadership, open communication and honesty.
- This was supplemented by awareness-raising in a wider organisational context – both Susanne and Angie had to bring other people on board in order to continue the work despite delays.
- Unpredictability means that it is quite challenging to have an accurate understanding of the resource implications of working together and respective areas, and levels of expertise.
- It is likely that we would have a better understanding of the implications and we certainly would have more awareness of each

other's strengths if we had embarked on a further joint project. However, there would still be a margin of unpredictability.

Lessons learned from this CUP that might be useful for others include:

- Different types of projects require different types of approaches and understandably possess different resource needs. Therefore, it is likely that unpredictability is at the heart of partnership working, and organisations embarking on this process will need to take this into account. The role of CUP in relation to community development is not going to be predictable.
- The findings of this research suggest that the task of reflecting on the role and limits of a CUP will be continuous. On the other hand, the findings also present that by sustaining a CUP, over time unpredictability reduces with the associated benefits for efficiency, and by working through any key challenges, the partnership will be strengthened in the long run.
- CUP working is both more time-intensive and more rewarding than going it alone. Through co-production partners can achieve better research and, most importantly, different research than would have been possible if they just do their project on their own. However, be prepared to take longer if project partners decide to employ a co-productive approach.
- Be prepared to challenge partners' assumptions and be mindful that CUP working is a continuous learning experience. Being conscious of this fact is a good starting point for enabling partners to transform difficulties into learning experiences.
- Partners should remember that benefits for the wider community and related community development often take longer to materialise and are predominantly indirect.
- Different forms of co-production in CUPs can create promising environments for fostering wider community benefits, provided the right stakeholders are involved.

Ultimately, we found that sustaining CUPs depends on individual leadership and commitment. It is perhaps not surprising that many of the benefits of CUP working accrue to the individuals who are directly involved and to their organisations.

References

Banks, S. and Armstrong, A., with Booth, M., Brown, G., Carter, K., Clarkson, M., Corner, L., Genus, A., et al (2014) 'Using co-inquiry to study co-inquiry: Community-university perspectives on research collaboration', *Journal of Community Engagement and Scholarship*, 7(1), 37-47.

Beebeejaun, Y., Durose, C., Rees, J., Richardson, J. and Richardson, L. (2015) 'Public harm or public value? Towards coproduction in research with communities', *Environment and Planning C: Government and Policy*, 33(3), 552-65.

Facer, K. and Enright, B. (2016) *Creating Living Knowledge: The Connected Communities programme, community-university relationships and the participatory turn in the production of knowledge*, Bristol, UK: University of Bristol/Arts and Humanities Research Council (AHRC) Connected Communities.

Facer, K., Manners, P. and Agusita, E. (2012) *Towards a knowledge base for university-public engagement: Sharing knowledge, building insight, taking action*, Bristol, UK : National Co-ordinating Centre for Public Engagement.

Hart, A. and Wolff, D. (2006) 'Developing local 'communities of practice' through local community-university partnerships', *Planning Practice and Research*, 21(1), 121-38.

Hart, A., Blincow, D. with Thomas, H. (2007) *Resilient therapy: Working with children and families*, London and New York: Routledge.

Hart, A., Davies, C., Aumann, K., Wenger, E., Aranda, K., Heaver, B. and Wolff, D. (2013) 'Mobilising knowledge in community-university partnerships: What does a community of practice approach contribute?', *Contemporary Social Science: Journal of the Academy of Social Sciences*, 8(3), 278-91.

HEFCE (Higher Education Funding Council for England) (2006) *Strategic plan 2006-11*, Bristol: HEFCE (www.hefce.ac.uk/data/year/2008/HEFCE,strategic,plan,2006-11).

Kindon, S., Pain, R. and Kesby, M. (2007) *Participatory action research approaches and methods: Connecting people, participation and place*, Abingdon, UK: Routledge.

Laing, S. and Maddison, E. (2007) 'The CUPP model in context', in A. Hart, E. Maddison and D. Wolff (eds.) *Community-university partnerships in practice*, Leicester, UK: National Institute of Adult Continuing Education, 8-20.

Manners, P. and Duncan, S. (2017) *Evidencing the impact of engagement: An analysis of the REF 2014 case studies*, Bristol: National Co-ordinating Centre for Public Engagement.

Martikke, S., Church, A. and Hart, A. (2015) *Greater than the sum of its parts: What works in sustaining community university partnerships*, Manchester: Greater Manchester Centre for Voluntary Organisation.

NCCPE (National Co-ordinating Centre for Public Engagement) (2011) *Partnership working principles*, Bristol, UK: NCCPE (www.publicengagement.ac.uk/do-engagement/partnership-working/partnership-working-principles).

NCCPE (2017) *The role of public engagement in the REF*, Bristol: NCCPE (www.publicengagement.ac.uk/news/role-public-engagement-ref).

O'Brien, D. and Matthews, P. (2015) 'Conclusion', in D. O'Brien and P. Matthews (eds.) *After urban regeneration: Communities, policy and place*, Bristol, UK: Policy Press, 199-204.

Wenger, E. (1998) *Communities of practice: Learning, meaning and identity*, Cambridge: Cambridge University Press (https://thesystemsthinker.com/communities-of-practice-learning-as-a-social-system).

FOUR

Community-university partnership research retreats: A productive force for developing communities of research practice

Josh Cameron, Beverly Wenger-Trayner,
Etienne Wenger-Trayner, Angie Hart, Lisa Buttery, Elias Kourkoutas,
Suna Eryigit-Madzwamuse and Anne Rathbone

Introduction

Etienne Wenger (1998) applied the term 'communities of practice' (CoP) to groups of people who come together to understand and respond to a shared topic of concern, emphasising examples from work organisations. This is something that human society has always done, but in analysing the process and exploring how to cultivate it, social learning theorists consider how to overcome challenges and support effective CoP collaborations (Wenger et al, 2002). Most published literature on CoP has reported on mono-professional contexts (Hart et al, 2013). However, the concept and approach lends itself to mobilising knowledge and experiences from more diverse sources. In our case, the diversity particularly related to culture, nationality, age, class and knowledge claims that drew on academic or personal lived experience (and in some cases, a combination of these).

Members of our CoP considered that the CoP approach was particularly well-suited to the broader *Imagine* project's 'community development approach' to the co-production of research, because we wanted to bring together our diverse experiences and sources of knowledge to deepen our understanding of what community resilience meant for us and how we could mobilise it for mutual benefit. We hope that this chapter will be of practical use to those who want to consider using CoP in other research collaborations involving diverse groups.

The literature also contains broader guidance on how to support the effective functioning of larger research teams, including those that involve interdisciplinary approaches (Thompson, 2009), mixed methods (Bowers et al, 2013) and lived experience collaboration (Abma et al, 2009). Many of these bring together collaborators in meetings often held over a few days, termed 'retreats'. However, most academic guidance and research has focused on retreats used by academics to produce written outputs (see, for example, Kornhaber et al, 2016) and not on the process of co-production by academics, practitioners and participants.

Participatory research: Intervention within a landscape of practice

Our programme consisted of a number of participatory research projects, all concerned with responding to some form of adversity. Over time our programme developed 15 such projects across seven countries (see the examples below). They addressed four main themes: child and family resilience; practitioner/teacher and school resilience; young adult/adult resilience; and resilience models for practice and research.

All our projects involved some form of collaboration between universities and community-based individuals and groups. This means that our CoP can be understood as entailing community development in the participatory action tradition of research (Stoecker, 2013). In particular, we strove for genuine co-production involving all collaborators in the full research process, including generating outputs. Co-production is not simply a politically correct term for academic researcher and participant involvement, but reflects a fusion of research and participant roles and a convergence of differing types of knowledge (Stuttaford et al, 2012), the purposes being to broaden the knowledge base that is brought to understand a research issue and also to use diverse knowledge and experience to identify how best to apply research findings in ways that respond to and that are sensitive to community needs and cultures.

Our focus was on resilience to adversity as a form of social participation (Hart et al, 2016). This social approach to resilience involves an array of different actors. It is an intervention, not in a single practice, but in a landscape of practice (Wenger-Trayner and Wenger-Trayner, 2014), which, in our case, comprised different cultures challenged by different forms of adversity. This called for a mixed research team, including academic researchers, community-based service providers and families, as well as young people with special needs.

Selected projects that were developed as part of the Imagine social programme

- In Brighton and Blackpool, young people worked collectively to create tools to support their resilience and improve their futures. A partnership with the School of Design from the University of Brighton led to a project called *Co-designing resilience*. Through active interventions by young people and community partners, our Resilience Framework was re-imagined in various digital and creative media.
- In South Wales, Newport Mind hosted a project that supported the development of family resilience. The project started with the facilitation of 'encounters' between the young people, their families and professionals (mental health and youth workers, teachers, police, fire service, academics) who work with them. Their work on family resilience has expanded to a training programme for parents/carers and collaborative work at primary schools to support children and young people with adversity faced at home settings, including domestic abuse.
- Peer trainers with lived experience of mental health problems collaborated with mental health practitioners and academics to co-design and deliver an eight-week 'Building resilience for wellbeing and recovery programme', offered as a Sussex Recovery College course.
- The *Imagine* social programme has also re-imagined assessment tools used in resilience research and practice. In collaboration with community partners and across countries, a novel assessment tool of the Resilience Framework is being developed. This tool will help target resources accurately, to improve the effectiveness of collaborative practices.
- School-based projects in Greece and Germany have created more resilient school climates, especially for those who are experiencing challenges in the schools. In a radical departure from traditional approaches in these contexts, acknowledgement of lived experience expertise has led to the projects being enriched by active parent involvement.

Boundaries in participatory research

The idea of an intervention in a landscape of practice brings into focus the multiplicity of practices involved and the differences or 'boundaries' between them. This prompts the need to find productive ways to learn and work across these boundaries, which makes them key learning assets, providing an opportunity to bring all relevant perspectives to bear on an issue. Our programme straddled several types of boundaries, including:

- Fields of practice (academic disciplines, professional practices, lived experience).
- Social and economic status (class, gender and race).
- Personal experience of the domain (different levels and types of experience of social and health adversity).
- Geographical location, culture and language (projects in different countries).

Looking through a landscape lens, it was clear that to members of our CoP who came together in our retreat meetings, we would have to respond to these boundaries in different ways in order to support our social learning processes. There were some boundaries we did not really address. For instance, we conducted all our formal sessions in English, requiring people whose first language was not English to cross the boundary into English-speaking. Over time we noticed that some of us were making more of an effort than others regarding this boundary. Other boundaries were central to our aims and were an integral part of our research approach.

Challenges

As Northmore and Hart (2011) pointed out, genuine reciprocal co-production is particularly challenging when the partnership involves academics and communities whose members are unlikely to have had formal relationships with universities.

Sources of knowledge

Our collaborations involved partnerships between people whose primary source of knowledge of some form of adversity came from different worlds:

- Academic (for example, researcher or university lecturer).
- Professional practice (for example, teaching or therapy).
- Lived experience (for example, personal experience of living with mental distress or family carer to someone facing adversity).

Issues of power

It is easy to assume that academics have the upper hand when it comes to producing knowledge. Partly because of the emphasis given to academia by research funders, academics tend to have more control over projects funded for research, as was the case for our programme. Recent literature on community-university partnerships (CUPs) (Hart et al, 2013; Davies et al, 2016) calls for some realism in terms of awareness of the power structures that exist in broader society within which such partnerships sit. To ensure effective collaboration we needed to understand the different external stakeholders (for example, employers, funding bodies, communities) that exerted power on all of us, and the expectations that this placed on our work (for example, what the outputs should be and competing priorities). For instance, collaborators from voluntary sector groups explained the pressures they were under to produce outcomes that would support future funding bids and that would also prove meaningful to the communities in which they were located.

Uncertainty

The differences in sources of knowledge and power created uncertainties about what the partnership could produce and what value it would have to various academic and non-academic participants. The research focus also created uncertainties about some participants' ability to contribute to research. We faced the need to address all these uncertainties as we proceeded.

Worldviews and audiences

Different practices come with different worldviews, different ways of talking, a different sense of what matters and different audiences with different needs. We had to be careful to recognise all these differences and organise activities that could serve the array of needs brought by various participants.

All this was mitigated to some extent by having a very open brief in terms of who the collaborators would be and by having broad research aims that could be applied to a very wide range of settings. Still, we had to fight the tendency for academic knowledge and associated roles to be privileged in research processes. We worked hard to help achieve a mutual recognition of the diverse forms of knowledge (Hart and

Wolff, 2007), including a valuing of tacit as well as explicit knowledge (Wenger et al, 2002).

Building a boundary-crossing community of practice

Hart et al (2013) argue that CUPs can mobilise knowledge across diverse partners by using a CoP approach and associated social learning theory (Wenger, 1998). CoPs can cut across traditional organisational barriers and hierarchies (Wenger et al, 2002). In CUPs they have been effective in combining research and practice development activities, and in addressing perceived and actual power differentials (Hart and Wolff, 2007). Given our challenges, our CoP approach helped us to build our capability to work across boundaries and to create research findings that address common concerns among diverse collaborators.

In this chapter we present our research projects within a CoP framework as an analytic tool and as an approach that steered our collaboration. Each individual project within our strand was cultivated as a CoP and we found it helpful to develop our overarching programme as a CoP across projects (hereafter central CoP). A key concern of this central CoP was how to conduct participatory research projects on resilience that involve a range of players and a community development endeavour. This central CoP helped the individual projects learn from each other and develop their plans. It also provided a way to bring together the diverse project findings and communicate them to the wider world in a meaningful way.

Stages of development through successive research retreats

The way this central CoP came together was through annual meetings, which later became known as research retreats. These were annual two-day meetings to share our experiences, good practice and challenges; support each other; and plan for the year ahead. Participants were our core international research community (approximately 25 to 30 people) who worked together using the underlying principles of a CoP approach. They included practitioners (for example, social workers and health professionals); academics (from various UK and European institutions and social sciences–related disciplines); and people with 'lived experience' expertise (for example, people from a mental health project and parents of children with special needs).

Traditionally, research retreats are academic events that focus on the production of academic papers (Kornhaber et al, 2016). We decided that our retreats were going to accomplish something different: build the capacity to move forward with a truly co-productive approach to our research programme, so we did not use the term 'retreat' until the final event, as will be explained below.

Cross-boundary maturity model for a community of practice

In their book on cultivating CoPs, Wenger et al (2002, p 69) outline a maturity model for the stages of development of a CoP. They propose that a traditional CoP goes through five development stages: potential; coalescing; maturing; stewardship; and transformation. Boundary crossing in our own programme is a central feature of our CoP approach, so we have reframed these traditional stages of development to include a description of each stage of maturity in relation to cultivating boundaries as learning assets (see column 3 in Table 4.1).

We use this updated version of the stages of development to frame the following summaries of our retreats and to show how our CoP progressed through the different stages as a boundary-crossing learning partnership to support the development of communities in which the different projects were located. Starting in 2013, we had four annual retreats hosted in different UK towns. The following accounts of each event are constructed from an analysis by the authors of event documentation (for example, agenda and presentations), notes taken by CoP participants (we ensured that a number of people keep reflexive summaries of sessions) and artistic and visual records/interpretations.

Retreat 1: Brighton 2013

The first retreat took place immediately after the launch event of the overall Imagine programme. The purpose was to bring together people who had already liaised in developing the project proposals or those who had expressed an interest in finding out more about our funded research brief and the overarching aims. One of the aims of the event was for possible collaborators to consider whether and how they might design or join an Imagine-Social community development research project.

At this stage, there were just embryonic ideas of specific Imagine-Social projects, but we wanted to start with the foundation of the potential stage, working to recognise the *potential* of boundary-crossing partnerships for all involved – seeing it not as an obstacle but as a key element of knowledge-building and mobilisation. To do this the retreat schedule was designed to demystify research and help people recognise that they all had skills and experiences to bring through

Table 4.1: A cross-boundary maturity model for a community of practice

Stage of development	Traditional CoP cultivation	CoP approach to cultivating boundaries as learning assets
Potential	• Loose network of people with similar issues and needs • Discover common ground and prepare for community	Project brings together people from different backgrounds and interests Careful design of activities helps people discover the potential value of crossing boundaries
Coalescing	• Members launch a community • Find value in engaging in learning activities and design a community	Members engage with each other's practice in concrete ways They experience how cross-boundary learning can be mutually beneficial
Maturing	• Form an identity, take charge of practice and grow • Set standards, define a learning agenda and deal with growth	There is an emerging commitment to: sustain engagement across boundaries develop areas of shared value and joint work
Stewarding	• Community is established and acts as a steward of its domain • Sustain energy, renew interest, educate novices, find a voice and gain influence	The community begins to push the cross-boundary partnership to optimise its ability to make a tangible difference in various contexts
Transforming	• Community has outlived its usefulness and people move on • Let go, define a legacy and keep in touch	The community creates a joint legacy to take back to members' respective contexts and to envision new ways of exploring boundaries in the future

interactive sessions in which people were prompted to introduce and share their experiences. Particular attention was given to recognising and emphasising 'lived experience' and practice-based experience as valid forms of knowledge on a par with academic knowledge.

We also introduced some frameworks that provided a common language across the diverse constituents. The Brighton team presented their 'Resilience Framework' as a common perspective. This framework takes resilience to be a process of social participation as well as an individual characteristic. It promotes the value of challenging sources of adversity as well dealing with issues and acts as a bridge between academic research, practitioner and lived experience expertise and knowledge (Hart et al, 2016). Etienne and Beverly Wenger-Trayner introduced the concept of communities of practice as an approach to learning across boundaries as well as the associated Value-Creation

Framework, which provides a shared language that allows participants from all walks of life to articulate the value that their communities create as they learn together (Wenger et al, 2011; Wenger-Trayner et al, 2017).

As we started to overcome fears about boundaries that include who is involved in research as well as the power of academics as legitimate producers of knowledge, and to recognise the potential of a shared language, the group started to move into the coalescing stage. For instance, young people from an arts-based mental health project envisioned themselves as people who had skills and experiences that could contribute to forming research questions about resilient responses to mental health stigma. The retreat closed with collaborators developing and sharing their plans for making progress on their initial ideas with each other.

Retreat 2: Durham 2014

One year later at the second research retreat the *Imagine* social strand had grown from an initially proposed 4 projects to 12 across several European countries. Approximately 25 people involved in these projects participated in the event. Again, it included a mix of academics, practitioners and 'lived experience' community partners. The agenda was drafted in advance by local project leads – which disproportionately involved academics. Some balance was restored by use of a distributed approach to leadership (see below) during the retreats and setting goals for the coming year. The Durham retreat was held in a residential education college for people with disabilities, which provided a meaningful, but largely neutral, venue for all involved.

The proceedings contained further elements of the *coalescing* stage. The retreat was the first opportunity for many to hear details of the range of our strand's projects and to get to know the people involved in delivering and researching these projects. Different projects were at various stages of development, which triggered some uncertainty and doubts – both on the part of members of projects who considered that they were 'behind' and on the part of more 'advanced' projects that considered they may have 'missed out' some important issues. However, the unevenness provided opportunities for projects nearer the beginning to learn from those at later stages, and for the latter to critically reflect on their development and consider adjustments. For example, academics and practitioners from the more developed schools-based projects in Germany and Greece reflexively reported that they felt constructively challenged by the developing approach of some of the other projects, and so decided to consider ways of introducing more 'lived experience' involvement of parents. One of our goals was to gain a better understanding of the cultural context of each of the projects and the cross-cultural approach to our work package. In particular, we explored how resilience is understood and fostered across cultures.

The community moved into the *maturing* stage as we committed to work across boundaries. Informed by discussions at the Brighton retreat, lead researchers from the sub-projects had refined the programme aims that were introduced and then adopted at the Durham meeting. These were:

1. To demonstrate the potential (or not) for CUPs to make better and more resilient collective futures.
2. To develop resilience theory and practice, particularly as they apply to communities and the potential to challenge sources of adversity.
3. To enable a cross-cultural comparison of 1 and 2 above.

Our commitment was further cemented as the community discussed and agreed on five activities/issues that each project would incorporate to enable cross-project comparison:

- Different perspectives working together.
- Applying the Resilience Framework into practice as a way to bring perspectives together.
- Challenging an adversity condition.
- Imagining better futures that worked across boundaries.
- Ending with what comes next in planning such futures.

On a more practical level we also shared an understanding of and commitment to a common set of research ethics standards, and planned a timetable of delivery for projects and research.

Retreat 3: Huddersfield 2015

In our third retreat, we continued to explicitly draw on social learning theory and spent some time in the *maturing* stage by:

- Exploring our philosophy of collaborative work across boundaries.
- Reflecting on the connection of different communities involved in our projects.
- Articulating how this differs from more traditional research approaches.

- Reflecting on the intersection of all the elements we needed to take into consideration in order to work on our shared topic of resilience from multiple perspectives; these included gender, age, personal differences, culture and social adversity.

In another discussion, the role of utopian ideas in our projects was emphasised. The theme of utopia (Levitas, 2007) energised collaborators to consider the role that imagining a better future plays in opening ways for various perspectives to contribute to a vision. As a sign of maturing, we noted that non-academic participants were developing the skills and confidence to work with academics and contribute to research, and that academics were recognising the value of this and feeling more comfortable with sharing claims to research expertise. For example, it was one of the peer trainers (people with lived experience of mental health problems who co-produced our 'Building resilience for mental wellbeing and recovery' course) who, in response to participant suggestions, confidently and very effectively presented the model we were using to track our research findings and impacts. This trainer had never been to a research event before and later said that the experience inspired her to enrol on an Open University psychology course.

This was also an example of *stewarding* that the rest of the retreat then focused on. We discussed how our outputs were going to reflect the cross-boundary work we had done, and how they would do justice to the diversity of perspectives in our projects. We identified a broad range of artefacts and potentially enduring processes or practices. Examples included:

- Individuals with learning disabilities developing the research skills and confidence to participate in conferences.
- A range of creative activities designed to support understanding of resilience and promote community development.
- Case study evidence of how the programme had influenced policy-makers.
- Research presentations and journal articles.

A key 'output' that was discussed, was the planned *Imagine* exhibition scheduled for the following year, that aimed to showcase the work of the overall *Imagine* programme. We wanted to convey both the products of our project and the process of collaboration that had brought these into being that led to the proposal to present the voices of people who participated in projects in a way that was linked to specific artefacts – the approach ultimately adopted in the exhibition.

Retreat 4: Sheffield 2016

The fourth retreat was our final scheduled meeting. It was the first event to be labelled in advance as a 'retreat', reflecting a level of confidence in our shared research identity across the diverse participants. Our two-day retreat was scheduled to take place just before the one-day *Imagine* programme's exhibition and conference, held at the Millennium Gallery in Sheffield (Imagine, 2016).

In full *stewarding* mode, we focused most of our time on producing creative outputs: finalising displays for the exhibition and writing collaboratively. The creative items for the exhibition had been produced in advance by projects under the co-ordination of one project member who was a community artist. The writing took place in small groups clustering around the four themes outlined at the beginning of this chapter. Time was allocated to plan, structure, develop ideas and get feedback on draft written outputs. Hart et al (2013) observe that community partners do not often have the same time or motivation to produce writing as academic partners. At the retreat, our focus was therefore on reviewing outlines of articles and co-producing plans of pieces not yet developed. In this way, we harnessed the input of lived experience and practitioner knowledge alongside academic skills, so that the latter could then work on producing fuller drafts after the retreat for re-circulation. Both academics and non-academics reflected that this was a more successful process than they had anticipated, and the consensus was that we, as a CoP, could have done more to increase the proportion of people who were not academics at the event.

Collaborators were encouraged to think of evidence for the range of impacts of our projects:

- The effect of interventions on children and young people.
- The influence on policy-makers arising from their participation in the *Imagine* policy seminar earlier in 2016.
- Evidence of changes in practice arising from the projects.

The Value Creation Framework (Wenger-Trayner et al, 2017) provided an effective resource for identifying impacts of various sorts and linking them to projects via individual or community 'stories' of resilience-building and challenging adversity.

Moving to the *transforming* stage, the group started to think about the future. Members considered what people had gained and where they were taking this collaboration beyond the initiative. They explored how partnerships might continue in new forms after the end of the programme, and how individuals and communities in their own contexts might make changes to the way they approach community development and production of knowledge in the future.

Discussion: Key enablers

How were we able to sustain a cross-boundary community over its five-year life and ensure that the products and transformations had the potential to leave an enduring legacy? Green and Kearney (2011) suggest this is more important than short-term community development outcomes. In this section we reflect on the factors that made this possible.

The key approach here was the positive use of boundaries (Wenger, 2000). In our discussions, activities and even the 'icebreakers', we enhanced interactions by making positive use of the different boundaries – for instance, by bringing different perspectives and experiences to bear on an issue. The role of the community was not to ignore or eliminate boundaries; rather, it was to find ways to harness boundary tensions positively in the service of deepening our collective learning.

Facilitated boundary encounters

Eib and Miller (2006) noted the need for a shared supportive and inclusive culture in the more homogeneous academic faculty CoP they reported on. When building a boundary-crossing community, either for collaborative research or community development purposes, this need to build a safe, inclusive social learning space is even greater.

Multiple modes of interaction

We tried to design agendas that allowed multiple modes of interaction. Within each retreat, we regularly used micro-*processes* to support our social learning such as 'icebreakers', cluster meetings and whole-group discussions. The various creative and interactive 'icebreaker' activities contributed to our attempts to 'cut across' boundaries, notably related to culture, role, identity, experience and power. In the first two retreats, academics had a greater influence on setting the schedule. This resulted in what many thought was a 'packed' timetable. Non-academics and people whose first language was not English used the 'distributed leadership' mechanisms described below to challenge this, resulting in revisions with more 'downtime' that demonstrated a recognition of the value of interaction, and learning that took place outside of formal meeting times.

Seeing each other's contexts

We built trust by promoting mutual understanding and challenging assumptions and stereotypes that people on different sides of a boundary may have of each other. One way that energy was released and mutual understanding was promoted was through introducing and sharing experiences and ideas that build community. For instance, in one retreat people were asked to bring two objects that represented their connections to resilience and their project. This was to help draw people into each other's worlds and establish meaning across boundaries in our social learning space. Everyone was interested in listening and seemed very engaged when people were talking about their chosen items. It helped people connect with and appreciate each other as individual people, not simply as their roles (or stereotypes of their roles). At the end of that retreat we reflected that we would have liked to have more time allocated for this exercise.

Disrupting comfort zones

To rebalance power relations and disrupt insider/outsider experiences, which is common in boundary-crossing contexts, we also created times when everyone was pushed slightly out of their comfort zone. For instance, we engaged the group in a dancing activity, called bio-dance, which forced people to express themselves and interact in ways that were unfamiliar to everyone.

Exploring emotional experience

Our retreats could open healthy relational spaces, partly because our topic entailed explorations of painful contexts. To understand and respond to this, collaborators emphasised the importance of establishing places of reflexivity (Hart et al, 2013) where emotions could be acknowledged, processed, and in some cases, harnessed, to support research processes and community development. These spaces were created by ensuring sufficient time was dedicated to reflection and feedback at the end of each day with the support of the 'distributed leadership' process (see below). Participants were keen to stress that this included more positive emotions too. Often these were identified as arising from the warmth and joy of human connection experienced in project collaboration.

Use of space

Davies et al (2016) consider the role of physical, virtual and relational spaces in CoPs. Bearing in mind how spaces can frame the behaviours of people and carry connotations of symbolic power, we selected physical spaces for our retreats that did not 'belong' to any of the collaborators – and in all but one retreat they took place in venues that were not 'academic'. One venue – a residential training college for people with disabilities – was appreciated for being a space where we could meet (formally and informally), eat and sleep, all on the same site. People found that this helped to focus attention – alongside a 'mobiles off' agreement.

Diversity of recording media

Our community decided to reflect the diversity of the forms of knowledge in terms of how we interacted and in terms of how we recorded our social learning. So as well as written notes, Lisa Buttery (a young person from a mental health arts project) acted as a 'community artist' and Jamie Hensley (a young person from a care leaver's project) undertook the role of community photographer. This generated a visual and creative record of the event that provided an alternative medium of interpretation and a balance to the verbal mode traditionally dominant in academic circles.

Responsiveness

Our intention to structure our meeting with a broad range of ways of interacting did not stop us from being responsive to the mood of the room by adjusting the agenda to meet people's needs. At an early meeting, anxieties emerged about 'doing research' among practitioners and lived experience experts. (This moment was captured by our community artist, Lisa Buttery, whose representation appears in Image 4.1.) We revised the agenda to give more time to demystifying research.

Image 4.1: Anxieties about 'doing research'

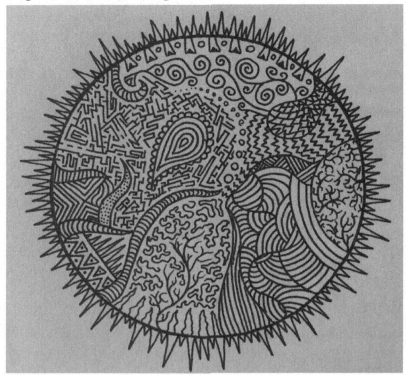

This was primarily achieved by increasing the opportunity for practical exercises related to people's projects.

Distributed leadership

Our ability to be both ambitious and responsive was enhanced because we involved members directly in designing and leading our community. Starting with the second retreat, we used a technique developed for CoPs called 'leadership groups' (Wenger-Trayner and Wenger-Trayner, 2012). The idea is to assign different community management tasks to small groups of members who take ownership of them: deciding what to focus on, making sure all voices are heard, watching for the negative effects of power relations, taking a critical look at the design of activities, thinking about external audiences, and so on. Given the boundary-crossing nature of our community, we made sure that these leadership groups included a diversity of members. These helped members to gain shared ownership of the community and its direction, in spite, and even because of, boundary differences, notably by providing a counter-balance to issues of power (actual and perceived). Table 4.2 provides some examples of the kind of feedback that these groups provided to help the community achieve its potential.

Table 4.2: Examples of feedback provided by the leadership groups

Agenda activists *Task:* Make sure that the community addresses all the issues that are relevant to the members *Example:* At the end of day 1 the agenda activists observed that some of the discussions about the research process – particularly in relation to data collection – had not fully engaged people who were not primarily from an academic role
Critical friends *Task:* Ensure that the process is well designed and collect feedback on what is working and what is not working *Example:* In accordance with the above observation, the critical friends suggested that the timetable for day 2 be adjusted to discuss further what, in various projects, is the 'research data' that we aim to collect and how we do it
Community keepers *Task:* Look after the social dynamics of the group and make sure that all voices are heard *Example:* The community keepers fed back to the group that some people considered that they needed longer breaks to help sustain their energy and attention; this was said to be particularly the case for people not used to such events and for people whose first language was not English
Public relations (PR) brokers *Task:* Explore how to communicate with external audiences *Example:* The PR brokers drew attention to the need to help participants from practice and community organisations communicate to their colleagues and senior people in these organisations the potential value of supporting people to be involved in the *Imagine* social project

Source: See Wenger-Trayner and Wenger-Trayner (2012)

Brokers

A key ingredient of our success was the presence of many people who lived in more than one of the worlds relevant to our community, for instance:

- Academics who had personal experience of a significant adversity related to one of the projects.
- Professionals with research experience.
- People with multi-national upbringings.

Because of their cross-boundary identities, these 'boundary spanners' were able to broker understanding across boundaries, translate perspectives and language, and be aware of how elements of one practice could be perceived, interpreted or misunderstood in another.

They also enhanced our ability to benefit from and build on existing networks and relationships of individuals and organisations constituting the three forms of knowledge. To some extent, by building on existing networks, we limited the potentially negative impact of academics controlling the power to select who would join the CoP, and therefore its starting agenda, which Glover and Silka (2013) suggest is an often neglected problem.

Boundary objects

A number of 'boundary objects' play a key role in helping our community manage and leverage boundaries between members. These take the form of *artefacts*, *discourses* and *processes* that are recognisable across boundaries (Wenger, 2000).

Frameworks

These included the Resilience Framework and the Value Creation Framework that provided a shared lens through which to view our diverse project work. Both frameworks are meant to act as boundary objects between constituencies, in particular between academic and non-academic participants (Wenger-Trayner et al, 2017). Associated with these *artefacts* was a common language or *discourse* – notably related to resilience and social justice, that helped our CoP to negotiate and share our experiences and interpretations.

Boundary production

Other *artefacts* were the joint products of our community. Our products took many forms – academic, practice-related and creative. They included toolkits, creative objects, practice guidelines, courses, presentations to various audiences, assessment tools and games, as well as academic journal articles:

- In Wales the Newport Mind project produced accessible activities and tools based on our Resilience Framework that they used to prompt parents and young people to think about how they could contribute to foster resilience in young people and the networks around them.

- The German schools project in Osnabrück reported that they had generated: significant teaching material and impacts with research projects being provided at Bachelor's and Master's levels, new modules on the topic of resilience and increased numbers of students reporting that they were more motivated to become teachers.
- The project in Fife, Scotland, was focused on supporting young parents and had produced a range of creative approaches to explore their resilience. These included games, role-plays and artistic creations that were displayed at the *Imagine* exhibition.
- The mental health recovery college project in Sussex developed and facilitated an eight-session building resilience course that over 100 people facing mental health challenges had attended at the time of writing this chapter.
- The Arts Connect project supported young people with learning disabilities to produce creative items (such as a board game) that were designed to help people (with and without learning disabilities) understand the challenges they faced in their daily lives and the approaches that could help them respond to these.
- Representatives from a range of our projects (including those above) contributed to an *Imagine* programme presentation of our emerging community development findings to an audience of policy-makers and charity sector lobbyists.

Some of our creative products were displayed at the *Imagine* exhibition in Sheffield that communicated the co-productive process, often through the stories that people told as well as the artefacts themselves (Phipps and Zanotti, 2011). Inclusion of this broad range of products meant that even when we devoted a large portion of our last retreat to producing written academic journal articles and chapters, we did not experience the same 'subjugation to the academy' that Stuttaford et al (2012, p 122) describe in their CoP. We found that lived experience, community and practitioner input alongside that of academics helped ensure the coherence, applicability and sharable nature of our work.

Effects or outcomes of the retreats

Mid-way through our programme, in a session that was noted for its high energy and level of engagement, participants considered the question of what good collaboration looks like in light of our experience. The following features were identified:

- Network of bridges.
- Shared understanding.
- Reciprocal benefits.
- Trust.
- Open communication.
- Good collaboration is evident when you've done something better than if you had done it alone.
- People connecting with shared vision.
- Requires precious time.
- Shared journey with synergy.
- Working to connect the disagreements to produce something new.
- An inspiring, equal and power-neutral partnership where all parties share experiences, workload and a commitment to a specific outcome.
- Making positive use of different knowledge bases (academic, practitioner, lived experience).

Our experiences support Wenger's assertions that, on the one hand, boundaries can be challenging places to inhabit. Yet, on the other hand, they are usually places of deep and significant learning (Wenger, 1998). Community development literature considers that the transformation of individuals is a key product of collaboration, especially in terms of becoming more reflective and active citizens (Recknagel and Holland, 2013). This is even truer when the formation of a CoP involves the renegotiation of significant boundaries. We, too, found that members of our community experienced personal transformations. Self-confidence grew among people who had hitherto not participated in research projects, with many undertaking untried leadership roles. Non-academics reported that they had developed new skills in writing, presenting, and above all, in conducting research that they felt able to integrate into their identity by the end of the project. Among academics, transformations showed in the ways they embraced deeper levels of co-productive research and learned specific methods to support this. For instance, some academics had doubted whether the collective approach to drafting research papers at the last retreat would work, but found our approach to have been very effective.

Building on these individual transformations we found evidence that they, in turn, were contributing to changes in people's communities and organisations. In a context where many 'third sector' organisations are experiencing negative impacts from having to compete with each other for funds (Mayo et al, 2013), involvement in the CoP provided an experience that reminded organisations and communities of the value of collaboration, as well as providing people with a methodology and enhanced leadership capacity to bring into fruition.

We were able to achieve these outcomes by sustaining our CoP over five years. This was done by combining structure, leadership and continuity on the one hand, with enough disturbance – often through the creative use of boundaries – on the other, in a way that allowed for experiences to be shared and new knowledge generated. More concretely it created new relationships and networks opening the door to future collaborations that were already emerging at the end of the *Imagine* programme.

Conclusions and lessons learned

At the end of these five years, our key message is that our CoP approach very effectively enabled diverse voices to be heard *and* to fully participate in our collaborative research project.

This was achieved in a manner that both developed us as a community and supported the development of the various communities associated with our multiple projects. We advance the following recommendations for people considering adopting a similar approach to collaborative community development–related research:

- In early stages of CoP formation consider how best to involve people who may span boundaries of different realms of knowledge. Similarly consider what 'boundary objects' may help communication and creative knowledge production across boundaries.
- Definition of knowledge – design activities that enable different collaborators to share their knowledge in a way that validates the different sources form which this may come. This is intended to increase collaborators' confidence in the legitimacy of their expertise, and to facilitate other collaborators' appreciation and understanding of that.
- Encourage explicit sharing of the expectations that different collaborators' stakeholders (for example, employers/communities) have of what the outcomes should be of their involvement. These should be discussed and agreement reached as to how to combine these in the overall plans of the project.
- Include a range of activities, formal and less formal, interactive and creative, to create a range of spaces where collaborators can contribute.
- Consider also the wider environment for the retreat – try to hold it in a space that does not feel like it 'belongs' to one set of collaborators

alone. Make sure adequate time is scheduled for 'downtime' and informal interactions and discussions.

• Make explicit use of social learning theory tools and frameworks – not just to analyse effective collaboration but also to guide it.

References

Abma, T.A., Nierse, C.J. and Widdershoven, G.A.M. (2009) 'Patients as partners in responsive research: Methodological notions for collaborations in mixed research teams', *Qualitative Health Research*, 19(3), 401–15.

Bowers, B., Cohen, L.W., Elliot, A.E., Grabowski, D.C., Fishman, N.W., Sharkey, S.S., et al (2013) 'Creating and supporting a mixed methods health services research team', *Health Services Research*, 48(6), pt 2, 2157–80.

Davies, C., Gant, N., Hart, A., Millican, J., Wolff, D., Prosser, B. and Laing, S. (2016) 'Exploring engaged spaces in community-university partnership', *Metropolitan Universities: An International Forum*, 27(3), 6–26.

Eib, B.J. and Miller, P. (2006) 'Faculty development as community building: An approach to professional development that supports communities of practice for online teaching', *The International Review of Research in Open and Distributed Learning*, 7(2) (www.irrodl.org/index.php/irrodl/article/view/299/639).

Glover, R.W. and Silka, L. (2013) 'Choice, power and perspective: The neglected question of who initiates engaged campus–community partnerships', *Gateways: International Journal of Community Research and Engagement*, 6(1), 38–56.

Green, A. and Kearney, J. (2011) 'Participatory action learning and action research for self-sustaining community development: Engaging Pacific islanders in southeast Queensland', *The Australasian Journal of University-Community Engagement*, 6(1), 46–68.

Hart, A. and Wolff, D. (2007) 'What we have learnt and where we might go next', in A. Hart, E. Maddison and D. Wolff (eds) *Community-university partnerships in practice*, Leicester: National Institute of Adult Continuing Education, 195–206.

Hart, A., Maddison, E. and Wolff, D. (2007) *Community-university partnerships in practice*, Leicester: National Institute of Adult Continuing Education.

Hart, A., Davies, C., Aumann, K., Wenger, E., Aranda, K., Heaver, B. and Wolff, D. (2013) 'Mobilising knowledge in community-university partnerships: What does a community of practice approach contribute?', *Contemporary Social Science: Journal of the Academy of Social Sciences*, 8(3), 278-91.

Hart, A., Gagnon, E., Eryigit-Madzwamuse, S., Cameron, J., Aranda, K., Rathbone, A. and Heaver, B. (2016) 'Uniting resilience research and practice with a health inequalities approach', *SAGE Open*, 6(4), 1-13.

Imagine (2016) 'Imagine Annual Event Gallery' (www.imaginecommunity.org.uk/imagine-annual-event-gallery).

Kornhaber, R., Cross, M., Betihavas, V. and Bridgman, H. (2016) 'The benefits and challenges of academic writing retreats: An integrative review', *Higher Education Research & Development*, 35(6), 1210-27.

Levitas, R. (2007) 'Looking for the blue: The necessity of utopia', *Journal of Political Ideologies*, 12(3), 289-306.

Mayo, M., Mendiwelso-Bendek, Z. and Packham, C. (2013) 'Community development, community organising and third sector-university research partnerships', in M. Mayo, Z. Mendiwelso-Bendek and C. Packham (eds) *Community research for community development*, Basingstoke: Palgrave Macmillan, 3-18.

Northmore, S. and Hart, A. (2011) 'Sustaining community-university partnerships', *Gateways: International Journal of Community Research & Engagement*, 4, 1-11.

Phipps, D. and Zanotti, D. (2011) 'It's the Basement Stories, not the Belt: Lessons from a community-university knowledge mobilisation collaboration', *Gateways: International Journal of Community Research and Engagement*, 4, 203-17.

Recknagel, G. and Holland, D. (2013) 'How inclusive and how empowering? Two case studies researching the impact of active citizenship learning initiatives in a social policy context', in M. Mayo, Z. Mendiwelso-Bendek and C. Packham (eds) *Community research for community development*, Basingstoke: Palgrave Macmillan, 19-39.

Stoecker, R. (2013) *Research methods for community change: A project-based approach* (Vol 2), Thousand Oaks, CA: Sage Publications.

Stuttaford, M., Glattstein-Young, G. and London, L. (2012) '"Dialogue, review and reflect": A spiral of co-learning and co-research to surface knowledge on the right to health', *Gateways: International Journal of Community Research and Engagement*, 5, 115-34.

Thompson, J.L. (2009) 'Building collective communication competence in interdisciplinary research teams', *Journal of Applied Communication Research*, 37(3), 278-297.

Wenger, E. (1998) *Communities of practice: Learning, meaning and identity*, Cambridge: Cambridge University Press (https://thesystemsthinker. com/communities-of-practice-learning-as-a-social-system).

Wenger, E. (2000) 'Communities of practice and social learning systems', *Organization*, 7(2), 225-46.

Wenger, E., McDermott, R.A. and Snyder, W. (2002) *Cultivating communities of practice: A guide to managing knowledge*, Boston, MA: Harvard Business School Press.

Wenger, E., Trayner, B. and de Laat, M. (2011) *Promoting and assessing value creation in communities and networks: A conceptual framework. Rapport 18*, Open University of the Netherlands, Ruud de Moor Centrum.

Wenger-Trayner, E. and Wenger-Trayner, B. (2012) *Leadership groups: Distributed leadership in social learning* (https://wenger-trayner.com/ resources/leadership-groups-for-social-learning).

Wenger-Trayner, E. and Wenger-Trayner, B. (2014) *Learning in a landscape of practice: A framework*, London: Routledge.

Wenger-Trayner, B., Wenger-Trayner, E., Cameron, J., Eryigit-Madzwamuse, S. and Hart, A. (2017) 'Boundaries and boundary objects: An evaluation framework for mixed methods research', *Journal of Mixed Methods Research* (http://journals.sagepub.com/doi/ pdf/10.1177/1558689817732225).

Part II
Co-creating through and with the arts

How does arts practice inform a community development approach to the co-production of research?

David Bell, Steve Pool, Kim Streets and Natalie Walton,
with Kate Pahl

Introduction

Kate Pahl

At the heart of this chapter is a recorded conversation between four people working at the interface between art and research. This Introduction, along with the Conclusion, is designed to situate the conversation within the wider context of arts practice and co-produced research.

Contemporary art practice has experienced a paradigm shift from the idea of art as sitting within the gallery to a more diffuse concept of art as collaborative and participatory (Bishop, 2012). These approaches involve people building knowledge together, and rely on a de-centring or de-materialising of the art object to suggest something new. This chapter sits within a tradition of dialogical approaches to knowledge production and draws on the tradition within contemporary art practice of the conversation as a form of engagement (Kester, 2004, 2011). Kester (2011, p 67) writes about such art projects:

> What is at stake in these projects is not dialogue per se but the extent to which the artist is able to catalyze emancipatory insights through dialogue. This requires an acute understanding of the many ways in which these insights can be constrained and compromised.

The conversation that follows is between an artist (Steve Pool), a chief executive of a museum service (Kim Streets), an arts educator (Natalie Walton) and a researcher (David Bell). All worked on the 'cultural' part of the *Imagine* project. This dialogue reflects their concerns about how they respond as individuals to a co-produced project, *Imagine*, with its focus on imagining better futures.

As a conversation, it explores the dialogic form (Banks and Armstrong et al, 2014). This enables the authorship to sit with more than one person, and be composed of multiple viewpoints. This situates a community development approach to the co-production of research within a conversation that lets in multiple viewpoints and points of difference (Mouffe, 2007). The discussion is personal but also political. Reading it provides a different kind of lens. The conversation reflects the lived reality of the project, the aspirations and pragmatic decisions, and it makes visible the problems and opportunities of bringing people together from different backgrounds, histories and expectations to try and build something together. It is socially produced. Stephen Willatts, a contemporary artist, wrote a set of propositions about art as a social model in a manual including the following statements:

Art and its dependency on relationships between people

> The realization that all "art" is dependent on society, dependent on the relationships between people, and not the sole product of any one person, is becoming increasingly important to the shaping of future culture. This divestment of authorship is seen as more relevant to an emerging culture founded on networks of exchange, fluidity, transience and mutuality, as it ultimately offers us the prospect of self-organization in person and interpersonal society. (Willatts, 2012, 2B)

Art, then, has something to contribute to a community development approach to the co-production of research in that it is socially produced, process-led and transformative as it can create and inform future cultures. The conversation now explores this further.

Hoping, capturing, remembering, imagining: A conversation between arts workers and a university researcher

David Bell, Steve Pool, Kim Streets and Natalie Walton

As four people who worked either on or for the *Imagine* project's cultural 'work package', we have been asked to reflect on our experience. Over the five years of *Imagine* we were not in close contact yet we explored common themes and ideas. Issues around collaborative and participatory methods, co-production and arts and humanities approaches to knowledge underpinned our research and our actions.

Our backgrounds vary. Our experiences are diverse. Our fascinations, hang-ups, biases, obsessions, hopes and frustrations clash, overlap, intersect and sail past each other. Our engagements with *Imagine* varied in terms of scope, project, employment and time committed. Our reflection started as a conversation. We decided this format would suit this chapter best – not in the Platonic sense in which discussion resolves itself in 'the truth', but rather as a means of capturing and working with these differences. In this, the chapter is itself in the spirit of much collaborative art and research, which – far from seeking a cosy, consensual conviviality – looks to explore (and reproduces) tensions, hierarchies, contradictions and differences that constitute our social fabric (Charnley, 2011; Bell, 2017). This is, of course, not simply a reflective mode but is productive as well: new individual and collective knowledges emerge in the in–between-ness of conversation, even as (and sometimes precisely *because*) the conversation diverges from the issues in hand.

Recognising the importance of such conversation, this chapter preserves the dialogic form. It is an edited version of a conversation that took place on 21 July 2016 at the Arts Council's office at Bretton Hall, Yorkshire Sculpture Park, where Natalie now works. Editing has included inserting references where works are directly cited, re-arranging the flow for ease of reading, and making general edits to wording and grammatical structures so the conversation is easier to follow in its written form. The participants were as follows:

David Bell: I joined *Imagine* around a year into the project. I worked as a part-time Research Associate exploring the relationships and tensions between contemporary arts practice in and around Sheffield and utopianism. This involved speaking to a number of artists (from a variety of backgrounds), curators and people involved in arts projects, as well as running workshops at *Imagine* events. I have a background in the interdisciplinary field of 'utopian studies', and I now work as a coordinator for Radar, Loughborough University's contemporary arts programme.

Steve Pool: I trained as a visual artist and now reluctantly describe myself as an artist who works in the social realm. I am artist in residence across the *Imagine* project, a role that was never really defined and never really had any edges.

Kim Streets: I am the Chief Executive of Museum Sheffield. In the *Imagine* project I collaborated with the team to conduct a series of interviews on the experience of the residents of the newly regenerated neo-brutalist Park Hill flats in Sheffield to produce a film about their lived experiences.

Natalie Walton: I was Head of Learning at The Hepworth Wakefield, a major contemporary art gallery in Wakefield, Yorkshire, UK, which opened to the public in 2011. In the *Imagine* project I worked with a group of young people from a rent deposit scheme, who had experienced homelessness. We used the gallery collection and the building as a starting point to explore conversations about the past, present and future.

This conversation begins with considering the idea of imagining better futures and making them happen, a theme that was central to *Imagine*. We explore the issues that emerge through co-produced research. Drawing on our direct experience of *Imagine* we ask what it is to answer a research question together, how to move through difficulty and where the best thinking happens.

The conversation

David: I guess, for me, a key question is not *how do* we imagine better futures, but *can* we imagine better futures? This might sound odd, but it's a key debate in utopian studies, which is where my academic background is. In these debates, it's sometimes held that actually no, we can't. Frederic Jameson's oft-quoted 'it is easier to imagine the end of the world than the end of capitalism' [2005, p 199] is indicative here. What I think he's trying to communicate is that we *cannot* imagine utopia because, by definition, it will be so radically different to the present. We cannot escape the social, material and structural forces of the present to imagine a world free from the various hierarchies, oppressions and tyrannies that constitute it because they constitute us too.

Kim: I like the idea of exploring the notion of 'better'. I think what we do in the museum is to give provocations, things that may inspire you to imagine the future differently and inspire you to question the present. I think there is something important about imagining; you need to be able to imagine something different to enable change to happen. Looking to the future can push you to achieve things, to an extent, occupy it!

David: That's closer to the position of [utopian studies scholar] Ruth Levitas, whose work on utopia inspired the framing of the [cultural part of the] *Imagine* project. She insists that although utopian visions don't give us blueprints for 'the good life', they play an important role in the 'education of desire': they help us desire more and desire better, particularly when they're connected to the material conditions of our contemporary world [Levitas, 2013].

Natalie: Much of the work I did at The Hepworth Wakefield was about exploring problems situated in the present so that we might think differently about futures. When we started the project The Hepworth had just 'landed': a futuristic building with a historical collection, a whole new organisation! It really did feel at the start, like we had landed. The project was a way of capturing what young people from the most disadvantaged backgrounds in Wakefield thought of the gallery, what it meant or could mean to them if we opened ourselves up to working with them, not just putting on programmes for young people and hoping that they will come to us.

Kim: I can see that the work done by Museums Sheffield has sometimes captured elements of stories, giving people an opportunity to reflect on or voice their hopes, their regrets, the showing and sharing of hopes and dreams. In the film we made for *Imagine* people are caught in time; we have captured their hopes and dreams and these, in a way, are suspended, fixed in time, in a display, but they're active in the present.

David: Yes, I'd also want to question whether artists and academics should seek to 'capture' enthusiasm for change. There's a danger of things being co-opted to the advantage of the academy/the artist with no material gain for communities.

Steve: I think there's a danger of getting too hung up on the words, though. You 'capture' a moment, you 'capture' a memory: that's not just containment, holding onto something so that people can collectively imagine from it, an archive of hopes that can inform the future, in the future.

David: Yes, absolutely. Jameson and Moylan, in particular, argue that utopianism requires a collective historical consciousness [Jameson, 2005; Daniel and Moylan, 2007]. Academia, the arts and museums are spaces – however problematic – where that might be forged, repositioned and reworked.

Steve: Park Hill has been central to the *Imagine* project.[1] Kim, you did work there with Museums Sheffield in 1999 – 'capturing', perhaps, young people's hopes for the future. Has that been done again with *Imagine*?

Kim: Yes. The film we made is about Park Hill's transformation, and for this we interviewed people who live in the redeveloped part that had been renovated by the Urban Splash developers. It's clear that they can see the future of the building and of a new community. People have moved there from three-bedroomed houses on the edge of the Peak District. So they can see a future, but perhaps in a different sense to the future Park Hill was intended to usher in…. In terms of the work in 1999: it makes me uncomfortable to use the word 'capturing' when reflecting on that, but I suppose we did do that. And looking back now I ask 'Why?' and 'What for?'

Natalie: Prior to *Imagine* I had worked on a pre-cursor programme with Kate Pahl to invite young people into The Hepworth Wakefield before it opened, to explore with them what this new gallery could be, what opportunities it could afford them and how they wanted to direct those opportunities once the gallery opened to the public. The young people were considered to be not in education, employment or training (NEET); this meant that they were constantly looking for work or being directed by youth workers to find opportunities in order to claim benefits. What we found while working with the group was affirmed in the *Imagine* project. We, the 'gallery experts', felt that these young people would benefit from the project and that discussions about the future would enable them to create a better future. However, the concept of the future for these young people was a pretty difficult thing to consider. In a chaotic life where the future looks pretty difficult and all they can do is to get through the present, we found that the future was not the best place to focus.

Given changes in education where perhaps we are losing a focus on imagination and where education is closing things down, perhaps the gallery is a place where we can open things up. As an adult I find 'the future' something quite difficult to get a handle on – even thinking about my own future is problematic. For me you need to feel embedded and confident in the present to imagine or even to think about the future. And when we worked with 'targeted' young people in Wakefield, we talk about making better futures. But whose *future* are we talking about? There are institutional futures, but what is 'better' for them is not necessarily young people's idea of 'better'. In our project we needed to depersonalise the future and make it about place, about Wakefield. In doing this we could bring in the gallery collection and Wakefield's history as a means to get to the present and eventually a future. We also talked about these young people informing how we work; we brought them into the gallery, gave them behind-the-scenes access and artists and researchers to work with who were respectful of their ideas and opinions. I worry, however, that once the projects run out of funds this respect, time and attention disappears, and we once again have let these young people down.

I think the agency of the young people – having them so centrally embedded in our project – allowed the institution to see how we can engage young people more deeply into our programming. So I think that's the main place where 'imagining futures' had an impact: on the institution. I don't know what the long-term impact of that has been since I left.

Steve: For me the idea of 'imagining better futures' was more of an ideological position. I saw it as stemming from the idea that we've reached a point in history where many people think things are getting worse. This is after a period – possibly mythical – where people thought things were getting better: from 1945 to the miner's strike, perhaps, and locally the Battle of Orgreave. There was a time period of post-war agreement where even consecutive Conservative governments presided over a period where things seemed to get more equal. Then the gap begins to widen again. But there's something else: to go back to what David was saying, there seems to be a limitation of alternatives – people can't imagine anything different, but they don't want to: they believe the status quo is actually as good as it gets.

As artist-in-residence on *Imagine* I didn't have to materialise anything, not like a project in an art gallery, so I could think of these questions in broader, less institutional contexts. So that gives me the scope to be naïve, perhaps optimistic, about the potential for culture to be transformative within society.

David: That's exactly it. In imagining the future it's often what *doesn't* change that's most revealing, because it reveals the limits of our imagination. And that doesn't have to be technology: it can be social norms and structures too. So we might *imagine* particular facets of the future differently on this project, but what does that mean if we don't also re-imagine the relationship between academia, the arts and 'community' (which I think we are also trying to do, of course)? And I think Natalie raises a really important point too: three of us in this conversation were precariously employed when working on *Imagine* – that changes how you think about the future. It's not just 'the communities' that face uncertain futures but also the 'professionals' engaged to work with them, albeit in different ways. The affective, material and imaginal consequences of precarious employment and unemployment are so often absent from these discussions.

Steve: Class is really important here. I remember previous work exploring the hopes of young people in Sheffield. A lot of the poorer kids had really impractical aspirations: 'I'm going to be a pop star or a footballer or a model', a route that is open only to a tiny, lucky minority. And when you work with asylum-seekers or kids leaving care, for example, the future just isn't an appropriate thing to consider in that abstract sense: they need a place to live *now*, a place they can feel safe *now*. Better-off kids, though, often have more practical future plans: 'I'm going to be a doctor', or solicitor or teacher.

This morning I was reading about Harry Brearley, who is often credited as the inventor of stainless steel. He grew up about 200 yards from where I live now in a poor area with seven siblings. In his autobiography he says how he was amazed his mum could even keep him clean. And he went on to do something so important! That time feels like the last days of wonder, when people felt like there were more possibilities. I think that, for me, wonder is the essence of the question about hopefulness, about possibility, about daydreaming. I know I'm being romantic here, but we need culture more than anything: capturing imagination and sustaining momentum are things that are lacking in the ways that we see the world.

David: There's a real difference in the kind of 'futures' we're talking about here: there's what you imagine on a personal level (what you want to be when you grow up, for example) and then a more collective level: what changes might we make to the way we organise society? These aren't absolutely opposed, of course: the fact so few people will go on to a life of making music isn't to do with their talent, but the structures of our world. So for me that's where we should intervene, and where utopianism tries to intervene: it's collective, and it imagines – or aims for – a large-scale transformation of social relations.

But I also want to come back to the class difference you just mentioned – and I think this is racialised and gendered too. The middle class (probably white) kids who wanted to be doctors or solicitors and so on – I suspect they weren't really 'imagining' anything different: it's more an expectation, or even a sense of entitlement. But the dream of being a pop star is imaginary: it's individualist, yes, but it's also transformative – a deep-seated wish for a life that's magical and free from the material problems that perhaps define so much of their lives in the here-and-now (that's not what being a footballer or a pop star is, of course, but it's how it's often imagined). For Ernst Bloch those wishes – 'daydreams' – even if individual, are key to any utopianism: the question is how we turn them into a collective force that re-imagines and re-makes the world.

Natalie: That's interesting in terms of The Hepworth. You've got 'the art gallery' – the symbol of 'high culture' – and then you've got disadvantaged young people. And connecting that (or not) is this broken logic of the institution. 'We build a gallery. It will represent culture! We open the doors and people will come and the whole place/the city will be culturally enriched.' But you need to consider all those people across the city who don't access the gallery. We can bring some of those young people in through the programme, but because of societal structures it's unlikely their work will ever adorn our walls. It's something I've found incredibly disjointed about working in art institutions. We were able to develop a programme in which we co-curated an exhibition of works from the collection with the young people, and it was made possible to showcase this work in an area of the gallery assigned to locally based or community-related exhibitions. Museums and galleries have a habit of putting 'community' work in a corner where it can be contained and framed within the hierarchy. I think we did manage to break ground in this instance due to the comments we had from members of the public who could relate to the ideas the young people had presented from the collection. The young people later made work that they wanted to place in the entrance to the office at the rent deposit scheme in order to show other young people their utopian idea of Wakefield.

Steve: Tear down the walls!

I've done workshops for kids at Leeds Art Gallery. I always ask the kids who they think the collection belongs to. They never know and are always surprised when I say it belongs to them. That's important! These collections belong to us, and sometimes just saying that registers something. It's not a massive thing, but this gallery is ours: this collection belongs to us, collectively, all of us. That sense of collective ownership can foster a sense of collective agency: the kids feel they should have a say in the future, and that helps them define themselves in relation to that future.

Natalie: Working with The Hepworth's collections with young people has really made me reflect on how shows are curated and how works are displayed. When they were in our stores and engaging in great depth on their own terms – often around place – they really started thinking through both history and the future. It was the start of something. It made me reflect on how we display works in the 'art world', how curators make decisions, who validates them, but then who the audience is. I still feel there is a disconnect between curator and audience. We have dialogues about what goes up for show, but it's very often on the terms of the 'art world': I think often we're not asking big questions or political questions, the kinds of questions that open up space for people to think about better futures. Working on *Imagine* has personally made me better at challenging the galleries I work with to ask those big questions in ways I wouldn't previously have thought of doing.

Kim: So this has been powerful in allowing you to change the things you are personally in control of?

Natalie: Yes, it's allowed me to ask questions I wasn't really able to ask and be confident that they need asking. I don't feel that learning has to be done in secret or that it needs to be behind people's backs in order to do the work you want to do. I now work more closely with curators and try to challenge them on what our local audience is seeing and how they, as curators, have a role to play in engaging with participants. I'd like to see equality in the development and delivery of projects.

David: I love what you say about ownership there, Natalie, and there's something wonderfully utopian about the idea that collective ownership isn't simply an end in itself, but a mechanism that opens up the imagination and thus the world to the unexpected. Something I'd like to raise here, though, is that we also need to situate that ownership globally and historically. So I don't know about Leeds Art Gallery, but a lot of public collections in the UK contain artefacts that have been stolen as Britain colonised the world. And this is something that always needs thinking through: how did (and does) Britain's status as a colonial power relate to our ability to imagine the future? So if we think about Harry Brearley again, we can't separate Sheffield's steel industry from colonialism: the city sold steel across the empire for munitions, railways and so on. And academia and the arts are implicated in this in a number of ways

Natalie's experiences of working with young people, though, remind me of some of the work I've seen with young people at contemporary art galleries. What's been good about much of this is that it's not just been framed around 'inclusion' in a present that is so often hostile to them for a whole host of reasons, nor simply in art world terms, but has been about increasing their agency: their ability to act on the world, and also to be acted on by the world.

However, I can't help but think of this in relation to thinking about class and entitlement. I watched a group of very middle-class young people talk to artists in a contemporary art gallery involved in the *Imagine* project. I'm sure they all felt teenage insecurity, but in the gallery they had a real confidence about them. I've no doubt most of them will go on to university, and I wouldn't be at all surprised if one or two of them became academics. But there's a sense of entitlement there too. I don't mean to say that they were bratty, or acted in a spoiled manner – in many ways their confidence was inspiring – but rather that there's a certain entitlement to how they felt so at home in a contemporary art gallery: they didn't need to be told this was a public space; they just felt that it was *their* space. They could instinctively navigate (and interrogate) its norms and expectations. That's in part because of the incredible work done by the curators and engagement team at the gallery, and the artist they were working with, but it's also a privilege of their class. And of course by working in the gallery in this way they were helping to reproduce that class and the privileges it brings: it's something that would look really good on a university application and will help orient them in the future.

Our conversation now turns to an exploration of methods and we question the current trends within collaborative research and how these can help us navigate the terrain of university-community partnerships (CUPs). Like many CUPs the project has worried around ideas and asks as many questions as it answers.

Steve: My experience working as artist-in-residence gives me a concern about the way 'social science' is used. A lot of the conversations

I've often been involved in are about institutions how museums, galleries can use social science to demonstrate 'economic impact' and 'audience satisfaction'. But I think social sciences can do much more than that.

Kim: At Museums Sheffield we're quite clear about the difference between data and qualitative research: we know there is more to social sciences than data. But we know how to use data to inform just about everything we do. I don't think we are so clear on other kinds of research.

Steve: I think it's important to look at why we're being asked to address this question, perhaps it is because the funding stream that *Imagine* emerged from [the Connected Communities programme] tries to 'co-produce' knowledge: to research 'with' communities rather than 'on' them. That's also related to the changing 'Impact agenda' and broader, ontological questions about why universities exist. There was a feeling that many people outside universities see them as ivory towers separated from the rest of the world.

Kim: I haven't perceived a change in the way universities do things. Co-production may make them reflect, but from where I'm sat it's about addressing the Impact agenda and the Research Excellence Framework and it's about funding. So on *Imagine* there are a set of questions that we've asked ourselves, but much of the co-production we've done has taken place with small groups for a very short period of time. I'm sure it makes a difference to those five or so participants for a time, but is that 'transforming the landscape of community research?' I'm not sure it is.

I still think there are problems when everyone outside the university is framed as a 'community partner': why don't academic researchers also belong to a 'community'? It creates a hierarchy. The academic is often framed as giving 'voice' to people who otherwise might not be 'heard'. I think we need to be really clear about what research is going to do in the first place: is it really going to affect policy? If it's actually designed to make a difference, then it needs to be designed with that in mind.

David: Yes, the word 'community' makes me uneasy, or at least the way it's often used makes me uneasy. I have two concerns. First, it too-often functions as a 'dog whistle' term for *particular kinds of community*, and in so doing makes them 'safe' for a middle-class paternalism to channel their interests in certain ways. Second, it often serves to impose a false unity on a collective that's constituted by difference, and functions as a point of exclusion as much as inclusion. That exclusion might be necessary, or even politically progressive, but I think it's too often disavowed by the cosiness we often associate with community. But I remember when I was considering whether to apply for the job I eventually got on *Imagine* I came across an essay you'd written, Steve, which I really liked. It addressed my final concern: you argued that community can never be assumed – it's always under construction and is always conflictual. I think you might have addressed my first concern too? That only certain groups of people are called 'communities' by academics?

Steve: I think some academics really do try to flatten those hierarchies, but even then you can't get away from the fact that they're a lecturer, a professor. Those titles have status and a degree of security that communities often don't have.

Natalie: I don't think our project had a transformative effect on the young people we worked with; it was too short and that meant we didn't get the depth of engagement you need to change structures. I feel there was a recognition, but not transformation.

I don't think this is possible until we unpick the language we use, its hierarchies and assumptions, like community or the way we talk about art.

David: Co-production certainly speaks a transformative language, and I think there's a genuine potential to do some good work within that, as well as examples – in *Imagine* and elsewhere – of that being done. But like Steve, I think it's really important to ask why the 'turn' to co-production emerged when it did. For me, it's really linked to the neoliberalisation of the academy. As people like Stuart Hall have pointed out, neoliberalism is very good at talking a democratising, even radical, language, but then turning that language and associated practices against the collective subjects who developed it. And I think there's a very real risk that the turn to co-production does that: it speaks the language of social movements and struggles ('research *with* not *on*') but often defangs them by channelling them through apolitical forms; and comes at a time when the working conditions of academics are ever-worsening. I've just written an article with Kate [Pahl] exploring some of these tensions [Bell and Pahl, 2017].

And going back to what I said earlier: I think it's important to interrogate what's not interrogated. What doesn't change in co-production? So, for example, we might try to break down the hierarchies between academia and 'community', but what about hierarchies within academia? What about the hierarchies between 'intellectual' labour and other forms of labour that are integral to academia? There's so much that goes into producing something like *Imagine*: administrative, cleaning, caring and so on. It's not just intellectual. One of the things that's really stayed with me from *Imagine* is when I when I co-organised a workshop at a conference. An administrator participated and said afterwards how much she'd got from it. Now that kind of thing should be so standard that it's unremarkable (the 'walls' between administrative and intellectual work should be challenged – even destroyed), but it really isn't.

Steve: I think that there was a real attempt to question hierarchies on *Imagine*, straightforward stuff like really listening to research assistants but also questioning where knowledge resides. I like David's more collective idea of production – I'd not thought about it like this – it sounds like a commune.

Kim: Experience can be a form of expertise too: people who've worked in different institutional settings can be really important because they'll know what works in different places.

Steve: I think we need some historical 'expertise' too. It's interesting to look at co-production's pre-histories. I've found it fascinating learning about the community development projects' histories that have been undertaken as part of *Imagine*, for example [see Chapter 2]. It's been really valuable to engage with this whole history that I knew nothing about: of people like me working in 'community regeneration'. There are lessons there that nobody gets to learn! You can imagine a think tank or someone in government now saying 'Let's do something a bit like the CDP [community development project] but don't show anybody any of that stuff because if they have the history they might work out how to really dig down deep!' So for me there's a real lack of historical information that helps us situate what's happening. Art, culture and research are forces we need to build a more equitable society – to 'transform communities' – but they get restricted and controlled. And then even the privileged people who work for institutions hate their work and lose faith in the very aims that took them to those places in the first place. So we can't let those forces end up completely in the hands of those institutions: it's that issue of 'capturing' again!

I've also found that institutional pressures limit the involvement of academics. There are projects that look so strong on paper, where academics' expertise and interests overlap with or are relevant to a community concerns, but in reality they struggle to connect them because they don't get anywhere near enough time built into their workload to engage. Then so much falls to research assistants, who normally didn't design the project in the first place, and then often leave to work elsewhere.

David: Yes, and often haven't had the chance to build lasting, deep and meaningful relationships of trust with non-academic co-producers, although the issue of that relationship runs deeper. Often, the relationship between academic and non-academic co-producers comes before the funding bid is put in. And then in whose interest is it to cultivate that relationship? Academics are ultimately answerable to universities as employers, and as employers they generally want to see the money and not the relationship. And communities often can't afford to put in the time for something that may not be successful.

Steve: I know some funders are beginning to address this by providing funding for early stage exploratory work.

In all this I'm reminded of a quote we used to use in the Creative Partnerships programme that worked with artists in educational settings. Something like: 'There is no point in waiting for the educational world to become perfect so we can do perfect work within it – this will never happen; what's important is what it is possible to achieve within an imperfect world.'

We could say nothing is possible and that there is no point in working with universities, but then I have discussions like this, with a combination of different experiences. This is a space of possibility! You are people who care and who are contesting things. And this is part of an academic project! This space is not incidental. And I think it's worth looking back: in a year or two maybe reflecting on this process and see what we've learned. What impact will this have on how we work? I'm interested not just in how research tackles a particular 'problem', but how it allows expansive new dialogues to happen. If not through projects like this, where do we get the space to step away and think differently?

Kim: I agree that these conversations are important. It's the type of conversation we should be having from the start of a project and right throughout its duration, but we're only having it at the end.

Natalie: I've found that the pressure of outcomes and time-limited projects gets in the way. If I got involved in this sort of co-production again I would ask for six months of these kind of conversations to happen so that we could share experiences as a way of moving forwards. We did have some really good conversations with the research assistant working on the project with The Hepworth but again, because of restrictions on everyone's time, they get squeezed! And I'm not sure how much of the conversations get captured. We seem to go round in circles, I spend my life having the same discussions and not getting anywhere. Because of this I spend my life thinking that someone is doing the same thing much better somewhere else.

Steve: I sometimes think that this must be working *somewhere else*, where they do things differently. But then perhaps that's just an impression you get through reading evaluation reports. I never really believe them, of course.

Kim: I think we need to 'capture' more of this – what we need to do better, what we need to do differently. But at the same time, I've been involved in co-produced projects where you have five meetings but still nothing is decided.

Steve: Yeah, is there a risk of too much talk? In *Small change* [2004] Hamdi says that people often talk for too long before they do anything, then act for too long before they stop and reflect. And there are questions about time here. Who's paid to have these conversations? To give up that time?

Natalie: Yes, we need to think about our capacity to deliver. We all have targets and expectations, but I've been involved in some projects that are structured around more informal conversations. That's incredibly healthy as a professional who's constantly expected to be in delivery mode: time to digest, to think about what we're doing.

Steve: Collective spaces are definitely important. I went to a talk recently about what 'excellence' means in relation to Arts Council England's framework. Nobody knew! But having a space to talk about it was really important: we could collectively work out a strategy for how to approach it. I think there are people who get into terrible habits of working because they're never able to find or create that collective space to talk through what they're doing. Galleries and museums are a case in point: people need space to discuss what they're doing and why.

Reflecting on the conversation and learning points

Perhaps, then, this conversation performed its own argument. It provided a space for those necessary discussions about the messy complexity of co-production. It illuminates the cramped spaces of possibility that emerge through such work and illustrates why those spaces are often so cramped (Bell and Pahl, 2017). Its dissemination in the form of this chapter provides a space of a different kind, a space for readerly reflection and further engagement. Preserving this kind of discussion – so often 'relegated' to precisely the informal conference chat of the kind described above by Steve – might also play a role in the construction of a collective memory: an archive of knowledge, frustration and hope that ran up against precarity and institutional demands.

Yet in another way this conversation performs its own failure. Since we had it (just over a year ago, as this is written) we have never again met up as a group. We've returned to it in intermittent, stolen, unpaid moments of panic, frustration and regret as the demands of new projects and new jobs take hold. There's so much we want to go back to, so much we could have done, so much we know we could say to each other and, perhaps, to you – the reader. That we cannot is indicative not of the *Imagine* project, but of the way the material structures of work (itself striated by class, racialisation and gender) mitigate against such sustained engagement, all too frequently cutting off imagination at its root, or just as its shoots begin to emerge.

Conclusion

Kate Pahl

In this conversation, key themes were explored: social class and the gallery, the importance of hope and utopia in the arts, but also the conditions of being in the arts world and a concern to make things better for young people. The authors address issues of social class and culture, and accept that the art world is not perfect. Natalie Walton talked about her experiences working with The Hepworth Wakefield and the glimpses of hope she had in developing a way of working that was about doing things a bit differently, giving young people ownership over the gallery in new ways. The difficulties of making change happen in the arts are articulated. This is a problem in practical terms – most artists are freelance, and money is tight everywhere. None of the people who wrote this piece did this in paid time. So what does this mean for the arts and community development approaches in those contexts?

Conclusions and lessons learned

The lessons learned from this that can be applied to a community development approach to the co-production of research include the following:

- The arts can look to explore (and also reproduce) tensions, hierarchies, contradictions and differences that constitute our social fabric.
- New individual and collective knowledges as opposed to truths emerge in the in-between-ness of conversations.
- Artists have important things to say about culture, communities and making things better, and this can be done in a number of ways, including participatory art.
- We need culture more than anything: capturing imagination and sustaining momentum are lacking in the ways we see the world.
- Art, culture and research are forces we need to build a more equitable society – to 'transform communities' – but they get restricted and controlled.
- Collective reflective spaces as well as lots of time are important ingredients to support these processes and may not appear where you plan for them.

To conclude, the arts can be collaborative and participatory. As a mode of being, the arts can help transformative change through imagining different communities, and this can contribute to a community development approach to the co-production of research with a focus on social change. Community, however, can never be assumed. One of the issues within *Imagine* were the different perspectives people brought to the visual, for example. Images were used in different ways, sometimes as 'aide memoires' to verbal data, sometimes as promotional, and sometimes to explore an idea through the visual mode. These perceptions can create shared spaces of contestation and/or make people feel uncomfortable. This conversation is situated within that debate. Here, we have created a dialogic form for a conversation that was concerned with the forming of community and the making of culture as part of a collective concern for a shared and hopeful vision of the future.

Note

1 Park Hill is a largely empty Grade II* listed former social housing estate built in the brutalist style overlooking the centre of Sheffield. Built to the revolutionary design of Jack Lynn and Ivor Smith, it sought to reproduce the social relations of the slums it replaced while providing a superior quality of life. Its success was mixed and its legacy is contested, although its symbolic power in the city (and beyond) is remarkable: its image is frequently reproduced on everything from fine art to tea towels and tote bags, and it serves as a totem for a nostalgic utopianism that laments the decline of social democratic modernism. It is currently being redeveloped, one section at a time: Chapter 6 makes reference to some work undertaken with residents of the first redeveloped section. For further reading, see Hatherley (2010), Banham (2011), Tuffrey (2013) and Ståhl and Östling (nd).

References

Banham, R. (2011) 'Reyner Banham on Park Hill', *The Architectural Review*, 21 September (www.architectural-review.com/rethink/viewpoints/december-1961-reyner-banham-on-park-hill/8618797.article).

Banks, S. and Armstrong, A., with Booth, M., Brown, G., Carter, K., Clarkson, M., Corner, L., Genus, A., et al (2014) 'Using co-inquiry to study co-inquiry: Community-university perspectives on research collaboration', *Journal of Community Engagement and Scholarship*, 7(1), 37-47.

Bell, D.M. (2017) 'The politics of participatory art', *Political Studies Review*, 15(1), 73-83.

Bell, D.M. and Pahl, K. (2017) 'Co-production: Towards a utopian approach', *International Journal of Social Research Methodology*, 21(1), 105-17.

Bishop, C. (2012) *Artificial hells: Participatory art and the politics of spectatorship*, London: Verso.

Bloch, E. (1986) *The principle of hope* (translated by N. Plaice, S. Plaice and P. Knight), Oxford: Basil Blackwell.

Charnley, K. (2011) 'Dissensus and the politics of collaborative practice', *Art & the Public Sphere*, 1(1), 37-53.

Daniel, J.O. and Moylan, T. (eds) (1997) *Not yet: Reconsidering Ernst Bloch*, London: Verso.

Hamdi, N. (2013) *Small change: About the art of practice and the limits of planning in cities*, London: Earthscan.

Hatherley, O. (2010) *A guide to the new ruins of Great Britain*, London: Verso.

Jameson, F. (2005) *Archaeologies of the future: The desire called utopia and other science fictions*, London: Verso.

Kester, G.H. (2004) *Conversation pieces: Community and communication in modern art*, Berkeley, CA: University of California Press.

Kester, G.H. (2011) *The one and the many: Contemporary collaborative art in a global context*, Durham, NC: Duke University Press.

Levitas, R. (2013) *Utopia as method: The imaginary reconstitution of society*, Basingstoke: Palgrave Macmillan.

Mouffe, C. (2007) *Articulated power relations: Markus Miessen in conversation with Chantal Mouffe*, Markus Miessen.

Ståhl, O. and Östling, T. (no date) '23,500T' (http://olastahl.com/23500t/).

Tuffrey, P. (2013) *Sheffield flats: Park Hill and Hyde Park – Hope, eye sore, heritage*, Stroud: Fonthill Media.

Willats, S. (2012) *Artwork as social model: A manual of questions and propositions*, Leeds: Research Group for Artists Publications.

SIX

Co-designing for a better future: Re-imagining the modernist dream at Park Hill, Sheffield

Prue Chiles, Louise Ritchie and Kate Pahl

Introduction

In this chapter we explore the possibilities for creative co-production, with Park Hill flats in Sheffield as the site of our enquiry. We describe how we collaborated with a small community of new residents in this newly regenerated and very well known 'housing estate'. We make a case for 'making', using drawings, models and images as a way to think about the residents' lived experience and how it might change and allow re-imagining. In this case we were thinking towards a future living in Park Hill and the opportunity the residents have to build a better community. Our aim was to offer a listening ear and design conversation with the residents, discussing their own particular ways of living in Park Hill. We explored themes around modernism and living differently; the residents themselves felt that they were living in a 'modernist dream', where modern architecture encourages modern life, 'to live out new roles and relationships ... providing a space in the modern world' (Friedman, 1997, p 17). Taking a historical journey, we trace a path from the people who originally made the buildings to the present and the people who now live in them.

Our co-inquiry was conceived through a number of events and encounters. This chapter reveals the insights and processes of collaboration. The first public event was a substantial exhibition visited by over 200 people at Park Hill; this was held half-way through the process of conducting in-depth interviews with 12 households and followed by two group workshops. The final event was the opening of the film made with Museums Sheffield, our project partners. We draw on experiential and materially situated methodologies, including the idea of material thinking from Paul Carter (2004), considering how *thinking through materials* can aid a co-productive approach to research.

Our thinking is future-oriented and considers the ways in which the residents themselves situated our thinking. Through this process their knowledge and skills combined with the possibility and potential of a new experience. As Ingold (2013) described, insights can come from the moment of making and discussing, in this case, whether in the interviews or in the workshop or looking at an exhibition together. These insights can help inform future thinking and decisions. Here at Park Hill, a making and 'joining in' epistemology helped residents make sense of their spaces both with each other and in their daily lives. However, we had to be realistic about what we could achieve. Of the households we worked with closely, only a couple were from a housing association rental home. Other residents who came forward to work with us in the more detailed workshops made a choice to change their lives and take a risk by moving into a relationship with modernity and a more open plan way of living.

Park Hill regenerated

Originally built in 1962, Park Hill was beginning to fall into decline by the 1980s and by 2005 was partially empty and seriously neglected. A partnership between regeneration developers Urban Splash and the government's English Partnerships with the local authority planned a new future for the estate. The project to regenerate Park Hill was controversial from the beginning, in as much as only parts of the scheme were to be re-let as social housing. At the time of writing, approximately one-third of residents are social tenants and residents have different tenancy agreements. This is changing all the time. Most apartments are for private purchase or have been bought and let out privately. Also, the very unifying and social element of the estate, the wide deck access at the front of the flats, is now closed off and private, with only entry phone access via the front door.

The scope of this project did not allow us to research in detail the economic and social demographics. Instead, it aimed to look with some residents at their homes and their relationship with their homes. The residents we worked with were from mixed ages and backgrounds, mainly couples, some single, and only one with children. There are children here again in Park Hill, but not many yet, although the on-site nursery is thriving and in new premises, catering for the children of people working and/or living in or near Park Hill. At the moment the community is new and hopeful of building a more secure and permanent community. All is not harmony but there is a robust tenants' association working to achieve this. Owen Hatherley, in his penetrating critique of Park Hill past and present in *A guide to the ruins of Great Britain*, acknowledges the stereotypes and controversies of the recent refurbishment, 'that obscures a deeply complex story, one which perfectly exemplifies Britain's tortured relationship with its recent past' (Hatherley, 2011, p 99). He is critical, for example, of the brightly coloured anodised aluminium panels replacing the original brick infilling the huge concrete frames – 'a direct repudiation of Brutalism's rough aesthetic'. However, for many, the colour gives visual relief, and is bright and optimistic.

The history of Park Hill, a huge modernist mega-structure

Park Hill is one of the most researched modernist structures in the world, with numerous dissertations, newspaper articles, books and commentaries written about it over the last 50 years. It has, more importantly, been home to thousands of residents throughout its 60-year history, and has spawned love and derision in equal measure. One past resident, a child in the 1980s, commented that, "if you have used this as your playground all your young life and loved it, why wouldn't you like modernism?"

It isn't just a modernist icon, however, it is a brutalist icon, due to its sheer scale and prominence. Brutalism, according to Alison and Peter Smithson (Rendell et al, 2007, p 184), 'tries to face up to a mass production society, and drag a rough poetry out of the confused and powerful forces at work.' It was much hated by the Liberal Democrats in Sheffield, who tried hard to demolish it in their short residence as leaders of Sheffield Council in the 1990s. It was swiftly listed, before even the Barbican in London, saved, and then a long and painful process of giving it a new life began. How could somewhere so compromised rise from the ashes and be given a new life? The scale, form and materiality of Park Hill proved to be a huge challenge.

Park Hill, was, however, built at a time when new solutions were urgently needed to improve the desperate housing conditions in the huge industrial heartlands of the North. Jack Lynn and Ivor Smith were two young architects who had recently left the Architectural Association and were employed by the new city architect of Sheffield in the then Housing Department. They were admirers of the Smithsons' idea of streets in the air. Lewis Womersley, the city architect who employed them, later wrote a book, *Ten years of housing in Sheffield*, that was tentative about the success of Park Hill, and presented it as an experiment they were cautiously optimistic about. Park Hill was one huge and radical solution to a huge societal problem.

Park Hill was originally a reaction against the early post-war failing, monolithic, high-rise blocks, isolated and lacking in street life. The architects were attempting to replicate the tightly packed street life of terraces and streets, but in the air. Street corners were included where the winding buildings twisted around, with the spaces around the blocks filled with shops, schools and playgrounds. From the lower end, next to the Victorian terraces, to the 13 stories at the highest point of the hill, Park Hill's modernity was praised, as was its community. "There's no stopping this collective thinking", a Yorkshire voice remarks in the original film of the new residents moving in to Park Hill.

Jack Lynn, in his description of the new Park Hill in the *RIBA Journal* of 1962, was concerned with providing the vitality and neighbourliness enabled by the pubs, corner shops and small businesses scattered throughout: 'The men and boys kept hens and pigeons and a few had pigs on top of the hill.' He asked 'what connection is there between housing, environment and community structure?', and discussed what no one had really addressed since Ebenezer Howard had done in the 1890s. The first complete layout was produced in July 1953, for 2,000 dwellings, nearly double the density of the area previously. A lot of thought was put into the programming of the development so the least number of people would be moved out of the area, and for the majority of local residents to be re-housed. The plan itself was ingenious, with different sizes of apartments and interwoven, interlocking plans, mainly two-storey, all having a double aspect, flooding all the apartments with light and views. For many of the new residents it was their first experience of internal bathrooms and modern central heating provided by the district heating system that is still in place to this day. The concrete frame with brick infill created a solidity and a permanence that looked far into the future.

'In an optimistic world Park Hill looked confident; as that world collapsed it looked intimidating' (Hatherley, 2011, p 94)

Our collaborations in the context of the *Imagine* project, Park Hill and the museum

The larger *Imagine* project is about the role of the imagination in building better futures. Evolving from the writings of Ernst Bloch, one of our conceptual concerns was to understand the history and legacy of what Bloch refers to as 'forward dreaming', the future worlds of daydreams and the imagination (Bloch, 1986) in the context of living in Park Hill. The original aim of this part of the *Imagine* project was to interview returning and new residents of Park Hill, and to develop an

Image 6.1: Park Hill, now

Photo: Prue Chiles

Image 6.2: Park Hill, then

Photo: Alan Silvester

understanding of what this iconic development meant to them. The project was conceived with Kim Streets, Chief Executive of Museums Sheffield, together with academics Prue Chiles and Susan Reid, and researchers Louise Ritchie, Paul Allender and Mathew Collins. We set out to find out about the lived experience of Park Hill, the concrete blocks, the feel of living there, as well as the decoration and home ornaments that made up the idea of 'home' (Miller, 2001; Buchli, 2002). The power of the design of Park Hill and its specificity led us to concentrate on their experience of the very fabric of modernity.

As part of the collaboration with Sheffield Museums, the most public and substantial outcome of this project was a film to match the existing powerful film on the residents of Park Hill made in 1996 that resides in Weston Park Museum. The film cut interviews with the new residents together with some of the historical archive material and an interview we carried out with Lord Hattersley in August 2016. This created a powerful link between the old and the new Park Hill.

Roy Hattersley was one of the commissioners of Park Hill as a very young man heading up Sheffield Housing Department. His wide-ranging and intensely knowledgeable recollection of this time was revealing. We asked what the climate had been like in Sheffield Council at the time Park Hill was built in 1957-60, and explored its attitude to the 'utopian modernist design'. Roy was interested in the notion of Park Hill being utopian, and said that it was never intended to be so; however, he was confident that it was completely transformative, and added that it was the most important and rewarding period of his life. He had clear memories of talking to the architects about the rough concrete – the marks on the concrete shuttering – and its radical newness. He said that Sheffield City Council felt like they were changing the city for the better. When we asked whether he thought Park Hill could be re-created to capture some of the early success of such a radical scheme in its second life, he said that he would have had it demolished. "Working-class people want to live on the ground in a traditional house with a garden and a fence."

In this project, with our small sample of collaborators, we found this attitude to tradition and modernity to be far more complex and nuanced. A number of personal histories from the 'old' Park Hill suggest how people loved living there, and that it was actually liked well into the 1990s. This suggests that attitudes towards the brutalist modernism as a huge failure were widespread but not universal. Stories of neglect and social problems are well documented, but mixed with more positive experiences.

The experience of living in Park Hill was, and is now, particular. It is a place of huge relentless concrete, and brick walls and edges form lines through the building. It has been argued that only young professionals and designers want to live in this modernists' dream (Orazi, 2015). The flats inside are modern in a way they never were originally – exposed concrete walls with crisp timber and white surfaces. Rooms were plastered with skirting boards, curtains and wallpaper. As we detail later in this chapter, we found from our interviews that most people were enjoying the new spaces:

> '… that's what Urban Splash have done, they've stripped it back and exposed all this concrete inside and they've given it anodised aluminium doors and all this sort of thing and they've kind of taken that and they've kind of made it more thoroughbred modernist than it ever really was before which is quite an interesting thing to do.' (architect, resident)

Five collaborative encounters

We now describe the experience of living in Park Hill drawing on five collaborative encounters, and articulate the ways in which we worked to co-create responses to the residents' living experience. The different collaborative encounters attempt to show how drawing on *a more materially based and embodied way of working and thinking together* can be understood as a form of re-imagining.

The interviews

First, we delve into a number of interviews undertaken with residents. Part of a two-year ethnographic research process (Pink, 2007) designed to empower residents to tell their stories and share their experiences, the interviews were recorded as 'oral histories'. These also formed the basis of one of the most highly visible outputs from the project, a documentary film that is soon to be part of the 'Sheffield Life & Times' gallery at Weston Park Museum, Sheffield.

Park Hill is a very over-consulted and researched development, and at the outset it became obvious that involving people who lived in the newly redeveloped part would be challenging. Park Hill residents had already been approached and had been involved in a number of research and media-related projects, and the research team faced issues with access to residents as well as interview fatigue. The team were particularly concerned with the need to include as many 'voices' as possible in the project, and the intention was to include both social tenants and private home owners. As previously mentioned, only a couple of social tenants took part, despite all residents living in Park Hill at the time of the research being invited. Invitation to the project was made in a variety of ways including by formal letter, leaflet drops, posters displayed in and around Park Hill as well as working closely with local stakeholders, including the tenants' association.

Residents who took part in the project agreed for their oral histories to be formally recorded. In nearly all cases these were recorded with residents in their own homes, and researchers met residents at least twice during the course of the project. When reflecting on the interview process one of the researchers noted, "I felt genuine relationships developed during the course of the research ... interviews were in depth and I felt residents really enjoyed sharing and talking about their lives in their Park Hill homes." Topics covered during the interviews included: why residents had chosen to live in a modernist development like Park Hill; what changes residents had made to their homes including decoration and storage; the modern feel of the space, particularly living at height and with light; how residents used the space within their homes; residents' feelings towards the emerging community at Park Hill; and residents' hopes and fears for the future of the Park Hill development. From the start the team engaged with key stakeholders not only the bigger players, that is, the local authority, councillors, architects, housing association and so on, but also those organisations that serve and are situated in and around Park Hill, including the local nursery school and tenants' association. The oral histories in this project were supplemented with interviews with these stakeholders as well as more informal chats with staff, and research observations made at Park Hill by research staff.

The residents we interviewed felt their newly developed flats and the spaces within them were easy to use, and described them as "light, airy and spacious". There was a real sense that residents had embraced the modern feel of their homes:

> 'I feel it's very iconic, I feel, I know it's an over-used word, but I think it's very cool; I feel it's very cool living here and I support, you know, that negative about the concierge and the little thing about the heating don't in any way colour my perspective. I've never lived anywhere that I loved so much as this.'

> 'Yes, we wanted…. I wanted to keep it open. So also I've tried to keep ornamentation to a minimum, you'll notice that there aren't any "pictures on walls".'

Each resident had 'spaces' they particularly enjoyed; for example, one resident referred to her seating area by the window, another the view from the bedroom, another the entrance to his flat and the very solid front door. The residents clearly love "living with light", thanks to the double-aspect floor-to-ceiling windows, although a minority found the lack of blinds and/or curtains in their bedroom spaces problematic:

> 'It's very very important to me. I've always been a summer-time person so I don't like the short days and the dark long nights … and so coming here, I mean, we did have quite big windows in the house we were in before, but coming here and having these HUGE windows from floor to ceiling just gives me the most amazing feeling…. It's invigorating for me…. I just love it.'

Some of the residents described how they had 'materially' adapted to their spaces. This included descriptions of belongings from previous homes that accompanied them to their modernist spaces and those that were discarded:

> 'Among the huge amount of stuff I had, there were about four lampshades and I could only use one of them, because the only light you can have a lampshade on is the one at the

stairs. So I put probably my most attractive lampshade on it. It does look nice, it goes with the theme of the flat and in these, I think it's similar to one or two of the lampshades I remember noticing in the show flat. I just like design like that, I'm quite keen on it.'

'I find stuff oppressive, I don't like having lots of stuff so again, that was another reason for me for moving here, it was just a good excuse for trying to get rid of things; I don't want loads of things.'

One resident described Park Hill as being "mind-clearing" as a space in which to live:

'I absolutely love it and I have to say that leaving that house and getting rid of all that stuff it, kind of, I don't know, my mind felt cleared. I love feeling uncluttered now that I can just ... cleaning is easier, I feel that the surroundings, there's more cleanliness. I just generally feel, I think, more comfortable.'

Articulating community through their experience of shared social space was a common theme. In the process of doing the interviews, residents discussed good and bad things about the experience of living in Park Hill. One thing we focused on was community forming and the residents' wish to create more communal spaces:

'I would really like to then, to have some more sense of social space and amenities within the development because I think that's very important to making it work a bit more. Just even having, like, somewhere where you can go down and have a cup of tea and even sit and work in a coffee shop where you could say "hello" to people. That would be nice, I think, for just to meet people a bit more, because at the moment, like, there isn't the opportunity to do that from here.'

Shared social spaces was a theme many residents brought up with us in the interviews:

'You see familiar faces as well so ... but it doesn't really lend itself to it, I suppose, not many.... I don't really know

what it is, it's not like there's no space for us to share like
a pub or something.'

In this way residents were 'thinking through design' – re-imagining
their spaces through talking about what 'could be'.

The exhibition

The exhibition entitled 'Park Hill Re-imagined' was funded through
the Economic and Social Research Council (ESRC) Festival of Social
Science. It was created half-way through the project to showcase our
emerging findings, but also to open conversations with residents who
lived in the newly developed Park Hill as well as those who had lived
there in the past. A co-production between residents taking part in the
research, the onsite nursery school (including the children), Museums
Sheffield and the research team, the exhibition took several months to
design. The idea for the exhibition stemmed from conversations held
between research and nursery staff. The nursery had a large archive
of objects and photos relating to the history of Park Hill that was felt
to be of public interest.

The exhibition was held in a ground floor empty space in a renovated
and inhabited block of Park Hill. It used to be one of the original pubs,
the Scottish Queen, overlooking the city. The research team invited as
many of the past and present residents as well as other interested parties
from Sheffield and beyond. When some people arrived at the Scottish
Queen, a shell now waiting for a 'fit out' – with its exposed concrete
and services – the building clearly evoked vocal memories of the pub
as it had been. The back of the old Scottish Queen had been removed
and is now a full-height glazed screen. We noticed many visitors just
staring out of the window, looking at the new empty landscape of Park
Hill, with quizzical looks on their faces. A very diverse set of people
came to the exhibition, new residents and original residents who had
grown up there. It was clear many people came to remember the place
and what it meant to them. We were surprised so many of the original
residents came and how easily the conversation flowed.

The exhibition was mounted by the research team with Museums
Sheffield and comprised of old photographs, video footage of some
of the interviews with the new residents, drawings of Park Hill by the
children of the Park Hill nursery, some items from the nursery archive
stretching back to the 1960s as well as paintings and art works of Park
Hill by local artists. Small groups collected around the old photographs
from the nursery and museum archives, and the power of these

photographs was immediate. Some visitors even recognised themselves in the pictures. There were clearly some very emotional responses and much laughter. Displaying people's histories through images is always a powerful experience. Pink (2007, p 17) argues that, 'photographic and video images can act as a force that has a transformative potential for modern thought, culture, and society, self-identity and memory…', and this was true of the Park Hill exhibition experience.

Manning the exhibition gave us a powerful insight into the past and future of Park Hill. The informal discussions gave us an opportunity to recruit residents to the workshops. People who signed up and wanted to work with us were clearly interested in the material fabric and meanings behind the iconic status of their modernist homes. They wanted to know more and perhaps to change things. These brief encounters at the exhibition changed our ideas and knowledge of the perceived wisdom and overriding image of Park Hill. This was a powerful glimpsed insight into the future of Park Hill, looking from the past.

The talk

To make residents feel they were part of a historical continuum, we held an informal event for residents where we presented an illustrated talk on remarkable modernist houses in the Yorkshire region built contemporaneously with Park Hill. We shared our knowledge of modernism in Yorkshire and the history of modernist housing that inspired us. We presented it in a very direct and 'architectural' manner. Books were passed around and the importance of some of these houses explored. One house in particular – Farnley Hey in the Pennines – is one of the most celebrated modernist houses designed by Sheffield City architect Peter Womersley for his brother in 1954 as a wedding present. It was one of the first of the post-war buildings to be listed and cited by English Heritage as 'the best of the 1950s in its lightness, sense of the picturesque and optimistic stance'. In this way, the style of Le Corbusier and Frank Lloyd Wright was brought to a dramatic site in the Pennines.

With a small group of residents, we discussed this house – the open plan living, interesting and exuberant use of materials, from wood to bright yellow Formica, and appreciated images of the light from the full-height windows, the long views framing the landscape and the rural and the urban. Everyone had a view or a comment, for example, something they liked or didn't, something that reminded them of the past or what they liked or were trying to create now in their homes in Park Hill. In effect, we gave residents unused to talking about the design of their homes confidence and 'permission' to give their views on design. This led to a productive sharing of material ideas, with a focus on things, objects, artefacts and ways of doing things. It became a reciprocal, equal exchange of different types of knowledge and experience, from established historical knowledge (residents and architects) to personal experience and views (residents and architects). For example, the idea of using raw exterior materials inside, like timber or concrete walls and the shelving as room dividers, were very present in the 1950s houses we showed. Both these modernist ideas were immediately commented on by residents as things they liked in their homes, and they were delighted they were part of a 'modernist design tradition'.

Image 6.3: Invitation to Park Hill

Source: Produced by Anna Cumberland, MA in Architecture student at Newcastle University

The first workshop

Making and creating together can be understood as a form of re-imagining. In the workshop we drew on the idea of 'collaboration as an art of placing' (Carter, 2004, p 11). Co-design becomes a creative process that is conducted collaboratively.

Six months after the exhibition and in the same space of the old Scottish Queen, now a temporary gallery at Park Hill, we held an afternoon workshop. After the talk (discussed above) and some lunch, we moved on to looking at the original drawings and new plans of Park Hill, and the way the architects had designed the new apartments, the changes and the ingenuity of the plans. When we started we were interested in how the residents thought through the design of the flats – it became a way of thinking about how things could be. This could be seen as a kind of thinking through design, as this resident, also an architect, described,

> 'Well, yeah we've got the bits that stick out, the bits they pinch from the street, so if you go out to the front of the flat again you see that concrete wall where the numbers are, that's the original street line, it's been built out with this kind of birch plywood to make that extra bay with the little corner window in it. So between that and the concrete wall that is the core where the stairs go down, that's where they've got the extra. So what I'm trying to say is the indent, that is where you get into the two-storey ones, you don't get all that, do you? So their stairs' on top of ours, but it's interesting the way they all interlock actually. There's a model down in the marketing suite which is quite useful for looking at that; it shows that the one bed below the two bed, or the other way round, anyway.'

We discussed first the different sizes of apartment, the number of bedrooms. The original plans and the new renovation became merged into one design. Every resident had strong views on their own homes and how they were living in them – where the plugs were, for example, and how they felt the architects had not wanted them to do things, such as putting a television in front of the windows. Relationship to space was one thing many residents described:

> 'I didn't particularly want to sit with my back to the window and I think you can, and I have seen people in a couple of

flats have the living room space quite facing in. So that you create … you almost create a line down to separate off the kitchen/dining area from the living room. And I decided that I didn't really want to do that, that I wanted to keep it quite an open space rather than blocking it off into two bits.'

We also brought models of the apartments and how they interlocked. The models were made for the workshop by two Master's Architecture students at Newcastle University who also came to join in with the discussion. The models were made to be dismantled and reconstructed, so were held together with pins. The complexity of the different plan forms was clearly shown in three dimensions. Working with scale architectural models of their apartments, the models provided a way of helping the residents order their view of reality. This was a small-scale co-design event, but some surprising findings came from the workshops – it became, around the table, a shared 'space of production'. The power of models situates the participant in a true scale model of their home, reading a three-dimensional reality.

> Models situate themselves somewhere between instrument, representation, object and sculpture. They hold the capacity to represent a diversity of intentions in a very direct manner. (Frascari et al, 2008, p 235)

At first, we were hoping the participants would want to mess around with the models more than they did, as they were only held together with pins, but they were too formal, crafted and pristine for the participants to change. However, we (the researchers) did move partitions, to poke into the tiny recesses and to understand scale and the use of the spaces. The residents actually helped us to understand the complexity and could clearly read the models. They were enabled enough to draw on drawings, so some sketched and drew lines on the plans of where they had inserted a screen or wanted to put in a wall or where they had added something. We learned that many of the residents were confidently changing their spaces. They were embracing the 'modernist dream', although there were issues with maintenance, cleaning, noise, and so on. In a discussion on a focal point to the apartments, all mentioned the lack of fireplace – a fundamental quality of living experience and different to their previous habitus. Ivor Smith, one of the original architects, said in a lecture in 2008 (recorded at the University of Sheffield) that the boldness of the structural grid

Image 6.4: Model of the different flat configurations and how they interlock, made from foamboard and printed actual scaled photographic images of Park Hill, by MA Architecture students, Newcastle University

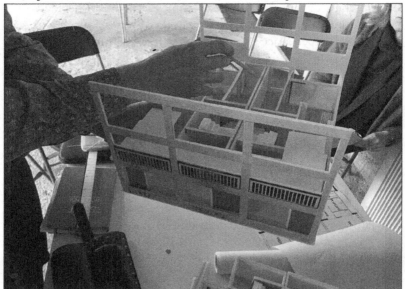

Photo: Prue Chiles

was intended to allow people to express themselves on their balcony as they wished.

The new residents showed an interest and willingness to go further to make themselves more comfortable. Examples included changing the bath to a shower, putting up shelving as room dividers and changing the interiors to their taste.

Comments on the small realities of everyday life became huge when dealing with the power of the structure they were living in. As we found in the interviews, the overwhelming plus points of the modernist structure were the views and the light. Curtains or no curtains on the huge glazed areas was a lively and important debate, and the no curtains won! We also discovered how aware the residents were of small details, but also in awe of the listing of the building. However, the interiors of the flats are not part of the listing ('the interiors [are] not of special interest', taken from the listing statement).

After a while some of the residents wanted to go further and explore the models. One couple had removed the 'superfluous' bath, which became a shower room, and other residents had devised storage solutions to the paucity of storage; this was a huge issue. A number of residents understood they could not change the internal spaces or paint the internal concrete. This is an ongoing discussion and one that the residents bring up again and again. The participants in the workshop talked about their desire for shared outside space as well as community facilities, of tool share schemes and of small allotments in the pristine landscapes. It was clear from our workshops that the time and politics of this community to come cannot be separated from the complexity of the scale of the operation, and the huge historical and political and social resonance of the place that is Park Hill. At Park Hill this could be called a 'community to come' (Blundell Jones et al, 2005, p 23).

The second workshop and the unveiling of the film

The final encounter sums up and concludes our project. It was at the same time celebratory and vital to the project, and included a few home truths. As a result of the first workshop we realised that the most important missing piece was to talk to the actual project architects who had drawn and designed and supervised on site the new Park Hill. We arranged for them to come up to discuss with the project team, the researchers and the residents what we had found out and to ask them questions. This discussion allowed direct questions of why the architects had done what they did, and they tried their best to explain. Two hours later and we had not taken a breath. We then all walked together to the screening of the film at the Millennium Gallery in Sheffield. We all enjoyed just 'hanging out' with the residents – waiting for them to get ready, taking their route from Park Hill to the city centre. Looking back at Park Hill over the valley one resident said, "That is our castle, there on the hill." We arrived at the Millennium Gallery and well over a hundred people were sitting down and all in anticipation of the film, chatting and drinking, again, a broad constituency of those involved and interested in Park Hill, past and present.

We wondered if the film portrayed an incomplete image, as it could not represent the complexity of Park Hill. One person's, the filmmaker's, eyes and ears were a little different to the researchers and residents. We thought the film discussed well what we were told by residents in the interviews. With Roy Hattersley's interview it also began to discuss the relevance of Park Hill as a historical continuum and a reflection of South Yorkshire's relationship with modernism. The wider audience at the film screening had criticisms about the lack of span of voices, that is, more social residents and ex-residents, and particularly the presence of children and the views of the nursery staff. Again, this was outside the scope of the funding – it was very much residents' views and their experiences of their homes.

However, we learned that a relatively short project as this could not really be the co-produced project we wanted, but it did allow us to get to know a small group of the residents and have a meaningful and valuable, genuinely for all parties, discussion on what the nature of living in Park Hill is for some, and how they are looking forward to a future, building their community and making the most of where they live. The interviews, by far the most in-depth personal discussions, were revealing in a different way to the workshop. This project is so site-specific and concerned with lived experience it was genuinely an experience of concrete and materiality.

Conclusions and lessons learned

In conclusion, this was an experience of working in a particular way – giving agency to the participants who already came in as experts in their knowledge of Park Hill.

If we were doing this again, these are some of the things we would do differently:

- We might consider using slightly different tools to allow more intervention by the participants. This could include more adaptable, rougher models and a more careful and considered use of images to have discussions around. For example, beginning with the modernist spaces from the talk, we could have looked closely at similar spaces in their homes and what these meant to them, and if anything specific needed changing.
- We could have focused more on the history of modernist architecture. If we had had more time we could have concentrated on a way of contextualising the residents' experience – they were trying to make sense of their more open plan space. A particularly successful part of the workshop was the talk – the residents were delighted to be 'talked to' about this architectural period, and were very appreciative of the links we made and then, in turn, that they made. Again, it is the enabling of a discussion on design and history to those feeling they do not know enough – everything is different with a veil of time.
- We would have empowered the residents to take their change-making seriously. What we discussed and possibly helped with was reassurance that they were doing something appropriate to their homes, even after the event. This involved nothing about whether something was right or wrong, just an opportunity to explore, to roam around to find connections, to be an architect. It was their

platform to start re-imagining the built fabric of their homes, building on what they liked in the first place.

- We would have worked in a more sustained way with the residents. Assembling the group to work with was by far the most logistically difficult part, and if we had managed to do this earlier we could have had more formal discussion on planning the workshop together. We had informal discussions at the exhibition in the Scottish Queen about the process of doing the project. In terms of a community development approach, it would have been more productive and indeed easier to concentrate on the external shared space and some of the residents' desire for allotments and tool share facilities, and to think about how the landscape could represent the new community and not the public face of the whole estate.
- We would also recognise the importance of 'daydreaming' when thinking about transforming communities. Perhaps our biggest role in these five events was to 'allow' the residents to dream and hope for building a successful community and home they wanted to stay in. Co-production early on and in short events, such as these described, can be a mode of thinking through dreaming.

Acknowledgements

With many thanks particularly to the residents of Park Hill, to Kim Streets and Lord Roy Hattersley, whose razor-sharp memory helped shape our thinking. Also to Alan Silvester, Museums Sheffield, and the whole project team.

References

Bloch, E. (1986) *The principle of hope* (translated by N. Plaice, S. Plaice and P. Knight), Oxford: Basil Blackwell.

Blundell Jones, Petrescu, D. and Till, J. (eds) (2005) *Architecture and participation*, London: Routledge.

Buchli, V. (ed) (2002) *The Material Culture Reader*, Oxford: Berg.

Carter, P. (2004) *Material thinking: The theory and practice of creative research*, Melbourne, VIC: Melbourne University Publishing.

Frascari, M., Hale, J. and Starkey, B. (2008) *From models to drawings – Imagination and representation*, London: Routledge.

Friedman, A. (1997) *Women and the making of the modern house*, New Haven, CT: Yale.

Harwood, E. (2015) *England's post-war listed buildings*, London: Batsford.

Hatherley, O. (2010) *A guide to the new ruins of Great Britain*, London: Verso.

Heynen, H. (1999) *Architecture and modernity: A critique*, Cambridge, MA: MIT Press.

Ingold, T. (2013) *Making*, London: Routledge.

Lambert, H. and the City Architect's Department (1962) *Ten years of housing in Sheffield, 1953-1963.*

Lynn, J. (1962) 'Park Hill', *RIBA Journal*, December.

Miller, D. (ed) (2001) *Home possessions. Material culture behind closed doors*, Oxford: Berg.

Orazi, S (2015) *Modernist estates, the buildings and the people who live in them today*, London: Francis Lincoln Ltd.

Pink, S. (2007) *Doing visual ethnography* (2nd edn), London: Sage.

Rendell, J., Hill, J., Dorrian, M. and Fraser, M. (eds) (2007) *Critical architecture*, London: Routledge.

SEVEN

On *not* doing co-produced research: The methodological possibilities and limitations of co-producing research with participants in a prison

Elizabeth Chapman Hoult

Introduction

To what extent is it possible to adhere to the principles of a community development approach to co-produced research, when the community involved resides in a prison? Pain et al's definition of co-produced research as 'research which is conducted together by a community, organisation or group with academic researchers' (2015, p 4) suggests parity between community and academic partners in the realisation of the project plan. Genuinely co-produced research is underpinned by the commitment to constructing research questions as they emerge around the concerns of the community. Where possible this is accompanied by a commitment to selecting and developing methodologies best suited to addressing those questions in collaboration with the communities concerned. As Durose et al put it, 'Co-production in research aims to put principles of empowerment into practice, working "with" communities and offering communities greater control over the research process and providing opportunities to learn and reflect from that experience' (2011, p 2). But what happens to this commitment when access to the community is regulated by rigorous, mandatory permissions procedures that have been carefully designed to protect the vulnerable participants from exploitative and insensitive academic studies?

The aim of this chapter is to illustrate the challenges of aspiring to work co-productively in a prison environment. I draw on the processes I worked through in coming to the decision to carry out a research project that eventually was unable to commit to co-production. Other, stronger methodological and ethical pulls – such as the structure of the permissions process and my growing awareness of the complexity involved in working with prisoners – made co-production very challenging to enact, or even request. In other words, this is a chapter about *not* co-producing research and the reasons why that might happen, even when the academic is highly motivated about, and committed to, the principles of the methodology. Although the aspiration to work in democratic, open ways with communities may be sincere and strong, I argue here that it is very challenging to implement co-production specifically. The participants are too vulnerable, the power dynamics too complex and the risks of doing harm are too great for co-production to work on a first-time visit, or for a one-off funded project, without the support of a third sector partner with expertise in the area. This is especially so when the academic does not have a background in criminology. However, I argue that there is space for such work, and the application of co-production in prisons is worth pursuing for all the reasons outlined elsewhere in this book.

Co-production: Specific challenges in prisons

The ethical and security protocols involved in requesting permission to carry out research in a UK prison are, quite rightly, stringent. Prison inmates are vulnerable in many senses, and the permissions procedures are designed to protect them from intrusive and exploitative research, as well as ensuring that all research in prisons has utility value. Any researcher applying to work with participants in a prison in the UK needs to first apply to what was, until 2017, called the National Offenders Management Service (NOMS) for clearance. NOMS has subsequently been re-named Her Majesty's Prison and Probation Service (HMPPS), but I will continue to refer to it as NOMS here because that was the body to which I applied in 2014 to carry out this project.[1]

Prospective researchers also apply for enhanced ethical clearance for permission to work with vulnerable adults through the usual academic institutional routes. The process requires that research proposals are robustly crafted and complete at the point of application. The researcher cannot contact the participants, or even the gatekeeper (for example, the prison governor), until all clearance has been achieved and the project design is tightly defined. This means that the researcher must identify the central aims and questions of the study for him or herself, as well as setting out a detailed methodology at application stage. Therefore, the process of developing links with the community in question, or even the gatekeeper for that community to identify concerns, cannot happen. Nor can the community have any meaningful input into the methodology or creation of research questions based around those concerns. The fundamental difference between research work carried out in a prison community and qualitative research work carried out in other kinds of communities then rests on access to the group in the pre-operational stage. Very little constructive, or even remote relationship-building work can take place before the project begins, and this would therefore seem to negate, from the outset, any possibility of co-producing research with the aim of supporting the development of the community.

Consequently, the project described here, which took place in a UK men's prison in the winter and spring of 2014-15, was not a piece of co-produced work with a community, nor did it ever attempt to be. The project 'Reading Resilience in a Men's Prison' was funded by the Economic and Social Research Council (ESRC) as part of the larger *Imagine* programme and, as the other chapters in this book demonstrate, *Imagine* was underpinned by a strong commitment to co-produced research with a focus on community development and social action. What constitutes co-production, what makes it possible and what limits its implementation were questions that were therefore alive in my mind throughout the time I carried out the work in the prison and made sense of the data afterwards.

One of the research questions that underpinned *Imagine* was, 'Is community research being transformed by developments in social research methodology, particularly the development of collaborative methods?' Interesting though the project was, it could not be described as transformational in any methodological sense. I was proposing a rather orthodox arts education methodology, which was essentially to run a study group and gather the participants' reflections on the films, together with their narratives about utopia, in order to understand the transferability of plural reading techniques. I was aware that this was slightly at odds with what other colleagues on the *Imagine* team were doing. Many colleagues were carrying out co-produced research, with a community development approach. I also suspected that the NOMS review team might want a more psychologically based 'scientific' study of resilience or hope. My dilemma, then, was how to execute an ethically sound and intellectually meaningful project with the prison community, while staying inside the conversation about the development of collaborative methods in social research with my colleagues in the *Imagine* team. I go on to illustrate these dilemmas with examples from the dialogues I had with colleagues and the panel in the planning process and the tensions that arose from both. I will show how these deliberations led to the decision not to go ahead with co-production. It is hoped that the account will contribute something to thinking about why the option of co-production is sometimes not taken up.

Vulnerability and the ethics of co-produced research in prisons: The permissions process

The application of co-produced methodologies is fundamentally more complex when it is applied to prison communities. In this case, however, the relationship was two-way – between the prison community (including the governor) and me as the researcher. Co-produced research with communities, as Kate Pahl puts it, 'involves a commitment to spending time with groups of people, for example, young people, youth workers, or artists, listening to their visions of what they would want to do. These visions are often located within concerns or problems' (2014, p 189). The operative word here is 'time'. Genuinely co-produced research depends on building relationships over an extended period of time. But in the project described here, this crucial preliminary listening stage was limited because of the need to articulate what the central aims and methodology of the project were in detail in advance of meeting any of the participants.

In addition to the requirement to articulate all the details of the project in advance, other aspects of the permissions process differentiated in context from other community settings where co-production was being employed. For example, there is the requirement to adhere to the standard NOMS policy of destroying all data after 12 months, unless an application for an extension is granted. There are strict guidelines about who has access to the data in the analysis stage. There is also the requirement for extra layers of ethical quality assurance that endure throughout the project, rather than finishing at clearance stage. An example of this was the commitment to the additional input from an academic colleague at my institution who would, as I put it in my application, 'take overall responsibility for the wellbeing of the research participants and act in a guardian role to ensure that the prisoners and prison officers' rights are protected with regards to informed consent and confidentiality.' This was a useful intervention and it made me think at every stage about the decisions I was making in terms of the development of the plan. Perhaps the most significant distinguishing aspect of prison work in terms of community research, however, is that the requirements to protect anonymity extend from the individuals to the setting itself. The location of the prison is not named here, and while this does not interfere with the presentation of the overall account or the argument, it does omit a defining aspect of community identity that accompanies other work of this type.

After submitting the original application, I was asked for more details. The letter from NOMS stated that the proposal had 'some strong foundations' but the level of prescription required to safeguard the participants was clearly a challenge. For example, in response to the original application, I was asked by NOMS to provide additionally illustrative ideas that demonstrated:

- the type of questions/discussions that will be generated during the reading group sessions; and
- a list of names of all reading materials/DVDs that will be distributed and discussed with the participants. ('Request for further information', NOMS research, 19 March 2014)

I had to draw on my own sense of what might be appropriate to the study without the valuable input of the participants themselves. I felt unsure of what to do next because pinning down the content and nature of the questions to this extent before commencement would effectively rule out a co-produced methodology, even in diluted form. I wrote to senior colleagues, Professor Graham Crow, then Principal Investigator of *Imagine*, and Professor Angie Hart, a Co-Investigator with extensive experience of the co-production of research. I had worked with Angie and Graham before on the South East Coastal Communities (SECC) project, a demonstrator project that ran from 2008 until 2011 and involved nine universities across the South East of England to investigate if it was possible for universities to collaborate with the aim of building capacity for community health and wellbeing. Both had a great deal of expertise in community-based research. The experience of co-leading SECC gave me an understanding of universities working in partnership with communities in the wider sense, but I had no experience of working with offenders in a prison. Angie and Graham were very helpful, pointing me to the work of Helen Codd (2008), Michelle Fine (in Fine and Torre, 2006) and Maggie O'Neill (2001 [2013]), academics who used a range of methodologies with marginalised or excluded communities, including participatory action research and feminist approaches, among others, so that I could immerse myself in work already done in prisons, which used a range of methodological approaches, even if not co-production. Angie Hart noted the reasonableness of the NOMS request and pointed out how thoughtful they were about the needs of the prisoners. She was straight-talking too:

> I think you should go back to them explaining more about why you want to use a co-production model, but if you do that you should probably argue that you are working with others who have experience of these approaches and who can help you. If you haven't done much of this before, you are really trying to start in a very difficult context without someone to help you. (email correspondence, 2 April 2014)

Graham wisely drew on his experience of the practicalities of time to help me decide. He took me back to the original case for support for the prison project that we submitted as part of the original bid, the aim of which would be to 'understand the potential for the imagination to build resilience and resistance in marginalised members of a separated community and to resist the harsher effects of economic and social disadvantage and to construct narratives of resilience.' Graham pointed out the flexibility that the aim afforded, both in terms of methodology and in terms of the cohort of participants, and drew my attention to the time factor (email correspondence, 1 January 2014).

I needed to develop a methodology that would both honour the case for support and contribute to the overall research questions for *Imagine*. I focused on the first and third overarching research questions:

- What are the best ways of thinking about, researching and promoting connected communities that can accommodate social and economic differences and diverse opinions?
- What role can imagining better futures play in capturing and sustaining enthusiasm for change?

The final note was added to the approval letter from the NOMS panel: 'In addition, it should be noted that we are not familiar with the reading materials/DVDs that will be distributed and discussed with the participants. We do note, however, that the DVDs are of an appropriate certificate (U/PG). We trust that all materials are appropriate to an offender population.' This has a profound impact on project design because the arts-based objects for discussion (in this case, science fiction films and books) had to be chosen in advance of the project, as well as questions for discussion and interview about them. In the end, when permission was granted, there was more leeway than the original requests for information suggested, as long as modifications to the research were communicated to the ethics committee and agreed with them before commencement. In the end, it took the best part of a year from my first submission of an application to NOMS to the point at which I met the participants for the first time – from February to December 2014. During that time I was working through the issues and re-thinking the proposal in light of these considerations.

Having set out my reasons for not pursuing co-production, I now set out what did happen.

'Reading Resilience in a Prison Community': The project that took place

The project that took place was underpinned by two ideas: exploration of imaginative and speculative representations of utopia; and a methodological commitment to the application of plural readings techniques to social research, especially around the subject of resilience. The two are not so far apart. Pahl draws together sociological methodologies that 'require a kind of imaginative engagement with the world' (2014, p 191) to make meaning. Likewise, here imaginative readings of the future world (indeed, universe) inspired by film texts were used to make sense of the world as it is and the near future. Science fiction, while providing wonderfully imaginative depictions of far futures, is saturated with dystopias, and it is challenging to find utopian futures represented, without irony. Given the relative dearth of film or television representations of hopeful utopias we – the participants and I – had to move utopianism to hope in the choice of the content of the films. Robert Zemeckis' *Contact* (1997), Stanley Kubrick's *2001: A Space Odyssey* (1968) and Andrei Tarkovsky's *Solaris* (1972) therefore formed the basis of the project. The centrality of the idea of utopia to the project had interesting methodological implications.

Theoretically, the most helpful work could be found in the intersection between Literary Studies, Community Adult and Prison Education. Steven Shankman's (2013) work is part of the renowned 'Inside/Out' programme, where he uses the philosophy of Emmanuel Levinas to teach the novels of Dostoyevsky to learners in US prisons. In his work, Shankman (2013) notes that the prison education environment provides an opportunity for authenticity both on the part of teachers and the learners – 'an honesty that is rare in a conventional academic setting, and that encourages students to be vulnerable and take risks' (Shankman, 2013). I also read Anne Snitow's (2011) experiences of teaching films to men in prisons in New York State, and learned from her exacting reflections on her own motivations for embarking on the project. Informed by this work, I applied the principles of plurality to the group appreciation of film texts, that is to say, the idea that while a single understanding of a text (or an idea or a person) is never able to be captured, deeper understandings may be gained through serious considerations of multiple readings. (This idea derives primarily from Derrida's notion of *différance*. For a longer explanation of how this idea relates to resilience, see Hoult, 2012, pp 12-16.) This notion had underpinned my previous work on resilience and adult learners, and here it was applied to the reading of film texts with a group of film viewers with the express intention of creating a group atmosphere that could tolerate and celebrate differences of interpretation.

In her extensive consideration of utopia as method, Ruth Levitas argues for the need to challenge the binary between sociology as 'knowledge' and utopian thinking as 'speculation' (Levitas, 2013, p xv). Instead, the encounter between utopianism and the methods associated with sociology, as in this project, 'seeks to legitimize utopian thought not as new, but as a repressed, already existing, form of knowledge about possible futures' (Levitas, 2013, p xv). I wanted to know if the participants could hold multiple interpretations of aspects of each film in play, and this led on to discussions that invited plural interpretations of the future. I asked each participant after watching each film was to "give me three different scenarios for what might happen to the world in 50 years' time." The question was not merely an accessory to the production of knowledge about how participants see their futures in 'real' terms. Ruth Levitas reminds us that 'utopia is a situated method in its operation in the world as well as in the conditions of its production' (2013, p 219). I was interested therefore in the way that the conditions of production of knowledge in these discussions that led to utopian thinking could lead into a more fully-fledged co-construction of knowledge, if not research questions and methods themselves. The resultant study was a small-scale qualitative, interpretative piece of research. The methods employed are set out below.

Methods

Once permission was gained I contacted the governor and discussed the plans with her. She was very supportive. She listened carefully and recommended that I read Shad Maruna's (2000) work on ex-prisoners who have reformed their lives, to inform my understanding of hope in this context. Core to Maruna's argument is that it is essential for ex-offenders to 'make sense of their lives' if they are to stay free of crime post-release (Maruna, 2000, p 7). The idea of activities, through art, which encourage the making of sense, would seem to have an application to rehabilitation and the reduction of recidivism, and in this sense, the project might have some application for uses within the criminal justice research community, as well as in the co-production literature.

Sample

Following that meeting with the governor, two potential participants were identified who agreed to recruit other participants to the group via a notice placed in the prison newsletter. Immediately the level of sophistication was evident in terms of their knowledge of the genre and the linguistic and social capital, and they differed dramatically from any stereotype I held of them. "Why are you excluding dystopias from the study?" was the first question the participant who became known as 'Bruce' asked me. He added that Ray Bradbury's (1953) dystopian novel, *Fahrenheit 451*, has added much to the investigation because of its central theme of the banning of books and the destruction of knowledge. I gave them each a copy of my own book that provided the theoretical framework of the project (Hoult, 2012), and Bruce read it before the project began. They listened to my account of what the project would look like and agreed to put an advert in the prison newsletter, which I drafted and they adapted. The newsletter contained creative writing, quizzes and information. I agreed to go back over to the prison in a couple of weeks' time when whole group of participants would be assembled. Potential participants responded to the newsletter item and attended an initial meeting in late 2014. The group comprised eight potential participants, but this reduced to five who were committed to attending all the sessions in the five-month project. All prospective participants received an information sheet and signed consent forms. Given the nature of the prison (Category D), flexibility about the timing of the sessions was built into the structure, to allow for time away for work and family visits for prisoners who acquired ROTLs (Release on temporary licence). In fact, in practical terms, a limitation of the methodology related to the category of the prison. As the participants earned ROTLs, outside visits disrupted regular group attendance. Therefore, longer sessions in a shorter time frame would have been advisable in a Category D prison.

Data gathering

The group watched the films and took part in researcher–led discussions about them, which were transcribed. The films included *Contact* (Zemeckis, 1997), *2001: A Space Odyssey* (Kubrick, 1968) and *Solaris* (Tarkovsky, 1972). Each participant was also given a copy of Philip K. Dick's novel *Valis* (1981) and invited to write responses to it along the same lines as the discussions. At the end of the project a follow-up interview was conducted with each participant and this was also transcribed. The interview focused on the ability to understand the films in multiple ways (in other words, to read plurally). It also explored whether participants could apply the plural reading technique to the narratives of personal and global futures. The data gathered comprised:

• Transcripts of the group discussions about each film.
• Transcripts of the semi–structured interviews with participants.
• Supplementary written responses to the films.

Data analysis

Thematic analysis of the transcriptions and the supplementary written data employed the following themes:

• Plural reading techniques.
• Hope.
• Responses to the alien.
• Explicit philosophies about the nature of the universe (including religious ones).

In total the project lasted from 2014–17, encompassing 11 months for the development of the project plan and acquisition of permissions and ethical clearance; five months of data gathering; 12 months of data analysis; and 18 months of writing outputs.

Tensions and limitations

Going into a completely new community is exciting and daunting, and this is especially true of a prison. There is a highly nuanced and complex power dynamic between visiting researcher and the group, as power and authority are not clearly demarcated or stable. Some of the group were much more erudite about science fiction than I was – as Bruce's opening comment about Ray Bradbury's text had indicated. One member of the group had even acted as an extra in a notable science fiction film. Ben Knights argues that 'there is a symbiosis between intellectual and pedagogic habits. Subjects are themselves produced in the arguments and dialogues of the corridor and the classroom...' (2008, p 5). The idea of alien was an ever-present member of the group – both in figurative and real terms, because of the nature of the films we were discussing and also because of the learning situation we found ourselves in – with me as alien visitor to their world and all of us finding ourselves in an alien environment that was probably not on any of their agendas as a temporary home. I write about this in more detail elsewhere (see Hoult, 2018).

Some studies of the impact of gender in the community adult study group suggests that some men tend to prioritise discourses of violence over accounts of their feelings in relation to fictional texts (Knights, 2008, p 28), and it is important to acknowledge that this might be a feature of the nature of the critique of the films in a men's prison. In fact, what I experienced in this case was not the resistance of nurture or discussions of affect – the participants were open about their feelings about their children and supported each other in stories of bullying as well as reacting emotionally to world events. Rather, in a pedagogical sense, the most challenging factor that guided the way that I managed the group was the potentially inflammatory (or indeed, dissolving) effects of the absence of structure. There was, after all, no curriculum or assessment requirements that we needed to heed. It was to the work of resilience literature (see, for example, Hart and Blincow with Thomas, 2007) on the importance of structure with vulnerable learners that I turned to for guidance. Prison itself is a highly structured environment, and although these were not noticeably vulnerable learners, the situation made all of us vulnerable. I was keenly aware that critical and philosophical disputes that were unresolved by the end of the session might carry over into the wings at night. Consequently, I took on a stronger, more directive pedagogical stance than I had planned for when I imagined that the project would owe more to co-production ideas than it did in practice.

Looking forward: Possibilities for co-produced research in prisons

My premise for understanding resilience is that the resilient adult has an ability to not only read in plural ways, resisting single meanings, but that they also resist single readings of their own lives. As I wrote in relation to a previous study, resilient adults 'engage in open readings, resisting closed meanings, and they take a playful approach to language' (Hoult, 2012, p 65). I had started out wanting to explore whether it was possible or not to teach these plural reading techniques as well as just to recognise them in the resilient. Previously I had argued that '(t)he ability to tolerate and cherish multiple readings and to resist fixed meanings is an important factor that emerges ... as a key commonality among resilient learners' (Hoult, 2012, p 67), and I had thought that the most pressing concern of this study would be to help nurture that ability in offenders. What I found, however, was that many of them could already do such work with sophistication, and the urgent concern was not about reading but *being read*. The challenge for the participants was how to resist the closed, single readings that would be imposed on them by communities because of their crimes. Most of us are not read through the lens of one single act (or a series of linked acts) in our lives, but many offenders have this experience. As Bruce put it:

> 'I mean the biggest issue for me is obviously, you know, whenever I – whenever I do anything people will Google me and find out what I've done. So, I'm going to have that stigma, if you like, attached to me throughout my life and I – that's the biggest issue, but – so again, you know, the easiest thing to do would be to retreat into my room and – and – do nothing, but you've just got to – you've just got to front it out and say, yeah, I made a mistake and now I'm trying to put it right and get on with it.'

It could be that this effect of being reified and cemented by an identity of crime limits the practice of hope. While individual participants could imagine personal and societal utopias with sophistication and grace, that ability is necessarily curtailed when they are read in closed ways by anyone who has access to the internet. I deliberately did not look up any participant until after the project was finished and the data was analysed. When I did, I wished I hadn't. The complex, kind and intelligent participants were reduced on the screen to one-dimensional cartoon characters by journalistic treatments of the events that had led to their incarceration. Throughout the project I was keen to insist that this was a research project that happened to take place with participants in a prison. Despite all the enhanced ethical and security planning procedures, it was a project that could have taken place with any community of adults. In the end, this was not a project about prisoners; it was a project that worked with participants who were currently residing in a prison.

Whereas I noted in previous work that unresilient learners remained 'stuck in a painful devotion to a fixed concept of truth' (Hoult, 2012, p 71), here the issue was that the participants might find themselves as the subject of those fixed concepts of other people. The lack of a right to erasure is an impediment to hope in a world in which digital accounts impregnate and regularly define material reality. The challenges of this are immense for the adult whose life has been written about as one single reading that is widely and perpetually available through the world wide web. How does the text of a life become open again when it has been closed in digital print? What are the reading practices required of a person in the resistance of prolific and authoritative scripts of their lives? I think that this is where a co-produced piece of work would be its most useful in a prison setting. If we take this widely distributed single reading of lives at the point of entry into the prison as the problem that needs to be addressed by the project, the research might profitably support the community participants in the development of a reading practice that helps them to challenge the closed single readings that others will apply to them. Such a project might take the theoretical stance of this project as its starting point – the encouragement of the toleration of multiple readings – and move from this into a 'writing' practice that enabled participants to provide multiple and plural versions of their futures that challenged the ones presented in the press and the internet.

The interrelationship between hope and plural readings of this project might then be applied more helpfully in a project that this group of participants had had a direct input into the design of. Returning to the wider *Imagine* focus on co-production, I was interested in what a project would look like if the participants had a chance to shape the questions and methodology. When I asked each participant what should I do next with this research, the issue of hope was paramount because that would be key to the ability to imagine alternative futures. 'Jim' identified directly that hopelessness would make a purposeful setting and focus for a second project,

> 'I would go to the most hopeless prison environment there is, which sounds like it's a [Category B]. I mean, people say it's a [Category C] but in the Category C you're a little bit closer to here ... and everyone struggles with their own bits and pieces in life and how they get over that, but it is – Category D is a more hopeful environment. You know, but certainly in – somewhere like [the Category B] I think

you would see a greater divide between the people really struggling, not that they wouldn't overcome it....'

The connection between the apparent escapism of the science fiction films and a benefit to the community of the participants was also identified by 'Chris' in relation to the main films *Solaris* (Tarkovsky, 1972), *2001: A Space Odyssey* (Kubrick, 1968) and *Contact* (Zemeckis, 1997). "The thing is, it's a nice release and an escape. Release isn't probably the right word, but then maybe it is. Everything you've done with us, and your questions, it's been nice, it's been appreciated." For 'Pete', however, the science fiction focus was a limiting factor in the work with the groups and potential groups:

> 'Can I be honest with you? I wouldn't pitch it as a sci-fi because I think you're limiting down the people with the genre.... I don't mean to be rude but that's not going to float their boat, you know, it's – what's going to float their boat is teaching them they can be more resilient, do you know what I mean, and become stronger people. Then that's, like, an empowering thing for people, isn't it?'

There is a place for pursuing methods that can occupy the space between the apparent inflexibility of the proposal and the complete shift to co-production in prison research.

Conclusions and lessons learned

So what would I change if I had the chance to do this project anew? These are the key learnings that came out of the project:

- Co-design from the start, drawing on the existing practices of participants:
  > I would draw on my learning from this project and the outputs from *Imagine* to re-design a proposal for a genuinely co-produced piece of work with the same prison. On a practical level I quickly found out that there was little appetite for reading, or at least reading the books that I had envisioned would be part of the project. Although members of the group were highly educated, very few of them took up the option of reading Philip K. Dick's *Valis* (1981), a science fiction classic, which I chose because of its supreme plurality and resistance to closed readings. Even those who

tried to read it gave up quickly, so I would work again with the fertile and open medium of film appreciation. All the copies of the book I had purchased ended up in the prison library.

- Work to the project partner's timescales:

  I would also make the project much tighter and shorter. I worked with the group over a five-month period because I thought this would help to build relationships and would enable a more democratic and community development approach to emerge – even if the notion of actual co-production had been jettisoned by then. In fact, in a Category D prison, things move so fast with the acquisition of ROTLs that they had people missing it most of the time. I would attempt to be there for an intensive week or two in future.

- Attend to the potential of co-production:

  My experience of submitting the proposal to NOMS was that the panel was encouraging and informed. I would be much braver about applying to the HMPPS for permission to carry out a co-production project the next time round.

- Attend to the grounded realities of the context and participants' ethical concerns:

  I would take seriously the core concern articulated in the groups and interviews, which was the participants' feeling that they will, for the rest of their lives, be 'read' in a single way (as a criminal), and their concerns for how this might affect their rehabilitation and re-offending rates, and make this the starting point for another project.

I conclude, therefore, that although the implementation of a co-produced research project in a prison environment is limited by the factors outlined throughout the chapter, it would be possible to carry out co-produced research with participants in a prison if the prison community is understood as a collective. In her sustained attempted to link collaborative ethnographies with literary criticism, Pahl points to the centrality of the practice of close reading that underpins both activities (2014, p 191). I would argue that such an approach can, and perhaps should, underpin meaningful work with prisoners is committed to a reform agenda. In this project, the close reading of the film texts took place as a group. The nature of the films made it impossible for the teacher to make authority moves in relation to those readings. Perhaps the texts themselves retained the mysterious authority to which we all adhered, in a way that echoes Ruth Raynor's assertion that in her work with community drama as co-production, the play is 'the boss' (Pain and Raynor, 2016), rather than herself as director/researcher or any member of the community of players.

A community development approach to co-producing research in a prison is very challenging because of the complexity of access arrangements and relationships, the enhanced permissions and ethical clearance procedures, and the transience of the prison community. It is not impossible, however, and it is worth pursuing. In the UK, the NOMS/HMPPS permissions system supports the process of project design, but the key issue remains that the researcher cannot begin to work with the community of participants until full permission is given. I would argue, however, that it would be possible to stretch the community development process across two groups of participants in the short term, so that, in fact, the project becomes two applications, the second of which uses the data gathered from the first group about core concerns and visions for social change to create the methodology for the second group. Research that is underpinned by a commitment to social justice and a democratic co-production method is possible if there is temporal divide between two sets of participants – those who co-produce at project design stage, informed by a sincerely delivered pilot, and those who participate in a second project that implements that design. In effect, then, the community is treated as more stable than its current inhabitants, which is clearly a problematic idea, but it is feasible to argue that the core concern of how to withstand the limiting effects of the single story, born out of the reporting of a crime and freely distributed on the internet, would remain the same. Although this may work against the timelines set out by funding bodies and accounting systems, there is the potential for deep and useful co-constructed research with a focus on building collective capacity for social change.

Note

1   The permissions process referred to is set out in full at www.gov.uk/government/organisations/national-offender-management-service/about/research

References

Bradbury, R. (1953) *Fahrenheit 451*, New York: Simon & Schuster.

Campbell, E. and Lassiter, L.E. (2010) 'From collaborative ethnography to collaborative pedagogy: Reflections on the Other Side of Middletown Project and community-university partnerships', *Anthropology and Education Quarterly*, 41(4), 370-85.

Codd, H. (2008) *In the shadow of prison: Families, imprisonment and criminal justice*, Abingdon and New York: Routledge.

Dick, P.K. (1981) *Valis*, London: Gollancz.

Durose, C., Beebeejaun, Y., Rees, J., Richardson, J. and Richardson, L. (2011) *Towards co-production in research with communities*, Swindon: Arts and Humanities Research Council (AHRC) Connected Communities.

Fine, M. and Torre, M.E. (2006) 'Participatory action research in prisons', *Action Research*, 4(3), 253–69.

Hart, A., Blincow, D. with Thomas, H. (2007) *Resilient therapy: Working with children and families*, London and New York: Routledge.

Hoult, E.C. (2012) *Adult learning and la recherche féminine: Reading resilience and Hélène Cixous*, New York: Palgrave Macmillan.

Hoult, E.C. (2018: forthcoming) 'Viewing the strange stranger as alien: An account of a science fiction film group in a UK men's prison', *Foundation: The International Review of Science Fiction*.

Knights, B. (2008) 'Masculinities in text and teaching', in B. Knights (ed) *Masculinities in text and teaching*, Basingstoke and New York: Palgrave Macmillan, 1–36.

Kubrick, S. (director) (1968) *2001: A space odyssey*, UK/USA: Metro-Goldwyn-Mayer [149 minutes].

Levitas, R. (2013) *Utopia as method: The imaginary reconstitution of society*, Basingstoke: Palgrave Macmillan.

Maruna, S. (2000) *Making good: How ex-convicts reform and rebuild their lives*, Washington, DC: American Psychological Association.

O'Neill, M. (2001 [2013]) *Prostitution and feminism: Towards a politics of feeling*, Cambridge: Polity Press.

Pahl, K. (2014) *Materializing literacies in communities: The uses of literacy revisited*, London and New York: Bloomsbury.

Pain, R. and Raynor, R. (2016) 'A soup of different inspirations: Co-produced research and recognising impact as a process, not an outcome', LSE Impact Blog (http://blogs.lse.ac.uk/impactofsocials ciences/2016/01/28/a-soup-of-different-inspirations-impact-and-co-produced-research).

Pain, R., Askins, K., Banks, S., Cook, T., Crawford, G., Crookes, L., et al (2015) *Mapping alternative impact: Alternative approaches to impact from co-produced research*, Durham: Centre for Social Justice and Community Action.

Shankman, S. (2013) 'Turned inside-out: Reading the Russian novel in prison, after Levinas', in S. Weil Davis and B.S. Roswell (eds) *Turning teaching inside out: A pedagogy of transformation for community-based education*, New York: Palgrave Macmillan (Kindle edn), Chapter 15.

Snitow, A. (2011) 'Dangerous worlds: Teaching film in prison', *Dissent*, Summer (www.dissentmagazine.org/article/dangerous-worlds-teaching-film-in-prison).

Tarkovsky, A. (director) (1972) *Solaris*. USSR: Creative Unit of Writers and Cinema Workers [167 minutes].

Zemeckis, R. (director) (1997) *Contact*, USA: Warner Bros [150 minutes].

Part III
Co-designing outputs

EIGHT

Co-production as a new way of seeing: Using photographic exhibitions to challenge dominant stigmatising discourses

Ben Kyneswood

Introduction

In this chapter I explore historic regeneration in Hillfields, an area of inner-city Coventry, UK, that could be described as suffering from 'territorial stigmatisation' (Wacquant, 2007, p 66). This work in Hillfields was part of the *Imagine* research project, forming a work package focusing on historical aspects of civic participation along with *Imagine North East* (see Chapter 2). Scoping interviews with current and former residents and community workers suggested that the poor reputation of the area developed in the post-war period, created by both outsiders and insiders, leading to Hillfields being perceived as a space, not a place, a 'potential void' and 'possible threat' (Smith, 1987, p 297) rather than a community of stable belonging. To develop interest, trust and capacity in the *Imagine Hillfields* project, community development strategies were used to identify the legacy outcome that community members wanted to see from the project. From this a co-produced output was designed: a photographic exhibition that illustrated complex community narratives of historic change, which sought to challenge stigmatising perceptions of Hillfields through positive media and public feedback.

This chapter proceeds with a brief introduction of the remit for *Imagine Hillfields*. An examination of historic regeneration initiatives in Hillfields explains the development of territorial stigmatisation in the area. An assessment of how the *Imagine Hillfields* project proceeded is then undertaken, with a focus on the emergent and iterative approach to inquiry. I conclude that co-production can be a sensitive and reflective approach for knowledge production, based in an understanding of the limitations of our enquiry and the potential of our community partners.

The *Imagine Hillfields* project

Imagine Hillfields sought to examine and understand historic regeneration in Hillfields, Coventry, UK. Its partner project *Imagine North East*, focused on Benwell in Newcastle and Meadow Well in North Shields. These three areas were identified as places of multiple, historic regeneration activity, with all three being locations for the community development projects (CDPs) in the 1970s (Loney, 1983; Banks and Carpenter, 2017) followed by multiple attempts to resolve perceived community problems. One aim of this *Imagine* work package was to 'chart the history of regeneration … from the perspective of residents themselves using creative media.' Co-produced outputs would 'develop community capacity' and generate a 'local archive of materials'. Finally, the findings would 'challenge all stakeholders, including policy makers and private sector organisations to re-imagine and develop better futures for these areas' (Banks, 2012, pp 1–2). By integrating creative practice to produce community outputs, *Imagine* sought to leave a legacy of community skills as well as impact in the public policy arena by presenting new knowledge and understanding to those in power.

Hillfields' history of territorial stigmatisation

Wacquant (2007) uses the concept of territorial stigmatisation to describe the fringes of 'the polarizing city' (2007, p 66). The 'advanced marginality' of residents of these spaces is 'fed by the ongoing fragmentation of the wage labour relationship, the functional disconnection of dispossessed neighbourhoods from the national and global economies, and the reconfiguration of the welfare state' (Wacquant, 2007, p 66). Wacquant's claim is that these areas are no longer hinterlands, that is, places for those who are not good functionaries of a capitalist system, but, with management and investment, may be resurrected. Territorially stigmatised spaces do not act as part of an economic cycle or traditional class model but are instead perceived by prosperous outsiders and precarious insiders as permanent 'badlands' (Wacquant, 2007, p 67). Both contribute to a stigma from above and below. Thus, to add to the marginalities of body, character and culture identified by Goffman (1963), insiders from below feel a disability of shame of residency and may deny the existence of a supportive neighbourhood. Outsiders from above see the areas as spaces not places, voids in their city that require external management (Smith, 1987). The concept is useful for exploring how Hillfields has been perceived in the post-war period, and particularly since the deindustrialisation of Coventry in the late 1970s. In the next section, using interviews from the *Imagine* project as well as documentary evidence, I want to explore how Hillfields became territorially stigmatised. In this way I hope to shed some light on why it was so important to those in Hillfields with whom I worked to challenge the stigma from which Hillfields suffers.

A brief history of Hillfields

Hillfields is a 160-acre suburb of Coventry close to the city centre. It was home to the Victorian entrepreneurs that gave Coventry the industrial base from which it thrived through most of the 20th century (Prest, 1960, pp 19-42). Much of its housing stock is Victorian, with a mix of terraces that housed factory workers and 'top shops', a local expression for three-storey properties with a large-windowed workshop for craftsmen on the top floor and accommodation on the ground and first floor. A shopping route through the area serviced a Victorian population of 20,000 residents and workers for manufacturers including Singer (bicycles) and Humber (cars), and linked the city centre to Highfield Road, home to Coventry City Football Club for 106 years. By the 1930s industry had begun to outgrow Hillfields. As Coventry became one of the most economically successful cities in the UK, manufacturers moved to new and expanded premises elsewhere. The workshops they vacated fell into disuse or became independent suppliers to industry, creating an insecure local employment market (Friedman, 1977). Hillfields began to falter just as the rest of Coventry was beginning to enjoy the prosperity of high productivity and high wages.

Up until the Second World War, Coventry was a city of mediaeval tight winding streets with timber-framed buildings alongside more imposing Victorian architecture. The destruction wrought by two blitzes, in November 1940 and April 1941, accelerated plans for its redevelopment. This vision was proclaimed through public exhibitions and in a government-sponsored film scripted by Dylan Thomas, *A City Reborn* (1945), which announced that 'there can be no thinking of returning to the good old days. The days of cramped houses and crippling streets. Of slums still living on in a lingering death from the last century' (Thomas, 1945). Because of a focus on rebuilding the city centre, the Cathedral and establishing new housing estates at Tile Hill, Wood End and Canley, Hillfields suffered 'the last century' longer than planned. Although it was named 'Comprehensive Development Area Three' in the 1951 City Development Plan, the necessary demolition and re-building schemes in Hillfields were protracted. By 1970, residents of Hillfields lived in among the worst property in the city, with contemporary research suggesting that over half of residential properties were without indoor toilets and heating, and reliant on the newly-built 'Slipper Baths' on Coronation Road (Bond, 1972). Thus, a diminishing local economy allied to the faltering redevelopment plan led to an increase in poverty, homelessness and crime, including prostitution and drugs. In this period, the process of 'de-placing' Hillfields began. Interviews with older residents explained it as a hinterland place where "people went through but didn't stop" (interview, 2015). That in 1960 the Council invested in public 'slipper' baths ahead of investment in indoor bathrooms is also illustrative. One interviewee explained that this was because "they thought the people would only put coal in the baths, that's what they thought of people in Hillfields" (interview, 2015). Yet interviewees also recalled that a sense of community was retained despite the ravages of war and redevelopment. Indeed, the 24 pubs, an RAF club and flourishing churches attest to local congregational activity. Nonetheless, from the outside, Hillfields began to be perceived as a 'potential void', requiring management and transformational change. For example, in Cabinet Office papers on the CDP, the Council was described as considering Hillfields a place of inadequate housing and home to 'yeoman stock ... immigrants ... and the socially inadequate (including fatherless families, meths drinkers, prostitutes)' (The National Archive, 1970). Carpenter and Kyneswood (2017) report that the local newspaper, the *Coventry Evening Telegraph*, quoted officials who described the area, including where 'a Councillor had described Hillfields as "a Dickensian slum", a Cathedral official "Coventry's twilight zone", and the police "Coventry's square mile of crime"' (Carpenter and Kyneswood, 2017, p 250).

The City Council saw the CDP as a vehicle for their management plan of Hillfields. During the 1960s, awareness of poverty amidst prosperity in Britain was generated by media activists, such as photographer Nick Hedges' work for Shelter (Allen, 2014) and filmmaker Ken Loach (Hayward, 2004), as well as photographers John Blakemore (2011) and Richard Sadler in Coventry (Clewley, 2017). The CDP was designed as an anti-poverty programme, involving action-research to improve welfare services and service use by communities (Banks and

Carpenter, 2017), with 12 projects across the UK, including those in Newcastle and North Shields discussed in Chapter 2 of this volume. In Hillfields, the action team worked with residents to improve their circumstances through providing support for access to welfare. This included opening a social services advice and support centre (called the Information and Opinion Centre, named to suggest listening rather than lecturing) and the creation of Coventry Law Centre (initially Coventry Legal and Income Rights Service) to provide free legal assistance (Partington, 1975). The action team also instigated a community magazine, *Hillfields Voice*. Despite these small successes, Coventry CDP director John Benington admitted that residents were ultimately left disappointed because the expected fundamental shift towards prosperity did not occur (interview, 2014). Although the CDP team offered temporary alleviation of poverty to residents, CDP could not fundamentally transform Hillfields because while the problems were in Hillfields, the solutions were not. The project, designed as an experiment in which the CDP acted as an intervention, did not develop community-level capacity from which Hillfields could thrive. The CDP team had been given the difficult task of achieving outcomes they had not promised using a formula that was not theirs. Hence their experience highlights the problems created by importing ideas into situations whose complexity can only be fully understood by taking into account the experiences of those living in it.

The immediate period after the CDP and through the 1980s saw "very little public investment in Hillfields", according to Coventry Council Development Officer John Payne (interview, 2015). Hillfields remained an area to avoid and took its first steps to becoming a 'badlands', territorially stigmatised by both insiders and outsiders. As champion boxer and former 1980s resident Errol Christie (2011, p 48) put it: 'Hillfields made most middle class people in Coventry shudder.' Interviews with residents from the 1980s reveal regular parties in tower blocks, where internal walls were removed to create a bigger space, as well as drugs being openly sold on the 'front line' of Primrose Hill Street, next to Sidney Stringer Secondary School. It took the 1992 riots that began in the Wood End Estate of Coventry and which continued into Hillfields, lasting in total around 10 days (*Coventry Evening Telegraph*, 1992), to revive local authority interest in the area. John Payne explained that the riots:

'Woke the council up because they realised they didn't know who to talk to. Who were the key decision-makers, the opinion formers? They didn't really understand what was going on.' (interview, 2015)

In response to a lack of understanding, Coventry City Council introduced area-based initiatives (ABIs) to address an increase in social unrest across the city. Area coordinators were appointed as "brokers between council departments, politicians, and the community" with a "long leash" to give councillors and senior council staff "early warning of things, insight to different situations, conversation, dialogue about particular problems, issues, networking and knowing who the best people to engage with are" (interview, 2015). The team in Hillfields was first managed by John Payne, who began by hiring former CDP worker Richard 'Slim' Hallett to assist a resident committee called the Core Working Group (CWG), convened to scrutinise Council decisions about Hillfields. Local decision-making appeared to make a difference, as CWG member Farid Noor explained:

> 'It wasn't your normal English-speaking white person running the show and doing everything for you. People made sure that there was a good cross-section from different communities, different faiths, and different genders, and it worked, it really did.' (interview, 2014)

While this appeared to reflect a willingness from the Council to tackle the stigma of Hillfields by working through a local committee, according to resident and chair of a Hillfields residents' association, Andy McGeechan, this did not last:

> 'It was lip service. You'd be invited to a meeting, and then they'd say thank you and the real meeting would begin without you. Even though it started off bottom up, it finished top down because residents haven't got the ability to manage the complexities of funding and the government will not give funding to local people.' (interview, 2015)

Andy suggested that projects would begin with community programming, capturing aspiration and support through offering small amounts of project cash, before pursuing corporate interests. This approach slowly sowed discontent and opposition, revealed, he suggested, through several initiatives. Despite its role in overseeing Council spending in Hillfields, the CWG was disbanded and replaced by a larger board that contained 15 professionals, including councillors and Housing Association officers, but only three residents. Andy also offered the example of the demolition of seven Hillfields tower blocks, which went ahead despite organised local opposition. Improvements that were demolished including a newly installed gated concierge and CCTV system that had cost more than £1 million several years earlier (interview, 2015). According to former councillor Arthur Waugh Jr, the owner of the tower blocks and local housing association, Whitefriars, compounded this action by reneging on verbal promises to build new homes. Instead the land was sold to create a new college, a centrepiece of a 'Learning Quarter' for Coventry (interview, 2015). Andy McGeechan also suggested other planning decisions that evidence a lack of resident preference. These include building a 63-bedroom homeless hostel on former residential land next to a nursery, primary, secondary school and college, despite Hillfields already housing Coventry's other two homeless hostels. Residents' concerns of an increase in anti-social behaviour in an area mainly designated for young people did not influence the Council (Simpson, 2012). And when the new boundaries for the city centre were redrawn in 2015, the Learning Quarter was absorbed into the city centre (Coventry City Council, 2015, p 5). Hillfields now begins at the homeless shelter and not the City College, which now claims a city centre address. As resident Dorothy Senior explained, "All we get now is the litter from the students and the [homeless] men hanging around" (interview, 2015).

These examples suggest an area that has been territorially stigmatised by outsiders. Yet insiders also began to contribute to the stigmatisation of the area. While the managers and users of community organisations I interviewed spoke of attempts to develop a sense of community through their activities, interviewees also spoke about how it was not like a community, as it had been in the past. Staff at Working Actively to Change Hillfields (WATCH) revealed that people completing job applications often missed Hillfields from their address because of the stigma attached to living there. Workers in local cafes also explained how they said they lived in Stoke, not Hillfields, because of the negative perceptions. This led to community fragmentation, something Trish Evans, manager at local charity WATCH, blames on austerity cuts. She spoke of the "constant need for community development" in Hillfields, but that the removal of grant funding and the introduction of new procurement now methods pits organisation against organisation. Collaboration and openness has now been replaced by secrecy: "I was at a partnership workshop. We've all had to sign non-disclosure agreements and everything is in confidence now so we're not allowed to share information. It was awful" (interview, 2015).

The Hillfields that I went into in January 2014 was at a low ebb. The organisations I had been told were partners in the project were struggling financially, with many of their volunteers also finding life more difficult because of the austerity agenda of the Conservative government. Food and clothing banks operated in multiple venues, often with long queues before the doors opened. Nonetheless, there were positives. New cafes had opened to cater for an influx of immigration from across the world, including from Kazakhstan, Iraq and Eritrea, and churches were also flourishing. Challenging how Hillfields was territorially stigmatised from above and below became the rallying cry of the residents, volunteers and workers who became involved in the *Imagine* project. The process of undertaking the project was not smooth, but the focus given to the project by those involved created an outcome of which we, as a group, were proud.

Imagine Hillfields: Community development and co-production

In developing the brief for *Imagine*, the University of Warwick team identified organisations to act as gatekeepers for the project. ACCOL, an Afro-Caribbean community organisation, the Herbert Art Gallery & Museum, WATCH and Foleshillfields offered access through how they worked in Hillfields. For example, Foleshillfields worked across communities, bringing groups together to discuss often–contentious topics. They were able to bring together African, Jewish and Muslim people on the topic of homosexuality. However, as noted above, when the *Imagine* project began in January 2014, the community organisations were working hard to survive the changes to working practices enforced by reductions in local government funding. Indeed, before the research project officially began, one community partner organisation closed. The manager at Foleshillfields explained that:

> 'After eight years, we decided to close down largely because it was getting increasingly difficult to get money for the things we really wanted to do, and we didn't want to become an organisation that just provided what we could get money for.' (interview, 2015)

Due to the long-term ill health of the manager, ACCOL could not be involved in the project, and asked that the elements of their project involvement, working with the Afro-Caribbean community, be operated by WATCH. By the start of the project in January 2014 we had two partners, the Herbert Museum and WATCH. The Herbert's outreach team had a track record in community-based arts projects while WATCH could act as gatekeeper through a strong volunteer base as well as ownership of Hillz FM, the full-time community radio station that operated from studios within the WATCH building.

The manager at WATCH, Trish Evans, asked that the *Imagine* project as a university/community partnership needed to support WATCH through a financial transition in which some staff had been made redundant. Trish Evans explained how, "Things have been so tight that some days we haven't even turned the lights on." This meant funding from *Imagine* was very much needed to maintain an important community organisation, but also that WATCH needed our support to achieve the outcomes they had agreed for their funding. I was appointed as the Research Fellow in January 2014 because of my past as a radio producer. This was also attractive to Trish. She was keen that I should build the capacity of volunteers at the community radio station. To achieve this, I adopted a community development approach. While the various and contested forms of community development cannot be dealt with in this chapter (for fuller debates, see Taylor, 2012; Kenny et al, 2015), the *Imagine* team discussed the best way to assign the capacity of university staff to support WATCH while achieving a successful research project. The first idea was to integrate stories of Hillfields life into existing and new radio shows on Hillz FM. I would support this by engaging in 'critical community practice' (Butcher and Banks, 2007) 'to identify concerns and opportunities, and develop the energy and confidence to work together' (IACD, 2015). This released management from supporting their radio volunteers to concentrate on restructuring and new partnerships. In this sense, *Imagine* was 'sharing responsibility for maintaining existing structures and services' (Gilchrist and Taylor, 2016, p 19) with WATCH staff, building capacity within the organisation through supporting the volunteers.

However, this approach did not get far with the volunteer broadcasters. As one broadcaster explained, "People have got nothing left to give. I do my show and work – that's it", while another suggested, "you've just arrived and you want them to do something for you. They don't know you. What's in it for them?" (interview notes, 2014). The idea, developed with management, was not developed with volunteers. These times at WATCH were stressful, with the relationship between management and volunteers strained. As staff numbers dwindled, more became expected of the volunteers. However, the volunteers were not engaged in what this meant, which led to a sense that their current efforts were not appreciated.

The first three months of *Imagine* became a listening exercise. I used WATCH as a base to understand the local situation and its effect on residents. I sought to build relationships with local people and discuss with them what working together could mean. Conversations with residents, workers and volunteers focused on their personal stories, often covering failed projects as well as their imagined future for Hillfields. These meetings were not recorded but noted later to avoid formality, and took place not only in WATCH but also in the cafes and other community venues in Hillfields. This period served as valuable reconnaissance as discussions led to context-specific questions about the buildings, the streets and people from the past and present. Community narratives were told in a way that connected people to their streets and buildings. People I spoke to highlighted how redevelopment could infringe on quotidian life in a way that enforces changes in daily practice, and could lead to the loss of community knowledge and spirit. These narratives also told how partnerships were forged between community workers and residents, and how improvements were achieved through close work with the local authority, but also that, as Andy McGeechan explains above, local people were never given the budget or trust to deliver their vision.

These conversations also began to create an emerging identity in the local community for what I had begun to call *Imagine Hillfields*. How to do research was often discussed, with trust and character the key factors. While I was introduced to new people, they still assessed my credentials for the community: "Why are you doing this?" "Who is it for?" were the two most familiar questions, the answers to which needed to be "for the people of Hillfields" if I was to get any of their time. Building these relationships mattered more to residents than documents containing promises about duty of care and phone numbers for complaint. That *Imagine Hillfields* gained some traction came from this period of listening, not just about failed initiatives but why they had failed, and why *Imagine Hillfields* might fail too.

After this period of familiarisation, a loose group began to form to give the project focus, drawn from WATCH staff and volunteers and a few other local people. A consistent theme of discussions with the public revolved around territorial stigmatisation (Wacquant, 2007). Those I spoke to wanted to challenge how Hillfields was seen by people from outside the area. These outsiders were cast as people who did not know the area and who did not understand its heritage. They were seen as people who blamed Hillfields residents for its status as a void place. Conversations also revealed how people in Hillfields could blame each other for problems. Newcomers to the area were described as having little interest in the area's heritage. The student population was blamed for littering and anti-social behaviour. Divisions were evident between tower block residents and terrace residents, as each preferred their choice of dwelling and prioritised it in public forums. Tentative steps were taken to encourage support around the idea of challenging the stigma. We started with a project about getting to know Hillfields, involving some members of the loosely formed group, as well as new recruits, by using photography to focus on what was perceived as positive about Hillfields that could challenge stigmatisation.

Photography and the Herbert Museum

To develop the concept around how Hillfields was stigmatised, an exploratory photography project was devised. Staff from the Herbert Museum recommended an approach with a social justice element to challenge the negative stereotype. Residents would photograph Hillfields as they saw it in September 2014. This approach is described by Johnsen et al (2007) as 'auto-photography' which 'illuminated "hidden" spaces that do not typically feature in public (or academic) imaginations' as well as providing a 'more nuanced understandings of the use, meanings and dynamics associated with other, apparently already "known" spaces' (Johnsen et al, 2007, p 194). By going out to walk their area and photographing daily life, residents also critiqued their understanding of how community life operated. They focused the cameras not only on the parks and streets, but also behind doors, between strangers, friends and family, and discovered new people and activities through collaboration. This was similar to Fink (2011), who, in an auto-photography project into inequality with two residents of a UK housing estate, found that 'visual research methods offer creative and participatory opportunities to generate locally produced knowledge about the nature of that connectedness' (2011, p 45). Working with a local photographer, the group presented Hillfields as a diverse place of hard work and enterprise, revealing different forms of relationship, illustrated by photographs such as that of a husband with his wife.

The photographs were exhibited at the Herbert Museum in Coventry on walls outside of the main Spring 2014 exhibition by Jason Scott Tilley, a well-known Coventry photographer. They presented a powerful counter to the territorial stigmatisation of Hillfields. Curation for the exhibition began with the process of sequencing photographs to tell a narrative: as one participant put it, "we didn't just hand these [photographs] over. We chose them and put them in the right order so it was our story" (interview, 2014). Taking responsibility for curation

Image 8.1: Husband and wife, Hillfields, Spring 2014

Photo: Mick Dabrowski

reveals how the group perceived the process of organising data as just as much an important step to achieving their goal as producing the photographs.

The group, buoyed by the photography project, began to discuss their next steps, with several members wondering whether similar projects had been also attempted in the past. This sat well with the *Imagine* project remit of tracking historic regeneration in Hillfields, and so the team sought to find new people in Hillfields to develop this idea.

Hillfields History Group

The Hillfields History Group is a community group that formed in the early 1980s. Their members came together in monthly meetings to discuss local heritage and document the physical changes in Hillfields through an archive of photographs, created out of their own work, donations and bequests. The five remaining members were elderly and the last of what was once a large community group. Every member grew up in Hillfields, and while several no longer lived in Hillfields, two did. Their photographic archive and collective knowledge were valuable in developing a visual narrative that tracked the physical changes and living conditions of post-war Hillfields. This provided a basis for understanding and developing community narratives about stigma in Hillfields. While the first photographic project had addressed

Hillfields and stigma today, through working with the History Group, *Imagine Hillfields* addressed historic stigma and its impact.

As with WATCH, the *Imagine* team adopted a development approach in which we sought to help the Hillfields History Group in exchange for their support. The History Group wanted to digitise their large print collection, and so WATCH volunteers agreed to scan the archive of photographs in exchange for their use on the project. The members of the History Group appointed a representative, Stanislaw-Jan Sakowicz-Librowski (known as Stas), to work with the loose group that had formed earlier, which included me as Research Fellow, Professor Mick Carpenter (University of Warwick), Isaiah Williams and Tanya Hayman, both volunteers at WATCH, Trish Evans and Ray Reid, both staff at WATCH, and Jason Scott Tilley, the Coventry photographer who had taken an interest in our approach to working in Hillfields.

Other opportunities arose out of the interest in photographic archives. Through his own contacts, photographer Jason Scott Tilley arranged for the members of the Hillfields History Group to visit the photographic archive at Birmingham Library to view a collection of prints of Hillfields from 1964 by the celebrated British photographer John Blakemore, who had lived in Hillfields at the time.

The Blakemore photographs identify how Hillfields had begun to be stigmatised, offering visual representations of the stories of dereliction I had been told by community members in the months before. Accounts of Coventry's post-war re-birth as the motor city of modernity such as Prest (1960) had ignored the poverty in Hillfields, yet here was visual evidence that illustrated those community stories. The photographs opened doorways to conversations about growing up in such conditions, and its effect on health, education and family life. These conversations could be serious in tone, a contrast to nostalgic conversations of an imagined past: the visual evidence of poverty lent a sobering effect to discussions.

Other photographic archives emerged from research. The list of professional photographers who had worked in Hillfields was impressive. It included John Blakemore, Richard Sadler, Victor Burgin, Vanley Burke, David Richardson and John Harris, as well as the commercial photography of three studios: Masterji's Art Studio, Tayler Brothers and ICA Studios. The past of Hillfields as a place of entrepreneurship, followed by its post-war dereliction, had led to this interest from photographers. Together with the discovery of three films, two created by the BBC and one by Channel 4, all recorded in Hillfields between 1973 and 2004, we began collating imagery that offered an insight into historic Hillfields life that was not within official accounts. The critical dimension to the investigations focused on how photographic archives of Hillfields offered an alternative narrative of post-war life and regeneration in Hillfields, giving the community explanatory power about how economic progress for Coventry had also led to the territorial stigmatisation of Hillfields. The multiple perspectives from the photographers added layers of complexity to the narrative of stigmatisation. For example, Blakemore's photographs, taken in 1964, and therefore over 20 years after the Coventry blitz, challenge the claim for Coventry as a city of modernity (Hodgkinson, 1970). Those taken by Richard Sadler in 1951 show his Victorian grandmother travelling the same derelict sites 15 years earlier, and with others taken by Clive Shayler of ICA studios for the CDP project in 1972 evidenced the same, but 32 years after the Coventry blitz.

These photographs resisted the celebratory and dominant narrative of a vision of a modern future for Coventry by highlighting how, between 1940 and 1972, poverty in derelict Hillfields persisted amidst city-wide prosperity. For community members, a new, historic, visual narrative supported their central aim of tackling stigmatisation, making the need to challenge how Hillfields was perceived today ever more crucial and timely. This issue was discussed as a new photography project, working with these archives and continuing a tradition by commissioning new work to continue the series of photographic archives. In doing so, Hillfields would have been regularly explored by professional photographers for over 100 years, beginning with

Image 8.2: Hillfields in 1964, over 20 years after the Coventry blitz of 1941

Photo: John Blakemore

the Tayler Studios in 1900. An exhibition of photographic narratives was mooted, with different archives used to prompt public discussion about how stigmatisation is created and sustained. Yet a major concern within the group was that an exhibition might not be taken seriously by the opinion formers in Coventry if there was not an element that attracted these people – that is, if it was not in the right venue or did not have star quality. The concern was that a community photography exhibition might be ignored. The idea began to form that a *serious* exhibition would attract major positive attention.

Image 8.3: Children on a derelict house, Hillfields in 1972

Photo: Clive Shayler of ICA Studios

A successful application to the Arts Council funded Jason Scott Tilley to work in Hillfields for three months during Spring 2015 to create the new work that continued the sequence of photographic archives. To strengthen the application, Coventry University offered him a Visiting Fellow position to enable him to use their photographic studios. In return for this in-kind support, Jason arranged for John Blakemore to give a masterclass in analogue printing to the photography students. The Blakemore sessions and Jason Scott Tilley's new photography (below, in Image 8.4) gave the *Imagine* project star quality. The development of these partnerships outside of Hillfields raised the profile of the exhibition, and it began to attract attention from officers in the local

Image 8.4: Mother and daughter, 2015

Photo: Jason Scott Tilley

authority. John Blakemore agreed to re-print his Hillfields series for exhibition, and this was followed by Richard Sadler's confirmation that we could exhibit the Minnie Sadler prints. Masterji, an Asian photographer, also confirmed his involvement. Added to this were three other archives chosen by the Hillfields History Group: a selection of the Hillfields History Group's own archive, the Tayler Brothers studio showing Hillfields at the beginning of the 20th century, and topographical photography of Hillfields from Coventry City Council's architecture department, which became available as the project began to be taken seriously.

The use of professional photographers excited the team but also excluded and challenged the community group in several ways. Community members, although agreeing to the value of the way the project developed, were not involved in the Blakemore masterclass, which was reserved for Coventry University students. Nor did Jason Scott Tilley need their support in making a new body of work of the people of Hillfields, or the other photographers in preparing their contributions. A partnership approach raised the profile and ambitions of the project but also led to less control over the outputs by the *Imagine* team.

As a response to this, the Hillfields History Group members suggested a second commissioned piece that they would oversee. This would be based on points of continuity and change in the architecture of Hillfields, offering a strong visual alternative to the black and white archive images, and the new collection of portraits by Jason Scott Tilley. We commissioned Nick Stone, a photographer who merges archive images with high-resolution photography taken from the same location as the original photographer. This commission extended the capacity of Hillfields History Group to conceive of and deliver arts-based projects, and resolved to some extent the marginality they felt. Nick Stone met with the Hillfields History Group who took him on a Jane Jacob's (1961) walk to sites of interest in Hillfields, showing him original photographs from their collection and locating the position from which that photograph was taken. The task highlighted how post-war regeneration had re-shaped Hillfields, including where entire roads had been removed to be replaced by new housing, as shown in Image 8.5. It took an hour to find the position John Blakemore was in when he took the original photograph in 1964.

Image 8.5: 'Top shops' in Vernon Street in 1964, replaced by a housing estate in 1975, which sits at 90 degrees to the original street plan

Photo: Nick Stone, using John Blakemore's original

These photographs visually demonstrated historic change and highlight the Victorian heritage in Hillfields. They proved very popular in the local newspaper as well as at the exhibition, where they were used as a provocation in the entrance to ask whether changes were for the better.

The *Imagine Hillfields* exhibition

We settled on the idea of an exhibition to achieve maximum publicity and policy impact, taking up public oxygen in a way that encouraged positive stories about Hillfields. The difficulty for the team was that there were no suitable venues in Hillfields large enough to accommodate an exhibition. The Herbert Museum also could not accommodate us at notice of less than several years. However, Far Gosford Street, a former Hillfields boundary with historic ties as part of the old shopping route, was at the centre of a multi-million-pound heritage regeneration project, with FarGo Village, a creative development of shops and cafes, a centrepiece project. The *Imagine* team presented the project to the developers who offered an exhibition space free for a month, during August 2015. Yet FarGo Village and its attempted gentrification caused unease among some in the team. Isaiah, for example, was concerned that we might be giving a controversial development our approval. We entered this debate, talking in pubs and with shopkeepers about the value of the exhibition as a way of understanding the history of the area. Their interest suggested that the exhibition offered a valuable contribution to the public debate about where Far Gosford Street had come from and what it was becoming with FarGo Village.

The energy for exhibition outputs grew once FarGo was secured as a venue. This period was intensive, with WATCH staff and volunteers offering insight and promotional support. The professional photographers contributed their works, including 94 year-old Masterji, who used Jason Scott Tilley to print his photographs of the South Asian community, and 90-year-old Richard Sadler who was visited in his Welsh home to collect the prints and directions for curation. The final additions to the exhibition came from Coventry City Council. Hillfields History Group was aware of negative slides of Hillfields by the internationally renowned Coventry Council Architects' Department (Gould and Gould, 2009). The slides illustrate how past visions of the future were planned but not consulted, including some which show the removal of the Victorian Hillfields in its entirety, replaced with high-rise buildings. A further addition was pictures of the Victorian and Edwardian entrepreneurs of Hillfields taken at the Tayler Brothers

Studio. Although these were not of the post-war period on which we were focusing, the story of Hillfields as a territorially stigmatised space begins with its period of prosperity, and this required representation. Finally, the Hillfields History Group chose six prints from their collection to focus visitor attention on what they do as a community group. These prints were from the CDP era, including several from the Victor Burgin collection, called 'UK76' by the photographer, but originally commissioned by the Home Office for the CDP in 1976 (they came to the Hillfields History Group from CDP worker Richard 'Slim' Hallett). An interpretation panel accompanied their installation that explained more about the group.

In total, the exhibition presented over 100 prints from seven contributors, each with their own explanatory interpretation panel. A public launch inviting all those involved, including those photographed by Jason Scott Tilley, was organised. This brought Masterji, Richard Sadler and John Blakemore together for the first time since the early 1960s, and drew in local news journalists to cover the event, ensuring that Hillfields received substantial positive local press coverage for the period of the exhibition.

The exhibition sought to challenge the dominant discourses of territorial stigmatisation by presenting the visual narrative through an historical continuum, revealing where change had failed residents and workers, who nonetheless continued to live their lives in Hillfields. Poverty and precarious living were as evident in the past as in the present. The curated photographs appeared to be in silent communion with each other: Blakemore's 1960s facades sat opposite those from 2015 by Scott Tilley, while Sadler's 1951 images of his Victorian grandmother looked across to the Masterji portraits of new migrants who had moved to Hillfields at a similar time. Businessmen's portraits sat next to schoolchildren, older and young people, mixing prosperity and poverty. This tension between potential and precarity illuminated and challenged the negative discourses of Hillfields as a place of social ills and problems, and instead depicted the social conditions created by policies that do not take situated life into account.

The internal walls were built to create different zones, with the sequencing taking visitors through the history of Hillfields. The dominant tower blocks of Jason Scott Tilley's oversized photographs, stuck using drawing pins, unframed and bare but printed in vibrant colour, reflect the temporality and austerity of the post-war tower blocks, designed to last but demolished in 2002. The framed photographs by Masterji were intimate, inviting the viewer closer into the lives of newcomers from South Asia. Blakemore's pictures were double-hung to ensure older people who had lived through those times could clearly see them. Indeed, plenty of people in wheelchairs were able to look in comfort at Hillfields in 1964. A similar approach was taken with Richard Sadler's prints of his grandmother Minnie. Incredibly, a very elderly and frail lady using a wheelchair knew Minnie Sadler as a young girl living on Bath Street. She was also able to give us the names of people in John Blakemore's photographs, including Pinky, the Rag and Bone man, whom she often fed at the family table, much to the chagrin of her mother.

Over 2,000 people attended the exhibition in the 18 days it was open during August 2015, with a further 500,000 mentioning the exhibition using social media. Visitors wrote in the comment book about single photographs, including identifying locations, lost friends and family. Some also shared contact details with us to tell their stories further. These included John Blakemore's Muslim neighbours from 1964 who explained how when John's house was demolished in 1975 the street filled with prints of photographs he had left behind in the top floor of his top shop, a story corroborated at the exhibition by John's first wife, Sheila.

A vision of Hillfields was generated by the route taken through the photographs. Visitors zig-zagged across the room, responding to calls from friends or spotting something familiar from afar. The

Image 8.6: Photographs were curated with the community to reflect community narratives

Photo: Jason Scott Tilley

chronological curation was blended, with past and present sliding together, as in Nick Stone's photography in the entrance. While reflections on the exhibition were positive, some visitors also expressed discomfort at how their perception of the area had been challenged. When I acted as an invigilator for the exhibition, while some visitors re-connected in a positive and affirming way, others reflected on an appreciation of the past but not of Hillfields today, as if to separate their heritage from what they saw in Jason Scott Tilley's images. In my notes, one visitor explained that her family had left in the 1960s. She expressed disappointment at the loss of the Victorian houses because of the value they would have today: "Some of those Top Shops would be worth a fortune now. But look what they replaced it with. It's terrible now, a real dive." For these visitors, the exhibition failed to challenge their stigmatisation of Hillfields today. Although we sought to present Hillfields across time, their evaluation was based not on life lived in hardship (and which they had avoided) but on the lost economic value of land and property in Hillfields.

Discussion

In this section I want to assess how the people of Hillfields were engaged to challenge the negative perception of the area through the *Imagine Hillfields* project and reflect on whether the project had a wider impact.

Early conversations in Hillfields with community members revealed stories about the relationship between the people of Hillfields and agencies from outside of Hillfields, usually those with status and power, who sought to transform an area considered damaged and out of date. Territorial stigmatisation developed in the immediate post-war era, with Hillfields initially performing as a hinterland in Coventry, markedly different from more prosperous suburbs, by offering sub-standard accommodation to the poor. Attempts to redevelop were protracted, and while the CDP intervention shone brightly for a short while, it did little to stem the territorial stigmatisation of the area. Subsequent regeneration attempts followed but with similar characteristics: some community engagement but ultimately major decisions were taken without community input. The perception from community members I spoke to was that past failures meant future interventions. Thus, what local people saw as an inequitable relationship contributed to a negative public perception that Hillfields required constant management. According to this narrative, the people of Hillfields were not to be trusted – their character was questioned, even when culpability for failings lay elsewhere.

Those I talked to were not against institutions coming into Hillfields to work with local people. They were concerned that *Imagine Hillfields* would not demonstrate a clear line of sight about how local people were involved in the inception, action and legacy of a project. Working with gatekeepers was no substitute for the kind of engagement that those I spoke to wanted. Thus, the volunteers at Hillz FM revealed not only the changing dynamics between volunteers and management caused by the retrenchment of the state, but also that their willingness to engage was predicated on how they wanted the research to be framed. The listening exercise, not formally recorded academic interviews but informal conversations, did not just explain their position in relation to historic projects and stigma, but also expressed through its form their expectations of the spirit of enquiry for *Imagine Hillfields*. Conversations revealed a methodological understanding of how original research should be conducted, based not on a contractual agreement of researcher behaviour, but on what kind of person the researcher is. From their perspective, co-production could only be defined through an exploratory process that began by addressing tensions between project partners and within the community. As those I spoke to critically assessed earlier interventions, and a co-produced partnership began to form, we also began to consider how to organise the project, and how this should reflect the needs of those involved.

The effect of changes to charity funding in Coventry, identified elsewhere as a national trend (Benson, 2014), meant that while WATCH received funding from *Imagine*, its contribution through gatekeeping and radio programming did not occur as planned. As the formal relationship between WATCH and myself dissolved, slowly, a loose group came together for *Imagine Hillfields* whose membership changed and evolved according to what people could contribute. This reflected the difficult times that people were living in, as well as their other commitments, but it also inspired a form of membership that included those with complex lives, and those who did not want to give up their other activities to play some part in *Imagine Hillfields*. This was very different from a formal agreement with the university because it was rooted in friendship ties and the daily practice of being in and from Hillfields.

The loose membership arrangement also accounted for multiple perspectives that found expression through photography, curatorial practice and community-based archival research. In this way, the project was rooted in the different paces of community lives, and created a web of intelligence about how local knowledge is shared, held and how it would be formed, or formalised, for the project. The concept of an exhibition took its time to develop because it had to be the correct form of expression for the local knowledge of many people. Yet the curated exhibition did not direct a singular community narrative. Equally valid was the knowledge developed from navigating the exhibition as a visitor, from people who were seeking out illustrations of a personal past. Visitors navigated their own route through, pausing at photographs of interest, beckoning friends to talk about something seen, or walking straight past other photographs. While the curated exhibition itself is visually catalogued, safeguarded for future researchers interested in how the exhibition looked, what is not recorded are the conversations between visitors that it prompted. Recording these memories would have been valuable too, reflecting the spirit of enquiry that we keep on looking to improve ways of seeing and of researching. We have the contact details of these people for future reference.

While Hillfields received positive press attention and attracted policy-makers to the exhibition, including senior Council executives, the impact was particularly felt at community level. A permanent exhibition of the John Blakemore photographs was placed in the St Peter's Community Centre. The local postmaster commissioned a series of History of Hillfields panels for the post office, working with Hillfields History Group to achieve this. Added to this, Masterji held his first solo exhibition the following year at the age of 94, with this exhibition travelling on to New York and Mumbai. In November 2017 his first photographic book was published. Hillfields, in the short term at least, appears to have claimed its place on the map.

Conclusions and lessons learned

By co-producing new knowledge with people from the Hillfields community, *Imagine Hillfields* tackled a single issue that was pertinent and persistent for many people: the territorial stigmatisation of an area. Co-production emerged as a methodology that resisted a structured approach to conducting university-community relations. Instead, an experimental and iterative process focused the project partners on the relationships around them to give impetus to the creation of new knowledge, born out of a shared experience of enquiry. In this sense, the spirit of scientific enquiry as a sensitive and reflective approach to knowledge production, was enacted – not by implementing the methods and methodology of others, but by challenging what enquiry is and can be.

Lessons learned from this project that might be useful for others include:

- Do not essentialise community. Community leaders and organisations might not speak for those you find most interesting or want to be involved.
- The pace of community life works differently for different people. Try to accommodate this in planning.
- Loose membership groups offer people a chance to be involved on their terms. This can work well for those with complex lives and for those who need time to think.
- Assume people might not share your thinking on why and how a project should proceed – focus on finding common ground rather than talking people around to your own view. Be prepared to consider and accept change.
- Community ethics revolves around trust, character and familiarity, not contracts. Be prepared to network and be seen.
- Ask people for help. Researchers do not always have to lead.
- Community outputs that are the product of many voices are provocative. Do not treat them as a single narrative.
- Focus on impact – how can you prove the worth of everyone's effort? Positive news stories bring out the policy-makers. Cultivate the media early and keep them informed.

Acknowledgements

My thanks go to the people of Hillfields, including those who stopped to chat and enquire, and those who were interviewed, but especially those whose influence was evident in the project. They are: Isaiah Williams, Trisha Evans, Sharda Taylor, Tanya Hayman, André Green, Mick Dabrowski, Ray Reid, Stanislaw-Jan Sackowicz-Librowski, Jason Scott Tilley, Mark Cook, Heather Parker, Andy McGeechan, John Payne and Ralph Butcher. I am also grateful to the Herbert Art Gallery & Museum, the team at FarGo, Mick Carpenter and Alice Mah, University of Warwick, who coordinated the project; the ESRC for funding the research; and the editors of this volume for their support and advice.

References

Allen, S. (2014) 'The sobering photography of Nick Hedges', *British Journal of Photography* (www.bjp-online.com/2014/10/nick-hedges-shelter-exhibition-science-museum/#closeContactFormCust00).

Banks, S. (2012) *Imagine: Connecting communities through research*, Internal policy paper for Work Package 2 of the ESRC *Imagine* project, Durham: Durham University (www.durham.ac.uk/socialjustice/imagine).

Banks, S. and Carpenter, M. (2017) 'Researching the local politics and practices of radical community development projects in 1970s Britain', *Community Development Journal*, 52(2), 226-46 (https://doi.org/10.1093/cdj/bsx001).

Benson, A. (2014) *'The devil that has come amongst us': The impact of commissioning and procurement practices*, London: National Coalition for Independent Action.

Bond, N. (1972) *The Hillfields Information and Opinion Centre – The evolution of social agency controlled by local residents, Home Office and City of Coventry*, CDP Occasional Paper No 2 [reprinted in R. Lees and G. Smith (eds) *Action-research in community development*, London: Routledge & Kegan Paul, 91-105].

Butcher, H. and Banks, S. (2007) *Critical community practice*, Bristol: Policy Press.

Blakemore, J. (2011) *Photographs: 1955-2010*, London: Dewi Lewis.

Carpenter, M. and Kyneswood, B. (2017) 'From self-help to class struggle: Revisiting Coventry Community Development Project's 1970s journey of discovery', *Community Development Journal*, 52(2), 247-68.

Christie, E. (2011) *No place to hide: How I put the black in the Union Jack*, London: Aurum Press.

Clewley, M. (2017) 'Photographer Dr Richard Sadler honoured by Belgrade Theatre' (www.atthetheatre.co.uk/2017/06/photographer-dr-richard-sadler-honoured-belgrade-theatre).

Coventry City Council (2015) *City centre area action plan: The preferred approach*, Coventry: Coventry City Council.

Coventry Evening Telegraph (1992) 'Terror on the streets', 13 July, 2-3.

Fink, J. (2011) 'Walking the neighbourhood, seeing the small details of community life: Reflections from a photography walking tour', *Critical Social Policy*, 32(1), 31-50.

Friedman, A (1977) *Industry & labour: Class struggle at work and monopoly capitalism*, London: MacMillan Press.

Goffman, E. (1963) *Stigma*, London: Penguin.

Gould, J. and Gould, C. (2009) *Coventry planned*, London: English Heritage.

Hayward, A. (2004) *Which side are you on? Ken Loach and his films*, London: Bloomsbury.

Hodgkinson, G. (1970) *Sent to Coventry*, Bletchley: Maxwell.

IACD (International Association for Community Development) (2015) *Annual Review 2014-15* London: IACD (http://www.iacdglobal.org/category/resources/annual-reviews/).

Jacobs, J. (1961) *The death and life of Great American cities*, New York: Random House.

Johnsen, S., May, J. and Cloke, P. (2007) 'Imag(in)ing "homeless places": Using auto-photography to (re)examine the geographies of homelessness', *Area*, 40(2), 194-207.

Kenny, S., Marilyn, T., Onyx, J. and Mayo, M. (2015) *Challenging the third sector: Global perspectives for active citizenship*, Bristol: Policy Press.

Loney, M. (1983) *Community against government: The British Community Development Project 1968-78*, London: Heinemann Educational Books.

National Archive, The (1970) *Cabinet Papers* [CAB 134/3291, 8], London.

Partington, M. (1975) *Recent developments in legal services for the poor: Some reflections on experience in Coventry*, CDP Occasional Paper No 13, London: Home Office.

Prest, J. (1960) *The Industrial Revolution in Coventry*, Oxford: Oxford University Press.

Simpson, C. (2012) 'Homeless shelter plan for Hillfields unveiled', *Coventry Telegraph*, 20 October.

Smith, D. (1987) 'Knowing your place: Class, politics, and ethnicity in Chicago and Birmingham, 1890-1983', in N. Thrift and P. Williams (eds) *Class and space: The making of urban society*, London: Routledge & Kegan Paul, 277-305.

Taylor, M. (2012) *Public policy in the community* (2nd edn), Basingstoke: Palgrave Macmillan.

Thomas, D. (1945) *A City Reborn* [script for film] (https://player.bfi.org.uk/free/film/watch-a-city-reborn-1945-online).

Wacquant, L. (2007) 'Territorial stigmatization in the age of advanced marginality', *Thesis Eleven*, 91, 66-77.

NINE

'Who controls the past controls the future': Black history and community development

*Shabina Aslam, Milton Brown, Onyeka Nubia, Elizabeth Pente,
Natalie Pinnock-Hamilton, Mandeep Samra and Paul Ward*

Introduction

What role does 'Black history' play in community development? This chapter discusses the ways in which Black and Asian minority ethnic (BAME) communities have been excluded from contributing to national and local histories, depriving them of resources that would enable them to develop coherent alternative perspectives on the British narrative. It focuses on the intersection of history and community development. It concentrates on local people and organisations and how they have used Black history in a variety of community-based activities in collaboration with the University of Huddersfield. Huddersfield, in the North of England, has a population of around 165,000, of which 76 per cent is White, 15 per cent is of Asian origin and 4.2 per cent is of African and African-Caribbean origin. This chapter explores how Black history impacts on community development bearing this demography in mind.

The term 'Black' as used in this chapter can be contentious and complex. The historian Onyeka states that:

> The term "Black" has been used in recent history to define individuals, communities, nations and their histories, etc. It has sometimes been applied to people that would define themselves in other ways.... "Black" is a political, ideological,[1] term used in reference and in opposition to "white" as a racial or ethnic construction because this has given rise to manifest destiny, white man's privilege, white power ... colonialism, imperialism and neo-colonialism. However, some academics and others use the term "Black"

only to apply to people of African descent, but that has not always been the case. A corrective is to use the term African or "African descent" when referring to people of African descent, and "Black" when describing a resistance or opposition to the white power just described. (Onyeka, 2017)

Black history has tended to be linked to the history of people of African descent. However, academics described as Black historians tend to describe their own ethnicity as African or/and African American, African (British), African Caribbean, or by other descriptions they feel reflect their identities. Not only is there a myriad of perspectives on Black identity but also differences in Black historical methodologies.[2] In this chapter we take account of but do not concentrate on those differences, but on how local community groups use Black history to challenge mono-ethnic white narratives of British history. The focus is on groups that have worked with the University of Huddersfield, which includes Let's Go Yorkshire, Kirklees Local TV (KLTV) and Building African Caribbean Communities (BACC), as well as Narrative Eye, a London-based organisation. They each illustrate how Black history can be used to support community development. They are small, community-based organisations that contribute to community development but rarely register in data sources or research. There are many other similar groups and more than 5,500 recognised BAME organisations exist in the UK (McCabe et al, 2010, p 9). The chapter used a collaborative approach to explore how some of these groups and historians have used historical narratives to underpin community development.

The authors of the chapter have a range of backgrounds. Shabina Aslam is a theatre maker and has been a creative producer and radio drama producer. She is based in Bradford where she particularly enjoys telling stories that challenge the status quo. Her practice involves working closely with communities to shape their stories into high quality theatrical productions. She is undertaking a PhD at the University of Huddersfield, on 'Bussing Out', an educational policy of the 1960s and 1970s. Milton Brown is a community activist and filmmaker. He founded KLTV as a social enterprise in 2010 to document the local community around Huddersfield and Dewsbury through film. He has been working with the university as a Community Research Fellow and is undertaking a PhD on how people of African descent have navigated Britishness since the 1960s. Dr Onyeka Nubia is an historian, writer and law lecturer as well as Visiting Research Fellow at the University of Huddersfield. He promotes the study of early modern histories to contextualise Black and world history. Elizabeth Pente was a doctoral student at the University of Huddersfield, researching public history, and has been an integral part of *Imagine* working with some of the community organisations involved in this chapter. Natalie Pinnock-Hamilton is a community activist, involved in a range of Black organisations, including BACC, and has been involved in a number of initiatives at the university. Mandeep Samra is a cultural historian, artist and heritage activist, part of Let's Go Yorkshire, an organisation that focuses on aspects of local cultural heritage hidden from and unrecorded by mainstream historical narratives. Mandeep has led on many projects, such as Sound System Culture, in which the university has participated. Paul Ward was a Professor of Modern British History at the University of Huddersfield and was head of the department that organised these collaborations. He is now Professor of Public History at Edge Hill University. All the people involved in this chapter have been seeking to further include Black history in the research, teaching and out-reach of the histories departments with which they work.

The work for this chapter was not undertaken through a formal co-inquiry or research group, but was conducted informally based on discussions that arose through working together in a variety of projects and activities. Additionally, Paul Ward conducted a series of interviews and wrote an initial draft of the chapter, which was circulated to all co-authors, for their comments and changes. Onyeka Nubia made substantial written changes, particularly in relation to the use of the terms 'Black', 'Black history' and others that define ethnicity. He also offered in writing and orally a very useful and critical counter trajectory to ideas in the initial draft that shaped subsequent revision. Other members of the group were also rigorous in offering their views orally. Many of these oral contributions were incorporated into the revisions and re-writing. Only about 20 per cent of the initial draft remains, which illustrates how oral contributions, written changes and comments from the group have made this a piece of co-produced research. The chapter is, therefore, an example of the co-production of history in that it involved university historians and community activists analysing issues, writing about the past together, and drawing on their expertise and experience. Those with experience of academic writing, such as Onyeka and Paul, took the lead in writing ideas, concepts and providing interpretations – but the chapter could not have been written without all the authors' contributions. We discussed issues of ethnicity and identity and the role of white academics in Black history. However, we agreed this chapter should not be about white agency but should remain an exposition on the role of Black history in community development.

The concept of co-production of historical knowledge involves thinking about how the past is interpreted better in collaboration and from different perspectives. Such public history provides resources for the development of new ways of understanding the past. It contributes to a community narrative on identity. We explore the ways in which a variety of history practitioners and community activists have used history to critique the imbalances in power of a society dominated by a normative whiteness. We delineate developments in Black historiography, inside and outside universities, to articulate a 'community development approach' to co-production – a collaborative approach to developing knowledge that involves examining and interpreting primary historical documents (Ward and Pente, 2017).

The chapter begins by examining the exclusion of BAME people from historical narratives, outlining the impact this has on the British narrative. It explores the imperative to develop communities to counter imbalances in power. It explains how Black history is used to identify needs and aspirations and enable BAME people to act to exert influence on decisions that affect their lives. This involves examining what is meant by Black history, the variety of forms it takes, the purposes it serves and the agency it entails, particularly in relation to community development. In line with other authors in this book, we consider that community development is a long-term value-based process that aims to address imbalances in power and bring about change founded on social justice, equality and inclusion.

Absence and exclusion

BAME exclusion from historical narratives has its roots in the need to justify colonialism, imperialism and the dehumanisation and enslavement of people classified as other than white, especially those of African, Native American, Oceanic and Asian descent. Paul Gilroy, in the first edition of *There ain't no black in the Union Jack*, argued that, 'This capacity to evacuate any historical dimension to black life remains a fundamental achievement of racist ideologies in this country...' (1987, p 11). BAME citizens of Britain, the Empire and Commonwealth found that when they visited their 'mother country', they were treated as immigrants and portrayed as anomalous and invasive. Roshi Naidoo and Jo Littler have noted that 'whilst the British *present* is now frequently thought of as being multicultural [by which they mean multi-ethnic], only too often is the British past, and British heritage, still imagined as being white' (Naidoo and Littler, 2004, p 330). In particular, people of African descent are excluded from their place in the past.

There is an important fact about higher education in Britain that underlines this exclusion. In 2011-12, only 85 out of 16,000 professors in British universities were of African descent (Ackah, 2014). Despite widespread awareness very little has been done since then to address this obvious disparity (Adams, 2017). Moreover, Black history has only rarely found its way into school curricula. Marika Sherwood conducted a survey of representation of Black history in education curricula in 2004 and concluded that it barely existed, effectively denying the existence of BAME people themselves in British history (Sherwood, 2004). Historical geographer Caroline Bressey notes that 'histories of a multi-cultural [again meaning multi-ethnic] London and the role of empire in the making and remaking of its many geographies remained stubbornly absent from popular culture and my school history' (2016, p 185). As well as education, the primary sources for African, Asian and minority ethnic histories have been largely unavailable in what are classified as 'mainstream' archives and repositories. Andrew Flinn, discussing the politics of archiving, suggests that:

> ... in reality the mainstream or formal archive sector does not contain and represent the voices of the non-elites, the grassroots, the marginalised. Or at least if it does, the archive rarely allows them to speak with their voice, through their own records. (Flinn, 2007, p 152)

Bressey proposes that assumptions are made about the 'whiteness of the British'. This has implications for how national identity and culture is perceived in the present. Bressey suggests the absence of references to race and ethnicity in many archives should not imply the absence of people of colour in British history, but that 'The *imagined Whiteness* of our national archives is one of the most blatant examples of the Whitening of Britishness' (Bressey, 2006, p 61). As Onyeka asks, 'Do we imagine English history as a book with white pages and no black letters in?' (2013, p vii).

Black history

The need for Black history is clear as people of African descent are an integral part of humanity and their history is a fundamental part of British history. Being able to interpret history is an integral aspect of being human, and it therefore relates to the place, space and context in which humans find themselves. The ways in which history is told depends on a series of power relationships. Michael Frisch, in his book on sharing authority in oral history, quotes a Nigerian friend of his:

> Why bother with history, when you're rich and powerful? All it can do is tell you how you climbed to the top, which is a story it is probably best not to examine too closely. No, you don't need history. What you need is something more like a pretty carpet that can be rolled out on ceremonial occasions to cover all those bloodstains on the stairs. And in fact, that's what you usually get from your historians.... For the rest of us, it's a lot different. We don't have the luxury of ignoring history. History is a giant stone that lies on top of us; for us, history is something we have to struggle to get out from under. (Frisch, 1990, p 20)

'History' – without any adjectives – is often interpreted as being objective and without purpose, other than to explain why things are as they are. In fact, the powerful often claim all history as their own. For groups excluded from power, history really matters. A group that has been marginalised will claim its own part of history, such as with Jewish, Native American and women's histories. In this way, people of African descent also take ownership of their own history. There are many roots to Black history, but one prominent strand originates in the US with Carter G. Woodson (1875-1950) and W.E.B. Du Bois (1868-1963), who tried to form a coherent methodology to define African diasporic history. In the early 20th century it was routinely stated that the 'negro has no history' (see, for example, Culp, 1902, p 51). For Woodson, Du Bois and others involved in the exploration of Black history, the purpose was community development and social transformation (Apple, 2013). Black History Month, which developed from Negro History Week in the 1920s, was not solely a commemoration of the past, but a call for change in the future, as was the development of a variety of African Studies and Black Studies programmes at US universities. Black History Month was introduced in the UK in the 1980s to draw together a variety of Black history initiatives. One co-facilitator of this mainstreaming was Akyaaba Addai-Sebo, who worked for the Labour-controlled Greater London Council. He explained:

I was very familiar with black history month in America, and thought that something like that had to be done here in the UK, because if this was the fountainhead of colonialism, imperialism and racism, and despite all the institutions of higher learning and research and also the cluster of African embassies, you could still find a six year old boy being confused about his identity even though his mother had tried to correct it at birth, that meant the mother had not succeeded because the wider society had failed her. (Addai-Sebo, nd)

There is a long tradition of the study of Black history in Britain by people of African descent and others. Much of their research is yet to be codified and some of it has been lost. Long before the 1980s Black History Studies were developing in a variety of locations outside mainstream institutions of learning. The findings of these studies were often dismissed as being polemical, political and divisive because they focused on oppression by organs of the state. As Kevin Myers argued, 'Scholar activists were critical in developing a culture of history and historical thinking in the struggles of immigrant and minority communities in post-war England. They helped to make those communities history minded' (2015, p 222; see also Waters, 2017). The Association for the Study of African Caribbean and Asian Culture and History in Britain was set up in 1991, becoming the Black and Asian Studies Association (BASA) in 1997. Its motto is an African proverb, 'Until the lion has its own historian, tales of hunting will always be of the hunter', signifying its attempt to tell the story that has not been told. Black history relied extensively on history already taking place in communities, for example, gathering evidence of the Black presence in archives across the country through BASA's newsletter (Bressey, 2006, pp 49-50). Colin Prescod, chair of the Institute of Race Relations, has said that for him, '"reparative history" has not been what you might call a "career choice". It has been an endeavour not so much chosen, as thrust upon me, given that I've found myself living in a society in which racism is ingrained' (Prescod, 2017, p 77). Prescod identifies the establishment of the Black Cultural Archives, the George Padmore Institute's archives, the formation of the Friends of the Huntley Archives at the London Metropolitan Archives and the development of the Black History Collection at the Institute of Race Relations as significant developments in reparative history. Yet Black History often continues to be considered as distinct from the 'formal' and academic history claimed by many university departments.

Priyamvada Gopal has remarked that 'It enables an ongoing historical amnesia which continues to segregate a majority "indigenous" history from that of … minority communities and as such, feeds into the hiving off of imperial history from British history' (2016, p 20). Gopal insists that:

> The project of developing a more demanding relationship to history – the very core of the reparative – must go beyond the notional largesse of "including" ethnic and cultural minorities in the national. The postcolonial must exist in a constitutive relationship to the national, not one of supplementarity – and in this regard, both agency and influence are central.

Objectivity and perspective

Many have argued for the need to overcome this separation. Hakim Adi has asserted the centrality of Black history in British history:

> It's impossible to study the history of Britain for the last 500 years without looking at the history of people of African and Caribbean origin, whether here in Britain, or in Africa and the Caribbean, because if the Caribbean and Africa were part of the British Empire, they were part of Britain. It is impossible to study British history without looking at those parts of the world. (Adi, 2007)

The veracity of this statement reveals that an intertextual philosophy is needed for academic rigour. But unfortunately, many historians claim that this is political and polemical. In what has been used as a standard textbook for history students, John Tosh attempts to resolve the tension between doing justice to the present while respecting the past. He argues that, 'Our priorities in the present should determine the questions we ask of the past, but not the answers' (Tosh with Lang, 2006, p 49). We can, then, think about writing, curating and using Black history with the present in mind. This emphasises the importance of foregrounding the phrase from Disability Studies that demands 'nothing about us, without us' – that people with disabilities should be involved in and central to academic studies about them, since they have the lived experience and embodied knowledge to understand their lives (Charlton, 2000). Similarly, there is a need for structural change in universities to end the disparity in the employment of BAME people to change the perspective from which 'minority' histories are viewed and studied. But there is also an imperative to think about what 'history' is for, and how it can be used to engage in social issues. Dr William 'Lez' Henry, for example, is clear about the social context of his academic work on reggae and dancehall deejaying, reminding his readers (quoting Professor Henry Lewis Gates) that Black histories have 'sustained these communities through centuries of oppression'. Hence, he says,

> ... there is no attempt in my work to separate the Deejay's lyricism from the worldview that spawned charges of "you're too close to the subject to be objective" [which] do not faze me in the slightest ... as we say in Jamaica, "who feels it knows it". I am not interested in spurious claims for objectivity, because often the best way to truly appreciate something is often to have the lived experience. (Henry, 2006, p 60)

Experience and emotion provide essential components of knowledge since they capture a perspective that emerges from the people's living history rather than just observing and writing about it. This draws the study of Black history towards community development. Ambalavaner Sivanandan considers that a Black perspective is an anti-racist perspective that 'derives not from some abstract academic definition, but from the living struggles of African–Caribbean and Asian working people in this country in the 1960s and 1970s, against an undifferentiated and brutal racism.' He argues, therefore, that 'a black perspective is a community perspective and not an individualistic one' (Sivanandan, 1993, pp 63-9). This is how the authors of this chapter view Black history – that it is a component in the development of community rather than solely an academic exercise.

A Black perspective is a community perspective

We take community development 'to start from the principle that within any community there is a wealth of knowledge and experience which, if used in creative ways, can be channelled into collective action to achieve the community's desired goals' (Gilchrist and Taylor, 2016, p 5). In this section we explore a series of projects that use Black history in different ways to think about collective and community development. Most of those discussed here are based in West Yorkshire, but the link between Black history and community development is national and international. As an example, Robin Walker, 'the Black History Man', has run an 18-week course called 'Black History, Personal Empowerment and African Cultural Studies' in and around London for at least two decades, which aims 'to turn out ... powerful, socially-focused adults who can move themselves and the community forward' (Croydon Voluntary Action, 2017). Similarly, Black History Studies seeks to 'Work with the community to develop its full potential' (Black History Studies, 2017; see also Black Studies Association, 2017). In the US, as a single example of thousands of activities, the programme officer for the Local Initiatives Support Corporation, District of Columbia, considered during Black History Month in 2016 that 'community development is an essential way to promote social justice for African-Americans' (Ali, 2016).

In collaborative work at the University of Huddersfield, the linkages between Black history and community development have taken a variety of forms. Milton Brown was awarded a Fellowship for People of African Descent at the United Nations in 2011. He has been involved in a series of community development activities since the mid-1990s based on sport, education and social media. He considers Black history to be "the historical journey of people of Black African descent" and that "the future is part of Black History, it's a continuum, it never stops" (quotations without references in this chapter are taken from the interviews conducted for the chapter). After a period in the Royal Air Force, Milton discovered Black literature and history, reading Malcolm X, Booker T. Washington, Marcus Garvey and Du Bois, and became a Pan Africanist, going to Uganda in 1995 and often afterwards. This led him, with others, to establish a variety of community organisations, such as a football academy based in districts of Huddersfield such as Brackenhall, Deighton, Sheepridge and Fartown, with high incidences of drug and knife crime. This resulted in working across the Atlantic with anti-gang initiatives in Los Angeles and Boston, and led him and others to establish the Parents of Black Children Association (PBCA) in 2006. PBCA, as Milton explains, aimed at "a world where ethnicity is not a barrier to opportunity, achievement and attainment." As well as advocacy and advice, PBCA offered validated Black Studies and Black History courses to its members. In 2008, faced with austerity, the local authority withdrew funding from PBCA and Milton established a new organisation called Kirklees Local TV (KLTV), a social enterprise that seeks to "document our local community" and uses film to provide audiences with access to people and perspectives rarely seen or heard. KLTV does not focus on BAME issues alone but through emphasising grassroots issues engages frequently with the African descent community in Kirklees. Milton suggests that "It's for people who don't have a voice. It's not about black, it's not about white, it's about humanity, it's about those who don't have a voice."

Another Huddersfield organisation, Building African Caribbean Communities (BACC), considers that history enables community development, but their view of what constitutes 'history' transgresses disciplinary boundaries without anxiety, destabilising the ways in which many in universities see the discipline. Explorations of the past and the town's spaces and places readily merge in celebrations of local, regional, national and international achievement by members of the community, such as at the Black History Month Showcase (in its fifth year in 2017), the Black Achievement Awards and Huddersfield Carnival, in its 30th year.[3] Knowledge is considered differently when its purpose is to build and celebrate communities rather than as an academic exercise. It enables knowledge to interact with townscapes and neighbourhoods that generate new ways of understanding. This highlights what Dolores Hayden (working in Los Angeles) explained as 'The Power of Place', in which 'combining research with community activism helped identify, interpret, and expand the intersections between everyday experience and the built environment, between the past and the present' (Meringolo, 2014, pp 419-20). Natalie Pinnock-Hamilton, a leading figure in BACC as well as many other community initiatives, says that:

> 'Black history should be for everyone. Everyone should know about the past, but it is about what's happening now and the future and as we move forward into the future. It's about highlighting that there are numerous black people out there who have achieved great things. We have doctors, nurses, lawyers and it is important for people, particularly young people to strive for, to say, yes, we can do it.'

As with Milton, Natalie considers Black history to be a continuum from the past to the future, and that BACC, as its name suggests, is about building community identity to develop the multitude of Black civic organisations into a more cohesive and therefore powerful entity.

Yet another approach comes from Let's Go Yorkshire, which is more firmly rooted in 'heritage'. In 2013, Let's Go Yorkshire initiated an arts and heritage project, led by Mandeep Samra, named Sound System Culture. For many years in Huddersfield a thriving sound system scene existed out of proportion to the size of the town (http://soundsystemcultureblog.tumblr.com; Ward, 2018). The project documented the lives and experiences of those who were involved. It was a project in which the participants sought to understand sound systems through an emotional attachment and to empathise with those who had gone before them, developing forms of cultural expression embedded in Britain's urban environment. Again, the project crossed the boundaries of academic disciplines and blurred past, present and future. As well as oral histories, it used photography, model-making, film and an interactive sound installation called Heritage HiFi built by Paul Huxtable of Axis Sound, which participated in African-Caribbean carnivals in northern England (Sound System Culture, nd). Mandeep was interested in the histories of different groups and the project emerged from going to school in Deighton and hearing stories of blues parties, listening to reggae on pirate radio and her pleasure on learning that the main reggae venue in Huddersfield had been owned by the Sikh Bhullar brothers: "I was really proud actually that a Sikh family owned this venue in town and when I found out that this committee used it for reggae dances, I wanted to know more."

Let's Go Yorkshire seeks to capture aspects of local cultural heritage hidden from and unrecorded by mainstream history. With Sound System Culture, Mandeep was working on capturing oral history, living history and memories. She kept saying to people that there was a need to capture and document this history because people were passing away and the memories were being lost. She emphasised the need to retrieve and retain first-hand accounts and archival documents because they were often absent, and that it was important to capture those who were part of the scene so that present and future generations had that knowledge if they wanted to do research. While Sound System Culture developed into a national project, its initiation in Huddersfield made a significant contribution to diversifying the 'history' of the town, ensuring that Black history came to be considered an essential component in community heritage. Equally importantly, the global nature of this local history highlights the ways in which the Black Atlantic reached into British society, culture and history. Such heritage projects capture the present with a mind towards creating future histories that underpin the identity of disempowered communities. To this end, the next phase of Sound System Culture, called Let's Play Vinyl, thinks about contemporary sound system artists as productive entrepreneurs, creating their own arts ecology in modern-day Britain. As Mandeep explains, "It's almost like telling the history and capturing the memories now, so that whatever's collated through this project will be a living history."

In different ways, these community-based organisations have drawn on Black history or contributed to it to assert the presence of African people in British history. Onyeka is one of only a few historians to research the African presence in early modern England. He is a Visiting Research Fellow at the University of Huddersfield and writer in residence at Narrative Eye. He approaches Black history from a different perspective. He has trained as a lawyer and as a historian, but spent most of his early life as an activist. He faced institutional indifference and ignorance from a range of UK universities. After 20 years of research he obtained his doctorate. The publication of *Blackamoores: Africans in Tudor England, their presence, status and origins* (Onyeka, 2013) contains only a small part of that research, but it has changed the way that people see diversity in Tudor England, and questions ideas of ethnicity, culture and identity. Onyeka learned a narrative of history at school and university, but instead chose to investigate using independent sources in archives across the country. He was dismayed by the lack of diversity being popularly portrayed in historical films such as *A Man for All Seasons* (1966), *Cromwell* (1970) and those about the World Wars. He explains that:

'I didn't grow up learning Black history. I discovered it myself by investigating history. Hitherto, the history I had been shown presented a world in which only white, upper-class, men existed. It wasn't even a world in which working-class men lived. It was missing social and political context. However, this history did give chronological dates, which were useful in a sense. We do need to know dates, times and places to give ourselves reference points for our understanding. Otherwise we may up end with only snapshots off history.'

Exploring the period 1485 to 1603, through systematic and rigorous archival research, Onyeka has found Africans in cities and towns such as Bristol, Hertford, London, Northampton, Norwich and Plymouth. He shows that African people in England were not all foreign and that most, whether born in England or elsewhere, were integrated members of their local parishes. They did not automatically occupy the lowest positions in Tudor society; this is important because the few modern historians who have written about Africans in Tudor England suggest that they were all slaves or transient immigrants who were considered as dangerous strangers and the epitome of 'otherness'. The multi-ethnic nature of Tudor England counters the popular narratives that suggest that Britain was mono-ethnically white until the Empire Windrush arrived in 1948 with nearly 500 West Indians on board, as well as countering associations that people of African descent only have histories as recent immigrants or within a narrative on slavery. As Gilroy remarked, people of African descent in Britain are excluded from history and become associated only with 'modern urban Britain' (1987, p 303). Many young people of African descent grow up almost hating what is shown to them of history because they feel the past is only about slavery, so they dwell in modernity. As Onyeka suggests, "Without name, language and identity, they are prone to destructive frameworks." By countering such conceptualisations, Onyeka's historical narratives are intended as a challenge to "the alienation and annihilation of self" and to draw people to investigate and research all over the world.

'Bussing Out', a project that spans community and academic boundaries, led by Shabina Aslam, deals with the experience of Black and Asian children who came to Britain in the 1960s and 1970s and were taken by bus to schools in outlying areas. The aim of the policy was partly to assimilate them into British culture and partly to assuage the alarm by white parents about the 'swamping' of *their* schools by 'immigrants'. This national initiative was advised by the Department of Education and Science through 'The Dispersal Policy 1965-1976', which recommended that no school should have more than 30 per cent 'immigrant' children on roll. This hidden history happened during a time when the term 'black' was coined to unify the common experience of racism and decolonisation. This period:

> ... inaugurated by decolonization and by the emergence of new non-white – "non-aligned" – nations, encompassing Civil Rights and Black Power in the United States, Garveyism in the Caribbean (although not only in the Caribbean), combining with Rastafarianism and reggae; the long struggle against apartheid; the black British "culture wars" and the mobilization of anti-racist movements in the 1970's. (Hall, 2017, p 100)

By examining the ambivalent experiences of the bussed children through oral history interviews and performance, Shabina's exploration of the 'othering' of the Black child and subsequent identity formation problematises the term 'black' by moving away from essentialising ethnicity through the examination of memory and imagination as played out through structural racism and diasporic influences to re-imagine recent history. Here, the use of community arts practice is an attempt to build a politics of criticism that aims to challenge power imbalances and empower communities.

Co-production and community

All those involved in writing this chapter have connections with universities but are critical of their exclusivity. All of us seek to change universities so that they better serve the communities in which they are located, and seek to address some of the intellectual imbalances of power inherent in educational institutions that have developed overt and subtle mechanisms of maintaining white privilege and racism. These mechanisms mean that only small numbers of BAME students and fewer BAME academic staff are admitted. This is a scandal! Of those who do go to university, there is an attainment gap, since while 74 per cent of white UK students achieve a first or upper second-class degree, only 47 per cent of African-Caribbean UK students do so. Similarly, only 7.3 per cent of professors are from Black or minority ethnic backgrounds. As part of the 'Why is my curriculum white?' campaign, now taken up by the National Union of Students, Mariya Hussain has argued that:

> In History classes the colonisation of India is taught through the lens of the business workings of the British, and the lives of the colonised [are] rarely mentioned; English Literature focuses on pre-1800 white writing; Philosophy and Religion are drowned by white, largely male thinkers and a Eurocentric perspective. The arts and humanities are the subjects that have the most work to do. They have the biggest opportunity to teach students a diverse range of interesting sources, and they do a great harm to our education by perpetuating the assumed authority of white euro centricity. (Hussain, 2015)

Here, Hussain considers that university historians have been central to maintaining an invisible but powerful whiteness. Many people have called for universities and university curricula to be decolonised involving addressing discrimination in employment and achievement and the dismantling the ideological apparatus of white supremacy. Undertaking collaborative research can be a step on the way to decolonisation. It develops a body of knowledge within universities based on BAME experience that complements the core vision of universities as places where knowledge is created. With Black Studies and BAME history on the curriculum, universities might be enabled to play a part in BAME community development. This is no easy task, since as Linda Tuhiwai Smith has argued, 'the term "research" is inextricably linked to European imperialism and colonialism.' Writing from 'the vantage point of the colonized', she continues, 'The word itself, "research", is probably one of the dirtiest words in the indigenous world's vocabulary' (Smith, 2012, p 1). This raises questions of power within collaborative research, and how individual academics within those institutions might relinquish authority to community organisations and activists rather than continue to control research directions.

There are many resources available to support Black history. The availability of Heritage Lottery funding (HLF) for BAME history projects is important since it encourages a primary focus on the needs of those who initiate the projects from the community, and there have been substantial numbers of innovative and inspiring Black heritage projects (Heritage Lottery Fund, nd). The HLF requires community participation in projects, using heritage to think about Britain's diversity. However, the unfortunate aspect of Heritage Lottery funding is that it is project-based and can often be ephemeral, with many projects maintaining no legacy, reinforcing the absence of Black history in archives. While many of the groups that have made this chapter possible have received project-based funding, it has not often enabled them to enhance their viability through expanding resources permanently. Collaboration between such community projects and universities offers the opportunity to sustain knowledge created in partnership and to open up resources for community development through new knowledge. For example, in the US, a partnership between academics and the African-American community in Muncie, Indiana, challenged a standard and influential sociological study written in the late 1920s by Robert and Helen Lynd (Lynd and Lynd, 1929). The Lynds decided that to portray Muncie as a typical US town they would need to exclude the town's African-American population from their data, which disseminated a myth about America's whiteness in subsequent sociological studies. In 2004, the academics Luke Eric Lassiter and Elizabeth Campbell worked with residents and university students to co-write and publish *The other side of Middletown: Exploring Muncie's African American community*. The book relied on collaboration with Hurley Goodall, born in Muncie in 1927 and who worked in the city's fire department. In 1976 he published *A history of negroes in Muncie, Indiana*, as part of his contribution to community development (Goodall and Mitchell, 1976). He had served on the Muncie Community Schools Board for Education and was elected to the Indiana House of Representatives in 1978 and was active in a range of community organisations. His involvement, and that of others in Muncie, in *The other side of Middletown* ensured that it was a genuinely co-produced book and had a transformative impact on pedagogy (Campbell and Lassiter, 2010; see also Lassiter et al, 2004). The involvement of universities and their students in community-based learning and research can make university education more authentic and relevant to Britain's ethnically diverse population, with the potential to increase the numbers of BAME students in Humanities subjects with the longer-term impact of increasing diversity among research students and academic faculties. To enable this social change, universities need to think about how to make their practices more transparent to enable engagement with BAME communities. This may mean that those already working in universities must be willing to give up some of their power and influence for social change to take place.

Conclusions and lessons learned

George Orwell contended in his novel *Nineteen eighty-four* that 'who controls the past controls the future' (1949 [2013], p 37). In this chapter we have explored how some groups have used Black history to contribute to community development, that is, they have used history to play a part in shaping the future. Sometimes this has foregrounded history, such as in Onyeka's engagement with the African history of Tudor England, whereas at other times the history of BAME exclusion and agency has underpinned organisations that have focused on specific aspects of community development, such as with the Parents of Black Children Association and Kirklees Local TV. All have addressed power imbalances in British society based on ethnicity and have drawn on global histories to understand how white privilege and racism operate. We suggest that there are advantages in collaborations between such organisations and individuals using Black history and university departments, although the relationships are not always straightforward and sometimes raise issues around indifference, nepotism, corporatism and exploitation. Nonetheless, a collaborative approach to developing knowledge, both historical and contemporary, can provide resources and open universities to greater ethnic diversity, which, in the long term, may begin to address issues of structural racism in British higher education. The inclusion of Black history into national historical narratives highlights how Black perspectives have avoided the individualistic approach of many academics and have emphasised community perspectives, with a potential role in community development and imagining better futures.

So what are our key messages from writing this chapter and the projects within it?

- Universities continue to underpin whiteness and power structures based on racism and colonialism.
- Don't stand back: use university resources to challenge racism and discrimination, which are historical and structural.
- Effective and principled collaborative and co-productive research enables better historical understanding – blurring the boundaries of university and community knowledge.
- Universities should be more civic in their presence and visible in their engagement with BAME communities. Universities have substantial resources that can be used for change and community development.
- Think about the purpose of history: who is history for? The co-production of historical knowledge can be radical and powerful enabling diverse histories.

Notes

[1] Of course, some see 'Black' as a cultural term too, such as Cheikh Anta Diop (1954). Maulana Karenga, Yosef Ben Jochannan and others have similar perspectives.

[2] For more on this, see Molefi Asante and Ama Mazama (2005); David Dabydeen and James Gilmore (2007), and Josna Pankhania (1994, pp 1-7). For Black Studies in the UK, see Andrews and Palmer (2016).

[3] The Carnival is organised by Huddersfield African Caribbean Carnival Trust (https://hacct.co.uk).

References

Ackah, W. (2014) 'There are fewer than 100 black professors in Britain – why?', The Conversation, 10 March (http://theconversation.com/there-are-fewer-than-100-black-professors-in-britain-why-24088).

Adams, R. (2017) 'British universities employ no black academics in top roles, figures show', *The Guardian*, 19 January (https://amp.theguardian.com/education/2017/jan/19/british-universities-employ-no-black-academics-in-top-roles-figures-show).

Addai-Sebo, A. (no date) Interview (http://everygeneration.co.uk/index.php/black-british-history/bhm-black-history-month/24-akyaaba-addai-sebo).

Adi, H. (2007) 'Putting the "British" back into Black history' (www.shunpiking.org/bhs2007/0402-BHS-HA-puttingbrit.htm).

Ali, A. (2016) 'During Black History Month, reflecting on community development' (www.lisc.org/our-stories/story/reflections-community-development-during-black-history-month).

Andrews, K. and Palmer, L.A. (eds) (2016) *Blackness in Britain*, London: Routledge.

Apple, M. (2013) 'Can education change society? Du Bois, Woodson and the politics of social transformation', *Review of Education*, 1(1), 32-56.

Asante, M. and Mazama, A. (eds) (2005) *The encyclopedia of Black studies*, London: Sage.

Black History Studies (2017) 'Educating the community to educate themselves' (www.blackhistorystudies.com).

Black Studies Association (2017) 'About us' (www.blackstudies.org.uk).

Bressey, C. (2006) 'Invisible presence: The whitening of the Black community in the historical imagination of British archives', *Archivaria*, 61, 47-62.

Bressey, C. (2016) 'Conversations with Caroline', in A. Burton and D. Kennedy (eds) *How empire shaped us*, London: Bloomsbury, 183-94.

Campbell, E. and Lassiter, L.E. (2010) 'From collaborative ethnography to collaborative pedagogy: Reflections on the Other Side of Middletown Project and community-university partnerships', *Anthropology and Education Quarterly*, 41(4), 370-85.

Charlton, J. (2000) *Nothing about us without us: Disability oppression and empowerment*, Berkeley and Los Angeles, CA: University of California Press.

Croydon Voluntary Action (2017) 'Free Black History course' (www.cvalive.org.uk/news/2017-february/18-02-17-black-history-dd).

Culp, D.W. (1902) *Twentieth century Negro literature; or, A cyclopedia of thought on the vital topics relating to the American Negro*, Naperville, IL: J.L. Nichols.

Dabydeen, D. and Gilmore, J. (eds) (2007) *The Oxford companion to Black British history*, Oxford: Oxford University Press.

Diop, C.A. (1954) *Cultural unity of Black Africa*, Paris: Editions Africans.

Flinn, A. (2007) 'Community histories, community archives: Some opportunities and challenges', *Journal of the Society of Archivists*, 28(2), 151-76.

Frisch, M. (1990) *A shared authority: Essays on the craft and meaning of oral and public history*, Albany, NY: State University of New York Press.

Gilchrist, A. and Taylor, M. (2016) *The short guide to community development* (2nd edn), Bristol: Policy Press.

Gilroy, P. (1987) *'There ain't no black in the Union Jack': The cultural politics of race and nation*, London: Unwin Hyman Press.

Goodall, H. and Mitchell, J.P. (1976) *A history of negroes in Muncie, Indiana*, Muncie, IN: Ball State University.

Gopal, P. (2016) 'Redressing anti-imperial amnesia', *Race and Class*, 57(3), 18-30.

Hall, S. (2017) *Familiar stranger: A life between two islands*, Durham, NC and London: Duke University Press.

Henry, W. (2006) *What the deejay said: A critique from the street*, London: Nu-Beyond.

Heritage Lottery Fund (no date) 'Be inspired by black British heritage projects' (www.hlf.org.uk/about-us/news-features/black-british-heritage/be-inspired-black-british-heritage-projects).

Hussain, M. (2015) 'Why is my curriculum white?', National Union of Students News, 11 March (www.nus.org.uk/en/news/why-is-my-curriculum-white).

Lassiter, L.E., Goodall, H., Campbell, E. and Johnson, M.N. (2004) *The other side of Middletown: Exploring Muncie's African American community*, Walnut Creek, CA: AltaMira Press.

Lynd, R.S. and Lynd, H.M. (1929) *Middletown: A study in American culture*, New York: Harcourt Brace.

McCabe, A., Phillimore, J. and Mayblin, L. (2010) *'Below the radar' activities and organisations in the third sector: A summary review of the literature*, Birmingham: Third Sector Research Centre.

Meringolo, D. (2014) 'The place of the city: Collaborative learning, urban history, and transformations in higher education', *Journal of Urban History*, 40(3), 419-24.

Myers, K. (2015) *Struggles for a past: Irish and Afro-Caribbean histories in England, 1951-2000*, Manchester: Manchester University Press.

Naidoo, R. and Littler, J. (2004) 'White past, multicultural present: Heritage and national stories', in R. Philips and H. Brocklehurst (eds) *History, identity and the question of Britain*, Basingstoke: Palgrave, 330-41.

Onyeka (2013) *Blackamoores: Africans in Tudor England, their presence, status and origins*, London: Narrative Eye.

Onyeka (2017) 'Black History Month: In retrospect', *Black History Month Magazine*, October.

Orwell, G. (1949 [2013]) *Nineteen eighty-four*, London: Penguin Classics.

Pankhania, J. (1994) *Liberating the national history curriculum*, London: Falmer Press.

Prescod, C. (2017) 'Archives, race, class and rage', *Race & Class*, 58(4), 76-84.

Sherwood, M. (2004) 'In this curriculum, I don't exist', History in British Education Conference (http://sas-space.sas.ac.uk/4334/1/In_this_curriculum%2C_I_don%27t_exist.pdf).

Sivanandan, A. (1993) 'The Black politics of health', *Race and Class*, 34, 63-9.

Smith, L. (2012) *Decolonizing methodologies: Research and indigenous peoples* (2nd edn), London: Zed.

Sound System Culture (no date) Blog (http://soundsystemcultureblog.tumblr.com).

Tosh, J. with Lang, S. (2006) *The pursuit of history: Aims, methods and new directions in the study of modern history* (4th edn), Harlow: Pearson.

Ward, P. (2018) 'Sound System Culture: Place, space and identity in the United Kingdom 1960-1989', *Historia Contemporánea*, 56, 349-76.

Ward, P. and Pente, E. (2017) 'Let's change history! Community histories and the co-production of historical knowledge', in K. Pickles, L. Fraser, M. Hill, S. Murray and G. Ryan (eds) *History making a difference: New approaches from Aotearoa*, Cambridge: Scholars Press, 94-112.

Waters, R. (2017) 'Thinking Black: Peter Fryer's *Staying power* and the politics of writing Black British history in the 1980s', *History Workshop Journal*, 82(1), 104-20.

TEN

Conclusion: Imagining different communities and making them happen

Paul Ward, Sarah Banks, Angie Hart and Kate Pahl

Introduction

In this book we have explored and developed the idea of a community development approach to the co-production of research. This approach emerged during the five years of *Imagine – Connecting communities through research*. Many communities are excluded from decision-making processes and are marginalised in relation to civic engagement and community participation. The *Imagine* project tried to imagine better communities and make them happen, but with a difference. We tried to do this together as a partnership between people based largely in universities and those based mainly in non-academic communities of place, interest and identity. This enabled the emergence of discussions about what this meant when academics in universities and a variety of people outside of them worked together. Everyone accepted that 'community' was difficult to define, but mostly we felt that the term symbolised a desire to live and work together for mutual benefit, rather than for the enrichment or accumulation of power by a few in society. Hence, community development, as a value-based process, which aims to address imbalances in power and bring about change founded on social justice, equality and inclusion, came to the fore as a way of understanding questions of civic engagement – people's participation in the communities in which they live. The notion of community development also implied the importance of not just seeing co-productive research as a quick process. The importance of developing longer-term relationships and legacies were issues we knew were important (Northmore and Hart, 2011).

Challenges and rewards of co-production

We have tried to bring to life in this book that the co-production of research, which brings experiential knowledge of people outside universities to the surface, enables them to create new knowledge that can lead to positive change in their communities. We consider that co-production can therefore give purpose to social sciences and arts and humanities research undertaken in universities. This might suggest that our book celebrates the co-production of research as unproblematic and exemplary. We hope it has not done that. As the reader should see from the chapters in this book, we have also tried to explain the difficulties we faced. We hope we have managed to convey something of the limitations and criticisms of co-production as an approach to research.

Working through community-university partnerships

There are numerous ways to critique the co-production of research and to think about its limitations. Certainly, within *Imagine*, some considered that the project and approach were having a limited impact on the ways in which universities operate, and that while there was a participatory turn in research, it was often done for the benefit of the universities rather than for communities outside academia. The increasing concern with the social and economic impact of research by the bodies that fund university research (as exemplified in the Research Excellence Framework) means that universities can derive quite considerable financial benefits from evidencing the impact of their research by working with communities. This does not necessarily 'transform the landscape of research' (which was implied in our fourth research question, as outlined in Chapter 1). It suits universities to have a superficial emphasis on impact and participation at the moment, but this is often achieved through short-term projects focused more on easily measurable outcomes, rather than being rooted in communities with real partnerships.

Yet as academics, the Principal and Co-investigators took the view that we had an opportunity to develop an approach to research that takes community development seriously. And while we are critical of much that happens in our universities, we also had a determination to overcome challenges rather than to focus on them, a view shared by many of our community partners (see, for example, Chapter 3). If we begin with an idealised version of the co-production of research that is impossible to achieve, we will not even be able to start a project. Yet, to quote the American historian and social activist Howard Zinn:

> If we do act, in however small a way, we don't have to wait for some grand utopian future. The future is an infinite succession of presents. And to live now as we think human beings should live, in defiance of all that is bad around us, is itself a marvellous victory. (Zinn, 2007, p 270; see also Hamdi, 2013)

Working through histories

A number of chapters suggest that an understanding of histories is an important resource in community development. In the 'historical context of civic engagement' strand of *Imagine*, the past really mattered in countering the stigmatisation of communities and places, so that Banks et al argue in Chapter 2 that looking to the past 'helped situate people and places throughout time and in the future' and that remembering enabled re-imagining. This happened similarly in the projects in Rotherham and Huddersfield (for Rotherham, see Campbell et al, 2018), where understanding history aided the development of a more confident community identity, empowered to challenge misperceptions. As Steve Pool suggests in Chapter 5, the capturing of a memory or moment creates 'an archive of hopes' as a tool for imagining the future.

Working through complexity and diversity

Imagine was a large, complex project that required a lot of work to hold together. It comprised four distinct work packages, each containing many smaller sub-projects, involving many people, with a wide variety of types of community partners. There were different kinds of organisations – smaller, less resourced groups and larger cultural institutions. There were people with diverse and overlapping identities and social positions, including children and young people, people with learning disabilities, working-class people, people who had been homeless, older and retired people, and people of different ethnicities, faiths and religions. It extended across the UK and into a number of other countries involved in the project. The 30 or so academics were also not a singular category – some were precariously employed research associates and assistants, others were doctoral students, others were permanently employed university staff. Each participant brought difference knowledge, experience and perspectives.

Imagine involved learning how to do things that many of us had not done before and learning from the varied experiences of different members. The ways of doing things – the research process – was important. It was not just about published outputs in a traditional academic sense; it was about the processes and practices of researchers working in collaboration. That is why description and analysis of how to do co-production are so important, as many of our chapters show. While we share common values and principles about why co-production is important and the ethics of how we should treat each other, as outlined in Chapter 1, we did not share a single methodology or set of methods of doing research co-productively. We used a variety of methods, some more defined than others. We readily crossed disciplinary boundaries. There was messiness and uncertainty, as emerges in Chapter 5 on arts practice and community development, and elsewhere in the book too. None of the chapters represent the end of the research processes, even if the particular projects are complete (as is necessitated by publication and the need to write a final report). The process of doing things together mattered. As Pool says in Chapter 5, 'it allows expansive new dialogues to happen', and these occur in different spaces and places, some facilitated by new ways of working, such as writing retreats, co-inquiry groups and writing workshops.

The existence of 'multiple readings' (the term used by Elizabeth Chapman Hoult in Chapter 7) provides a rationale for co-productive research, but throws up potential difficulties. Working collaboratively means that there are likely to be diverse viewpoints and disagreements, some of which cannot be resolved but must be accommodated if people are to feel their contribution is valued. Crucially, this recognition of multiple perspectives is linked to people's sense of agency. If no one listens to people in communities facing difficult circumstances, then their agency is severely limited. Co-production can often entail community development outcomes if people do feel increased power and agency – but that is not easy and straightforward when imbalances in power are so embedded and can be reproduced by universities in their relationships with communities.

One of the aspects of the *Imagine* project that we have struggled with is methodological diversity. In 'Co-designing for a better future' (Chapter 6) Prue Chiles, Louise Ritchie and Kate Pahl describe a process by which residents in the Park Hill flats in Sheffield re-imagined their spaces through a material process of design. Likewise, in Chapter 5, arts workers across a number of settings describe the process, in a conversation, of imagining better futures in the art world. Co-production can happen in conversations; it can also happen in material objects, in visual images and in poetic language. We recognise the diversity of people's approaches to working together, and in this book this diversity is highlighted by the number of ways people have worked together producing books, exhibitions, models, art works and creative objects.

Capturing the *Imagine* process

Inspired by the research retreat format developed by a group of *Imagine* researchers as described in Chapter 4 by Josh Cameron and colleagues, we decided to have a 'writing retreat' for people drawn from different parts of the *Imagine* project at the end of the programme. At the final *Imagine*-wide event in September 2017, over the course of two days, we produced a booklet to summarise the process, findings and outcomes of the project – a 'book in a breath' constructed by the creativity of the 20 or so people involved, which is freely downloadable from the web (Imagine, 2017). The co-creators of the booklet found the experience intense yet productive in turning collaborative thinking into a concrete product that made sense of the complexities of *Imagine* and, even at the end of the funded period, looked to the future and how others might also use some of our methods based on a community development approach to co-producing research between community partners and university academics.

Such a productive event highlighted some of the obstacles and difficulties in co-production. Holding a two-night residential event is both expensive and time-consuming. It was not possible for everyone involved in *Imagine* to attend for reasons of time, costs (paid by the project) and practicalities (writing a book with 100 authors in two days would have been too challenging). It required sensitivity to how people *felt* in relation to their previous involvement in the research process and how they might be engaged in the creation of a booklet during the two days. Working with others – the fundamental condition of human society and essential in co-production – involves investment of time for co-inquiry by academic and community partners that goes beyond what is normally expected of them.

Conclusions and lessons learned

The original, official title of our project was 'The social, historical, cultural and democratic contexts of civic engagement: Imagining different communities and making them happen.' This title suggested that although it was a 'research' project, one of its aims was to see change occur. It was not the most inspirational name for a project, and so we gave the project the working title: *Imagine – Connecting communities through research*. We wanted to place the emphasis on hope for the future, on creative ways of understanding communities of place, interest and identity as they exist now, to make change happen. We wanted wonder, hope, daydreams and utopian thinking to play a part. These ideas are about human agency, about involving people in imagining the future on their own terms. Bringing these themes and aspirations together, through a community development approach to the co-production of research, is important in imagining better futures and making them happen.

The *Imagine* project generated many successes and many challenges, but above all it was a learning process for all those involved. At the end of the *Imagine* writing retreat (Imagine, 2017) participants wrote messages to those following in their footsteps in the journey of co-produced research, of which the following is a selection:

- There's no such thing as perfect co-production, but don't let that stop you taking the first steps.
- Your voice, your knowledge counts.
- Don't be scared of disagreements and tensions – create a space where they can be aired. Use them to generate ideas and bring energy.
- Be generous, it's not always easy, stick with it, it's worth it!
- Stay positive and value differences.
- Let your passion be your energy and hope in tired times.
- Spread tales of what works when things seem impossible.
- Embrace the unexpected.
- Try to think of yourself as a 'we'.

We hope that this book has gone some way to make the argument for research to be understood and practised as co-research. We hope we have given some fuel to those readers who are struggling through difficulties with co-production to help them keep on their journey. But most of all, we want to stimulate others to begin to develop co-productive research communities. For us, the '*Imagine* journey' was certainly worth the effort. Of course, with all the complexities and tensions involved, we are fully aware that there is no such thing as perfect co-production. But do not let that stop you taking the first steps in trying to think of yourselves as a 'we'.

References

Campbell, E., Pahl, K., Pente, E. and Rasool, Z. (2018) (eds) *Re-imagining contested communities: Connecting Rotherham through research*, Bristol: Policy Press.

Hamdi, N. (2013) *Small change: About the art of practice and the limits of planning in cities*, London: Earthscan.

Imagine (2017) *Invitation to Imagine* [booklet] (https://files.acrobat.com/a/preview/7d91c091-780d-49e5-a051-30c3c21616fd).

Northmore, S. and Hart, A. (2011) 'Sustaining community-university partnerships', *Gateways: International Journal of Community Research & Engagement*, 4, 1-11.

Zinn, H. (2007) *A power governments cannot suppress*, San Francisco, CA: City Light.

Index

References to images and tables are in *italics*

Made in the USA
Monee, IL
11 January 2022

88698417R00129